ANCIENT
HISTORY

The Author

Albert Hyma received the bachelor's, master's, and doctor's degrees from the University of Michigan. He has taught history at that institution for thirty years. In addition, he has both studied and lectured in various foreign universities; in 1936 he was knighted by Queen Wilhelmina of Holland for his work in Dutch history. He is the author or coauthor of more than twenty books on historical and scholarly subjects, including the College Outline *Ancient, Medieval, and Modern History.*

COLLEGE OUTLINE SERIES

ANCIENT
HISTORY

by Albert Hyma
Professor of History
University of Michigan

BARNES & NOBLE, INC. • NEW YORK

PUBLISHERS • BOOKSELLERS • FOUNDED 1873

Printed in the United States of America

Preface

This outline is intended for the use of students and instructors in courses covering the whole field of general world history, or in other courses devoted entirely to the history of the ancient world. A survey of ancient history such as this should provide a useful supplement to the prescribed textbook, particularly for students who are easily confused by detailed discussions of numerous subjects which seem to follow in rapid succession. Often the reader of the text in question does not have time to digest the subject matter as quickly as would appear desirable or necessary. In such cases the use of the present work may well prove a great boon, resulting in the saving of much valuable time.

The author has often watched his students wander through the labyrinths of ancient history, seeking desperately a real "shortcut" to the desired goal—a thorough understanding of a wonderfully interesting subject which sometimes loses nearly all its charm because simplicity and clarity are lacking in the picture perceived by the bewildered student. Unlike other outlines formerly in use, the present one reads like an actual textbook, although it still remains an outline or digest. It will lighten the task of the student in preparing for daily recitations, and will greatly facilitate the difficult work of reviewing.

Each chapter has been introduced by a brief list of important dates, which will focus the attention of the reader upon what is most significant in each assignment. The paragraph headings printed in bold type and the list of dates following the last chapter, will prove helpful in reviewing for either daily quizzes or final examinations. The bibliography at the end of the book may be used as a guide in extra-curricular readings.

The author wishes to express his cordial thanks to Professor B. C. Clough of Brown University, and to Mr. Morriss H. Needleman, for many constructive criticisms of the original manuscript. The author also wishes to thank the editorial staff at Barnes & Noble, Inc., for valuable suggestions.

—ALBERT HYMA

Ann Arbor, Mich.

Table of Contents

Maps

ANCIENT HISTORY

Tabulated Bibliography of
Standard Textbooks on
Ancient History*

The following list gives the author, title, and publisher of the standard textbooks referred to in the table on the next page.

Boak, Hyma & Slosson, *The Growth of Western Civilization*, Vol. I, 4th ed., Appleton-Century-Crofts, 1951.

Caldwell, *The Ancient World*, Rinehart, 1949.

Ferguson & Bruun, *A Survey of European Civilization: Ancient Times to 1660*, Rev. ed., Houghton Mifflin, 1958.

Robinson, *Ancient History*, Macmillan, 1951.

Sanford, *The Mediterranean World in Ancient Times*, Rev. ed., Ronald Press, 1951.

Smith & Moorhead, *A Short History of the Ancient World*, Appleton-Century-Crofts, 1939.

a. Swain, *The Ancient World*, Vols. I & II, Harper, 1950.

b. Swain, *The Harper History of Civilization*, Vol. I, Harper, 1958.

Trever, *History of Ancient Civilization:* Vol. I, *The Ancient Near East and Greece;* Vol. II, *The Roman World*, Harcourt, (1936) (1939).

Van Sickle, *A Political and Cultural History of the Ancient World*, Vols. I & II, Houghton Mifflin, 1947-1948.

* Tabulated Bibliographies are exclusive features of the College Outline Series and are fully protected by copyright.

QUICK REFERENCE TABLE TO STANDARD TEXTBOOKS

Bold face type refers to pages.   Light face type refers to chapters.

CHAPTERS IN THIS BOOK	TOPIC	BOAK et al.	CALDWELL	FERGUSON & BRUUN	ROBIN-SON	SANFORD	SMITH & MOOR-HEAD	SWAIN a.	SWAIN b.	TREVER	VAN SICKLE
I	Introduction	1	1	1	3-30	1-2		Vol. 1 3-56	3-37	Vol. 1 1-2	Vol. I 1-2
II	The Kingdoms of Ancient Mesopotamia	2	2	16-19	33-53 83-85	3	3-4	59-95	39-48	3	3
III	Ancient Egypt	2	3	19-23	54-82	5	1-2	96-129	49-63	4-5	4-5
IV	The Hebrews, the Aramaeans, and the Phoenicians	3	95-103	24, 25	86-96	6	7	130-164 202-243	64-67 80-89	6	6
V	The Assyrian and Persian Empires	3	103-113	17, 25	97-113	7 171-181	5-6	165-199	69-79	7-8	7-9
VI	The Background of Greek History	3, 4	68-81 114-123	23-25	117-140	81-85 8	8	247-280	93-104	9-11	10-11
VII	The Greek City-States	4	124-128 8-13	2	140-294	9-10 12, 13	9-13	281-474	104-120	12-28	12-32
VIII	Hellenistic Civilization	5	15-16	3	295-432	14-16 18-19	14-20	475-544	121-147	29-33	33
IX	The Roman Republic	6	18-20	4	435-549	17 20-25	21-29	Vol. II 85-407	151-170	Vol. II 1-14	Vol. II 1-18
X	The Roman Empire under the Principate	6, 7	21-23	5	553-638	26-31	30-32	411-452 495-535	171-230	15-26	19-25
XI	Fall of the Roman Empire	7	24	6	638-682	32	33, 35	536-583	230-245	27-29	26-28
XII	The Rise of the Christian Church	9	505-507 525-528	7	682-684	507-509 547-575	34	453-494	251-294	30	426-427 552-555
XIII	The Germanic Migrations and Kingdoms	8		8	658-665	539-548 558-570		425-427	242-245 406-412		626-628
XIV	The End of the Ancient World		528-530		643-657			584-613			

See preceding page for list of complete book titles.

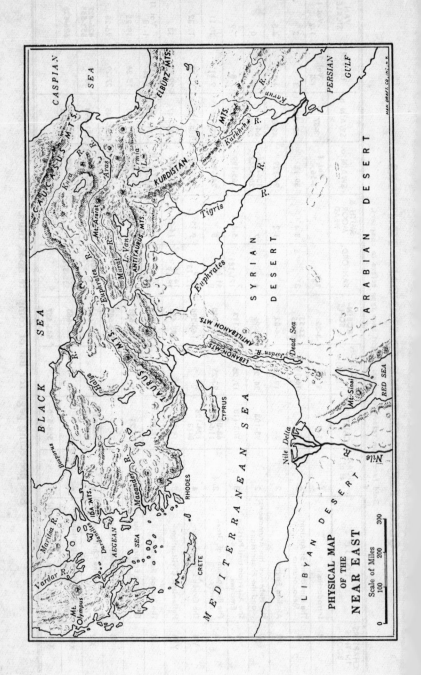

PHYSICAL MAP
OF THE
NEAR EAST

Scale of Miles

0   100   200   300

Topics

Nature of Preliterary History
Stone Age Civilization
The Age of Metals
How Europe Became Civilized
Rome and the Barbarians

Chapter I.

INTRODUCTION

Webster's *New International Dictionary* defines history thus: "A narrative of events connected with a real or imaginary object, person, or career. . . . A systematic written account of events, particularly of those affecting a nation, institution, science, or art, and usually connected with a philosophical explanation of their causes. . . . The branch of knowledge that records and explains human progress." From this excellent definition we gather that the purpose of history is to tell the story of human beings from the earliest times to the present day. It describes their political institutions, their social customs, their economic interests, their intellectual achievements, their artistic products, and all other experiences that constitute the story of mankind.

The Nature of Preliterary History. Preliterary history covers that section of history in which human beings were not interested in writing, or not able to develop writing. Until the second half of the nineteenth century some scholars assumed that writing was not known anywhere in the world before 2000 B.C. Today it is generally believed that some of the most ancient peoples knew how to write before 3000 B.C. Consequently, the period of history covered in the present chapter precedes the year 3000 B.C.

I

The Sources of This Early Period. It follows, therefore, that in order to determine what kind of lives the earliest people of antiquity lived, we must rely upon sources other than written records. A student of history is aided in this task by the researches of geologists, anthropologists, archeologists, and zoologists. Skeletons, of what are regarded as prehistoric human beings, have been found in many parts of the world. Thousands of implements used by early man have been collected in museums and other buildings. Interesting drawings have been found inscribed upon rocks in caves and elsewhere. Geologists have told us how old are those layers of earth beneath the surface in which skeletons and tools of human beings have been found. Finally, zoologists have attempted to determine if and how human beings were developed out of a certain high type of animal.

CIVILIZED AND UNCIVILIZED LIFE
BEFORE 4000 B.C.

Stone Age Civilization. Whenever peoples were making use of crude stone implements, they are said to belong to the Old Stone Age. Those, on the other hand, who had learned to make use of finer and sharper tools, are said to have lived in the New Stone Age. In the Old Stone Age it is believed that man wore no clothing, except perhaps a girdle at the waist. Nor did he have a fixed abode, but sometimes he sought shelter in caves or in trees. When the use of fire was discovered is entirely unknown, nor can we speak with much assurance about the food that the earliest human beings used. No doubt they were often engaged in hunting, and they may have had some domestic animals. Some scholars also mention a Middle Stone Age, during which time human beings had weapons made out of flint, with pressure-chipped edges. They also made use of the bow and arrow, together with the spear. Presumably the weather was now colder in various regions, for more meat was now eaten, and more skins were prepared for clothing, while caves became the homes of many persons. Perhaps in this time man knew more about drawing, painting, and carving. Undoubtedly he also entertained certain religious ideas. In the Late Stone Age or the New Stone Age the weather is said to have been still colder, and more clothes were needed. More use was made now of agriculture, and various domestic animals were pastured. Along the shores of some of the lakes in Switzerland houses have been found which contained furniture made of wood, pictures, pottery, spoons, and vessels likewise constructed out of wood. Mankind now depended less upon hunting and more upon agriculture and the use of domestic animals.

The Age of Metals. About 4000 B.C. the inhabitants of ancient Mesopotamia knew how to make use of bronze, copper, and iron. This has been proved by the most recent excavations in that region. But at the very same time the peoples in Europe seem to have been in the Old Stone Age. Between 4000 and 3000 B.C. a great deal was done in Egypt and Mesopotamia in the direction of scientific agriculture and industry. Irrigation was perfected in the valleys of the Nile in Egypt, and those of the Euphrates and the Tigris in Mesopotamia. Since it was impossible for a few men to control the course of those great rivers, it became necessary for the inhabitants to band together and to establish a government. Laws were drawn up, various articles produced were exchanged for others, a distinction was being drawn between servants and masters, and a number of persons were set aside as a separate class to function as priests. When excavators reached the lowest level of land upon which civilization once flourished in Mesopotamia, they found that metals were already in use, that is, between 5000 and 4000 B.C.

The Rise and Fall of Nations. The latest researches in Egypt and Mesopotamia clearly reveal that a period of a high degree of civilization would be followed by one of much less culture. In some instances from twelve to fifteen different layers of soil were laid bare, indicating that upon various urban levels a high degree of civilization had been reached, while some later cities were much less highly civilized. After the destruction of such cities, it may have taken centuries to restore the level of prosperity and culture that had once existed upon that site. We all know, for example, that Rome, the greatest city of the ancient world, was invaded many times, so that during the sixth century of our era the records state that not a single human being was left in the town. Exaggerated though this account may have been,

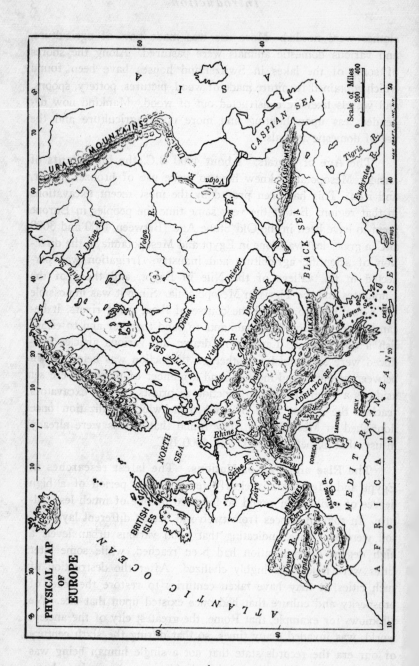

PHYSICAL MAP
OF
EUROPE

Scale of Miles
0   200   400

we may say at least that the population declined from more than a million to less than a thousand. We also know that in western Europe during the third, fourth, and fifth centuries of our era, civilization underwent a terrible decline. An economic depression, lasting about two hundred years, witnessed the ruin of the ancient world from Mesopotamia westward to the shores of the Atlantic Ocean. Is it then surprising to learn of the same fate experienced by the cities of the ancient Near East? And is it surprising to learn that when the highly cultured inhabitants of that region ventured forth to invade other countries and to settle there, under less favorable conditions they lost many characteristics of an earlier and more highly civilized age? This must undoubtedly have happened to those peoples who went from Mesopotamia southeastward into India, eastward into China and to Central Asia, northwestward into Asia Minor, and still farther north-westward into Europe. Thus it may well have happened that certain peoples retrogressed from the metal age type of civilization to the stone age form of civilization. Europe was probably peopled by persons from the ancient Near East, who were not able to maintain the high level of agriculture, commerce, and industry to which their ancestors had been accustomed. On the other hand, many peoples rose from a relatively low level of culture, as was the case with the Teutonic peoples, to a much higher level. This may have been done in some cases independently of others, while in other cases the barbarous peoples received most of their culture and information from highly civilized neighbors. This happened to the Franks, the Angles and the Saxons, who invaded respectively Gaul and Briton.

How Europe Became Civilized. It is clear to all historians that Europe was originally barbarous, and when it finally emerged out of barbarism to receive the first gifts of civilized life, they were transmitted to the Europeans by the inhabitants of the ancient Near East. We know now that the first homes of civilized man were Mesopotamia and Egypt. Between 3500 and 2500 B.C. the extreme southeastern part of Europe was illuminated by the culture of ancient Egypt and Mesopotamia. After this region had basked for a time in the light of Oriental civilization, barbarians swooped down from the north, destroyed part

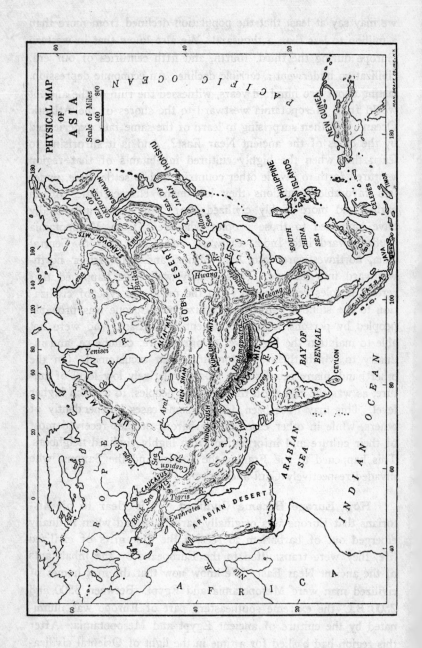

PHYSICAL MAP
OF
ASIA

Scale of Miles
0   400   800

PACIFIC OCEAN

MAN. DRAFT CO. INC. N.Y.

INDIAN OCEAN

of the highly civilized life they found there, and then became civilized in turn. These barbarians, these invaders, were the Greeks, who afterward proudly spoke of themselves as the torch-bearers of civilized life, whereas they had been originally nothing but barbarians and destroyers of civilization. Everything that they had had in the field of civilization, they had received from other peoples. Although afterwards the Greeks referred to these peoples as "barbarians," they could not hide from posterity the knowledge that they themselves had been the original barbarians. The Greeks in turn fell before a people that was located still farther to the west.

Rome and the Barbarians. The Romans also at one time had been barbarians, but they had been instructed by various peoples in the Italian and Balkan peninsulas. When the decline of Rome came at last, the Germanic barbarians invaded the great empire from the north, destroyed various towns, sacked libraries, and for a time were content with a mediocre degree of culture. But eventually they learned to live side by side with the highly cultured Romans, they adopted highly scientific agriculture, they developed industry and commerce, and later they in turn constructed great nations and a high type of civilization. The time was to come when Germans and Englishmen would look with scorn and contempt upon peoples farther to the south and east. They would also use the term "barbarians" and would sometimes seek to hide the fact that originally they also had been barbarians.

Significant Dates

Oldest Cities Founded . . 4500 B.C.

Golden Age of Sumerian
 Civilization . . 4000-3000 B.C.

Age of Sargon I . . . . 2700 B.C.

Reign of Hammurapi . . 1950 B.C.

CHAPTER II.

THE KINGDOMS OF
ANCIENT MESOPOTAMIA

Since the most recent excavations in the ancient Near East tend to prove that civilized life flourished in ancient Mesopotamia before it did anywhere else, the present work begins as it should with a description of the earliest kingdoms founded in the valley between the Tigris and the Euphrates rivers. It was in this region, according to the Bible story, that the earliest human beings lived. Also in this region, according to the interpretation of many archeologists, cities were constructed (*ca.* 4500 B. C.) before any in Egypt. It can also be demonstrated very easily that from the same region civilization first reached India and China. The extreme southeastern corner of Europe also received from Mesopotamia, as well as from Egypt, its earliest knowledge of civilized life. In southern Mesopotamia the famous city of Ur was built from which Abraham set forth to find a new home in another country, and to become the progenitor of the Hebrew race. Here a number of important nations grew up and declined in turn, to make room for others. Among these were Sumeria, Babylonia, Assyria, Chaldea, and Persia. Here were produced the oldest known written records of the human race. Here also was found

8

evidence in the form of silt deposited to the depth of eight feet that at one time a huge flood covered the whole of ancient Meso potamia. The stories of the Creation and the Flood written in this region seem to prove that even ancient Egypt received some forms of civilization from Mesopotamia.

THE SUMERIANS

The Land and the People. Ancient Mesopotamia is the valley of the two rivers known as the Euphrates and the Tigris. They have their sources in the mountains of Asia Minor, and they flow toward the Persian Gulf in a southeasterly direction. To the north of this valley lie the Black and the Caspian seas and to the south beyond the Persian Gulf is the Indian Ocean. To the southwest extends the huge peninsula called Arabia, bounded on the west by the Red Sea and on the south by the Indian Ocean. To the west of the valley lies the high land of Syria, including ancient Palestine. Although much of Syria, and almost all of Arabia, is now a desert, in the period from 4000 to 3000 B. C. there was a stretch of fertile land in the form of a crescent— hence called the Fertile Crescent—which extended in a huge semi- circle from the Persian Gulf on the east around the northern portion of the Arabian peninsula to Palestine on the west. It witnessed the rise and fall of many nations and the migrations of many peoples from east to west and the reverse. The high lands of Arabia and Syria were barren throughout almost the whole of each year. The valley of the Euphrates and the Tigris, however, became increasingly fertile because of the silt that was brought down each spring and early summer from the melting snow in the mountains of Asia Minor. In Mesopotamia itself the amount of rain that fell was but small, averaging about three inches annually. But the absence of rainfall in the valley was made up for by great amounts of water brought down from the eastern and northern mountains. These streams would flood the low- lands, but soon were checked in their course by man-sewn net- works. Canals were dug and dikes were constructed along the banks of the tumultuous streams. Here lived between 4000 and 3000 B. C. a people that was more civilized than any other of that time. Just who they were and whence they came is not known, but they are called Sumerians. Even before 3500 B. C. they were highly civilized. They made use of metals. They lived in cities, around which they constructed walls, partly to protect themselves against the rising waters, and partly to ward off enemy attacks. Practically nothing was known about them before the opening of the twentieth century, but, owing to the arduous labors of archeologists during the last two decades, the wealth of material brought to light has compelled many scholars to give up their former opinion that Egypt was the home of the oldest civilization known.

Political History of Sumeria. The Sumerians were ruled by a king who lived in an immense palace. But just how he ruled can not be ascertained. He and his people fought wars against neighboring tribes, until for a time the Sumerians seem to have dominated the whole of ancient Mesopotamia. Berosus, the Chaldean historian who flourished in the third century B. C., mentions ten patriarchs or kings who ruled before the great Flood, which must have occurred between 3800 and 3500 B. C. Kish, Nippur, and Ur were among the chief cities of Sumeria, and in the last-named has been found a royal palace made of sun-dried brick. But after 3000 B. C. the Sumerians underwent a decline, and about 2630 B. C. the valley of the Tigris-Euphrates fell into the hands of another tribe of people, belonging apparently to the Semites. The kings of ancient Sumeria made use of chariots and their troops were armed with copper helmets and spears. Since arrowheads and parts of bows have been found in their tombs, we must conclude that they also made use of such. The Sumerian troops were well organized, marching in compact units, and were also disciplined, contrasting favorably with the troops employed by the Semites.

Sumerian Society. The Sumerians had priests who exercised religious functions for the people. According to many present authorities, the Sumerians were originally monotheistic in their belief, for the most ancient written records state clearly that they believed in only one God. This is a very important fact to note, because until very recently (1937) a large number of historians believed that mankind originally was polytheistic and that gradually as human beings became civilized, they formed a higher conception of the deity. The social classes among the Sumerians included the aristocrats, to whom the government officials and the priests belonged, the free landholders, the traders, and the slaves. There seems to have been little distinction between slaves and freemen. The laws, considering the time, were remarkably liberal, penalties were as a rule justly prescribed, marriage was monogamous, and women possessed a considerable amount of freedom, contrasting favorably with Greek women of a much later time. However, the husband had the right to sell his wife and children to pay for his debts. This, by the way, was also the custom among the primitive Germans of the third and fourth centuries of our era.

Agriculture, Commerce, and Industry. The Sumerians were very skillful in agriculture, taking full advantage of the fertility of the soil and of the water supply. They raised great crops of grain, vegetables, and dates. They kept such domestic animals as cows, sheep, and goats. For plowing they made use of oxen while the donkeys pulled their carts and chariots. They also had a flourishing dairy industry, as indicated by their sculpture. Commerce was thriving even before 3000 B. C. The land appears to have been owned partly by the ruler and partly by the priests and soldiers. The land was worked by tenants, who rented the land; by free laborers, who worked for wages; and by slaves. Unlike the peoples of the Stone Age culture, they used sickles made of any of three materials—stone, baked clay, or copper. Their bread was baked in about the same fashion as the Arabs do it today. The people constructed ovens with domed brick with a fire within, so that the dough could be plastered on the side. Wool and flax were produced in great quantities also. From the flax, linen was made, while the sheep and the goats produced the wool. Very remarkable was the metalwork, not only in copper and silver, but also in gold. The Sumerians also used ivory, fine stone, and precious woods. A great many records of Sumerian businessmen testify to the remarkable height that commerce reached before 3000 B. C. Both men and women signed receipts, accounts, bills, notes, and letters. They were all inscribed on clay tablets, the chief source of knowledge of this early type of civilization. We also learn from these tablets that money was lent at from 20 to 33⅓ per cent interest, as regulated formally by law. So extensive was Sumerian trade that their merchants had agents in places as far away as Asia Minor. These representatives made use of letters of credit. Salesmen traveled from one city to another, for hundreds of miles. Although coinage was not yet employed, commerce was carried on successfully through barter. However, before 3500 B. C. gold and silver were used as mediums of exchange, and there is no doubt much truth in the Biblical record that Abraham bought a cave for which he "weighed out" four hundred shekels of silver. The ratio in value between gold and silver was at that time eight to one. We also have interesting records of a transaction for the payment of a cargo of a ship that sailed from the city of Ur about the year 2100 B. C.

The Fine Arts and Architecture. Most of the buildings were constructed of sun-dried brick, but bricks were later baked in kilns. The masses lived in very low houses, with roofs constructed of mud or of reeds. But the homes of the wealthy were rather large, being made up of at least two stories, and constructed around a court. Some of the homes were beautifully furnished, possessing lovely chairs, tables, chests, baskets, vessels of wood, copper, or stone, and beds. Impressive are the remnants of the royal palace in Kish, constructed about the year 3500 B. C. It was built of brick, and provided with huge staircases, large columns, and paneled walls that were decorated with both human and animal figures. The Sumerians before 3000 B.C. knew how to construct not only the vault and the arch, but also the dome. They made use of sewers made of baked brick. Between 3000 and 2000 B. C. a large number of square, pyramidal temple-towers were constructed, called *ziggurats*. They were built upon a raised platform, one terrace being constructed above the other, and each being a little smaller than the one below. Ur also had one of these ziggurats, constructed as usual of sun-dried bricks upon a lower level of baked brick, that was 200 feet long, 150 feet wide, and 70 feet high. (It is interesting to note that the Bible tells of the building of the Tower of Babel, which may well have happened about the year 3000 B. C.) Extraordinary was the skill of the Sumerians in metalwork, wherein their casting was perfect. Furthermore, their sculpture was truly magnificent

In many of their graves have been found delicately carved ornaments and weapons. One of the royal graves dates back to 3200 B. C., and from it has been taken an object made of gold showing hair tied with a fillet, a golden lamb, a dagger, pins, beads, earrings, and bracelets. Beautiful, also, is a silver vase dating from about 3000 B.C., and illuminating is the figure of an eagle with a lion's head above two stags made of copper, its size being nine by seven feet. Some authorities are even of the opinion that two female heads, dating from about 2300 B. C., are almost as perfect as those produced by the greatest Greek masters during the fifth century B. C.

Literature and Writing. The Sumerians seem to have been the oldest people that made use of writing. They employed pictographic symbols, but afterwards they changed these symbols into conventional signs which represented syllables. They had about 300 such signs, so it cannot be said that they originated our alphabet. They impressed their writing upon soft clay tablets, making use of a stylus that was provided with a triangular tip. This tip gave to the strokes the shape of a wedge, and for that reason the system of writing was called *cuneiform,* that is, wedge-shaped. In addition to the many thousands of business letters left by the Sumerians, must be mentioned the religious literature. It includes the mythical epic poem describing the Creation, that of the Flood (the Epic of Gilgamesh), and that of a certain shepherd who tried to fly to heaven on the back of an eagle.

Science. In the field of science the Sumerians made even greater contributions. They bequeathed to the Babylonians and the Assyrians a system of astronomy and mathematics. They divided the circle into 6 x 60, that is, 360 parts or degrees. They also divided the day into twelve double hours, each of which was subdivided into thirty minutes, so that one of their minutes was equivalent to four of ours. They used the same system in their weights, for their talent was equal to sixty minas, and each mina was equivalent to sixty shekels.* The Sumerians also made great progress in calculating the areas of intricate geometrical figures. They divided the year into lunar months of 29 to 30 days each.

---

* These terms later came to refer to money rather than weight.

Each year for that reason was only 354 days long. Occasionally a thirteenth month was added, in order to make the moon year harmonize with the sun year. Much was also accomplished in the field of astrology; that is, an apparent connection was shown between the course of the various planets and the lives of human beings.

Religion. As stated previously, the Sumerians originally believed in only one God, but after 3500 B. C. they developed various forms of polytheism. They began to worship a large number of gods, from among whom they transmitted to the later Babylonians their chief god Marduk. The government of Sumeria was really a theocracy, for the ruler was also the chief priest. The other priests were divided into three classes, namely, the singers, the magicians, and the sooth-sayers. From certain omens, such as the flight of birds, they would derive events of the future. The Sumerians had a vague conception of a future life, but do not appear to have believed in a heaven or a hell. They were accustomed to bury each deceased person with his personal objects, in order that the spirit of the dead person would thereby be pleased. It was felt that the spirit not satisfied with the burial would haunt the house and its inmates.

ANCIENT BABYLONIA

Political History. When shortly after 3000 B. C. the Sumerians began to decline, other peoples made ready to take their place. Among these were the Akkadians, a Semitic people, who had constructed the city of Akkad in the northern section of central Mesopotamia, and were ruled about the year 2700 B. C. by King Sargon I. They intermarried with the Sumerians, and were instructed by them in the art of warfare, agriculture, commerce, industry, science, and religion. Several centuries after the reign of Sargon I another Semitic race called the Amorites began to dominate the inhabitants of Mesopotamia. By making the city of Babylon their capital, they became known as the Babylonians, and their state as Babylonia. The plain in which Babylon was located is known as the Plain of Shinar. Here was constructed a new nation (between 2300 and 2000 B. C.) of great political power, but one which added practically nothing to the marvelous contributions to civilization made previously by the Sumerians.

MESOPOTAMIA

SHOWING MOST IMPORTANT CITIES
CONSTRUCTED BY THE SUMERIANS,
THE BABYLONIANS, THE ASSYRIANS,
AND THE PERSIANS

Scale of Miles

0   100   200   300

The Reign of Hammurapi (Hammurabi). This was the sixth king of the Babylonians, who, like the Akkadians, were instructed by the Sumerians. They adopted from the Sumerians their laws, system of writing, literature, art, and learning. Thus it happens that the famous stories of the Creation and the Flood written in Mesopotamia between 3000 and 2000 B. C. are said by some scholars to be Sumerian works and by others Babylonian. The accounts differ from the story told in the Bible by reason of their polytheistic character and their relatively low moral standards. The same features belong to the famous Code of Hammurapi, who reigned apparently in the twentieth century B. C. This king ruled wisely and collected taxes carefully. He made the Euphrates navigable once more and also improved the calendar. The laws he codified have been so widely discussed in historical literature that they deserve a separate paragraph.

The Code of Hammurapi. This collection of laws was inscribed upon a large stone cylinder seal. It contains 282 articles, preceded by a prologue in which Hammurapi recognizes seventeen gods and goddesses. He subscribes to the familiar dictum of "an eye for an eye and a tooth for a tooth," but unfortunately he does not apply this retributive principle justly to all classes of people, thereby showing himself much inferior to the Hebrew lawgiver Moses. Hammurapi decrees that if a "man destroy the eye of another man, one shall destroy his eye," but when a wealthy person destroyed the eye of a freedman, the former knew that he would merely have to pay a fine (see Articles 196 and 198). Have not the wealthy persons of later ages known also in advance that they would receive far better treatment than if they were poor? Hammurapi's wealthy subjects must have been pleased with his eighth article, which stated that a thief who could not repay a person from whom he had stolen something should be put to death, but that all others merely repaid more than they had stolen. Very important also is the unfair discrimination made by Hammurapi between employers and servants or slaves. He ordered that if a person destroyed the eye of a man's slave, he would have to pay one-half of his value. On the other hand, Hammurapi's code reveals striking superiority when compared with the political and social customs of other peoples of the ancient world.

Babylonian Society. From the Code of Hammurapi we also learn that agriculture, commerce, and industry were carefully regulated by the government. Those persons who failed to cultivate their fields were penalized, while those who neglected to keep the canals and the dikes in proper condition were also punished. Although a large number of persons owned land, much of it was the property of the government and of the nobles and the priests, exactly as had been the case among the Sumerians. Those who rented the land had to pay for it two-thirds of the crop. All business agreements required written contracts with the signatures of witnesses. Those who borrowed money had to give cattle as security in the place of money. Farmers received liberal treatment, and women enjoyed a relatively favorable position. Slaves were treated reasonably well. They were often set free, and it was stated in the code that a child of a slave and a freedwoman was free. Workmen were restricted by contracts, while the Code carefully prescribed what their wages should be. Between the poor laborers and the nobles and priests there were the men and women who comprised the middle class. Among them were the ordinary businessmen, clerks, teachers, and skilled workers in the industries. The latter were organized into guilds. The Code also recognized monogamy as proper and binding. But in case the wife was ill for a long time the husband was permitted to have another wife or a concubine. The bridegroom presented his bride with a gift, while the bride's father presented the bridegroom with a dowry. In case of divorce, which was permitted, the wife took charge of the children and the husband had to return the dowry. Wives could inherit property on equal terms with the children. They could bequeath their property as they saw fit. Many women participated in the trades and professions, while some of them even served as priestesses, but husbands were permitted to sell both wives and children for debts.

Babylonian Religion. The Babylonians resembled the Sumerians in that they were polytheistic and regarded their gods merely as supermen. The gods were believed to share with human beings their passions and many of their ordinary habits of life. Sacrifices were given, not in order to insure for oneself a better future in the life beyond the grave, but only to derive advantages for this life. The temples were the property of the state, and were instituted not merely as places of worship, but often as banks and business establishments. Many were the magicians and diviners who thought they could foretell the future by studying the liver of a sheep slain in sacrifice. Schools were conducted as were those among the Sumerians, with the pupils using the clay tablets in much the way that ours use paper tablets.

ANCIENT ASSYRIA

The City-State of Assur. About the year 3000 B. C. a Semitic people constructed a new state called Assur (Ashur), from which name the word "Assyria" has been derived. This was a city-state located in northeastern Mesopotamia, on the banks of the Tigris River. It retained its independence for perhaps six or eight centuries until Babylonia grew so powerful that it annexed Assyria (*ca.* 2100 B. C.). Affected no doubt by the highly civilized Sumerians, the Assyrians long before the reign of Hammurapi possessed advanced political institutions and a flourishing commerce and industry. They traded with the inhabitants of Asia Minor and Syria. Large numbers of cuneiform records indicate how extensive their commerce was. They made use of small silver bars which carried stamps indicating their respective weights. These bars were used in preference to barter, but letters of credit in the form of clay tablets were also extensively employed. On one of these tablets it is clearly stated that Assyrians used to lend money to peoples in Asia Minor at the rate of from 20 to 30 per cent. It is not surprising that money was first used in Asia Minor, where the early Assyrian merchants had been so active ages before.

The Kassites Conquer and Rule Mesopotamia. About the year 1785 B. C. a tribe of invaders called the Kassites conquered Babylonia from the north and afterwards extended their rule over other sections of Mesopotamia. Under Babylonian domination the Assyrians had continued their lucrative trade with districts to the north and northwest, but it seems that the Kassites did not appreciate a high degree of civilized life. For several hundred years after 1785 B. C. Assyria declined together with Babylonia.

The Hittites. One of the most mysterious and at the same time one of the most powerful peoples of the ancient world were the Hittites, who inhabited Asia Minor and northern Syria. About the year 2000 B. C. they were the dominant people in eastern Asia Minor, and in 1750 B. C. they invaded even southern Mesopotamia and sacked the city of Babylon. Although during the sixteenth century B. C. they temporarily lost their political power, shortly after 1500 B. C. they created an empire in Asia Minor and extended their sway over the regions to the south-east. Thus they were able to hold in check the Assyrians, who were bent upon conquest again. These Hittites were not Semites, nor do they seem to have been closely related to such peoples as the Sumerians or Egyptians. Their language was Indo-European in relationship, as is the Persian language. Originally the Hittites seem to have inhabited the plains to the north of the Black and Caspian seas. They resembled the Kassites. The Hittites were ruled by a king, whose power was not nearly so great as that of the Babylonian or Sumerian king. Their military organization was so highly developed that they were able to hold the Assyrians long in check. From the peoples of Mesopotamia they borrowed the cuneiform script. Some of their records show that they used to make treaties with the rulers of Egypt. They seem to be the first people in the ancient world who developed the iron industry, and it was from them that the Assyrians learned to use iron in the manufacture of weapons. Before 1500 B. C. the Assyrians had been dependent upon a copper supply, but copper was not nearly so hard and durable as iron. The Assyrians also acquired from the Hittites an interesting style of architecture used in the construction of royal palaces. These were built of brick and stone, and had a porch provided with numerous columns flanked by two square towers. On each side of the entrance was a huge stone figure of a lion, while the porch was also decorated with sculptures in relief.

Subsequent History. From 1785 to 1169 B. C. Mesopotamia was largely dominated by the Kassites. But during the twelfth century B. C. the Assyrians were favored by a number of circumstances which enabled them not only to secure complete independence, but also to build an empire of their own. At that time the power of the Hittites and of the Egyptians was declining, and that of the Kassites was easily overthrown. Consequently, the Assyrians, with their improved arms and renewed ambitions, conquered the whole of Mesopotamia and northern Syria. During the next four centuries they also extended their sway over the region directly to the north of Mesopotamia, while during the seventh century B. C. they ruled even Egypt for a short time. From about 750 B. C. to 612 B. C. Assyria was the greatest power in the ancient Near East. This empire and its civilization will be discussed in a subsequent chapter.

CHAPTER III.

ANCIENT EGYPT

Egypt is a land of romance and mystery which, unlike ancient Mesopotamia, was seldom disturbed by invasions and foreign wars during the period from 3400 to 1700 B. C. It was the first country in the ancient world to bring about political unity and thus become a great state. Besides, no other country in the ancient Near East enjoyed so long a period of union and independence as did Egypt. Here were constructed the famous pyramids, sphinxes, and obelisks, which form the delight of all tourists today. Egypt was also a commercial country of the greatest importance, and its scientists were able to surpass others in some branches of mathematics, while they also were the first to perfect a solar calendar.

POLITICAL HISTORY

The Land. Egypt was practically nothing else but the Nile River and its valley. The Nile has its sources in east central Africa, in Ethiopia, or Abyssinia. The valley of the Nile River has an average width of about ten miles, but the width varies from six or eight to thirty miles. The total area is about ten thousand square miles. On each side of the valley there extend desert plateaus, except near the mouth of the river, where it enters the Mediterranean Sea in the north. Here the valley broadens into a delta, with an area of about 350 square miles. At the southern border of Egypt is the so-called First Cataract (waterfall). From this point to the coast of the Mediterranean Sea the length of the Nile Valley is about 650 miles. As a result of the abundance of spring rains in the higher regions to the south and of the melting of the snow in Abyssinia, the river rises rapidly in the month of May and continues to rise until early October, when it reaches its greatest height, that is, from twenty to forty feet above the normal level. During the first week of November the waters begin to recede, and in January the river level is once more back to normal.

The People. Although the inhabitants of ancient Egypt were, strictly speaking, not Semites, they were closely related to the inhabitants of northern Arabia, Mesopotamia, and Syria. From the paintings and statues left by the Egyptian artists of the period before 2500 B. C. we gather that the Egyptians possessed deep-set eyes, large cheek bones, fairly thick lips, and a comparatively short nose. Their hair seems to have been always black and straight. Their skin had been white, but powerful rays of the sun quickly turned the color to tan.

The Union of Upper and Lower Egypt. Before 3000 B. C. there seem to have been two kingdoms in Egypt, the southern half or Upper Egypt, and the northern half or Lower Egypt. Little is known about Egyptian history before their union, which occurred between 3400 B. C. and 3000 B. C. For many centuries a Stone Age culture flourished in Egypt, but it is difficult to determine its dates. It may be that side by side with highly civilized areas there were others in which there existed little civilized life. It may also be that civilization was preceded or sometimes followed by a Stone Age culture. At any rate, there can be no question about the numerous remains of the Stone Age civilization in Egypt.

The Dynasties. According to an Egyptian historian called Manetho, who wrote in Greek, the rulers of Egypt were divided into thirty groups, or Thirty Dynasties, the first "Lord of the

Two Lands" being King Menes. The last ruler in the long list
that Manetho prepared was Alexander the Great, who conquered
Egypt about the year 330 B. C. Menes seems to have ruled
shortly before the year 3000 B. C., while other important rulers
were Khufu (Cheops), who belonged to the IVth Dynasty and
reigned about the year 2850 B. C.; Amenembet III, whose reign
occurred from about 1938-1903 B. C.; Amenhotep III, who ruled
from 1411-1375 B. C.; Tutankhamon, whose magnificent tomb
was discovered in recent years; and Rameses II, who ruled from
about 1292-1225 B. C. Rameses II belonged to the XIXth Dynasty
and was one of the strongest kings in the history of Egypt.
He was followed by a long list of weak rulers, but after Assyria
had conquered Egypt in 672 B. C., two important kings, Psamtik
I and Necho, who belonged to the XXVIth Dynasty, set Egypt
free again.

The Old Kingdom and the Middle Kingdom. The Egyptians reached their highest level of civilization in the period from
2740 to 2270 B. C., that is, the Age of the Old Kingdom. In this
time the greatest of the pyramids was constructed, and the arts
and sciences flourished. Egypt was ruled by a king whose title
was Pharaoh. He wielded autocratic power, and was believed
to be descended from the gods. He was regarded both a god and
a king. Although he cannot be said to have been responsible to
the people, nevertheless, as king and as god, it was his duty to
take the best care of them. He was responsible to his ancestors,
whom he had to worship and who were his protectors, and to
the gods above. He appointed both the civil officials and the
priests. He was head of both the church and the state, one might
say. Consequently, the government of Egypt was a theocracy.
But it must be noted that the king as a civil ruler was really above
all priests in more than one way. He was in charge of the irrigation works which were necessary to conduct the waters of the
Nile River and its silt to all parts of the valley. The land belonged to him alone, and those who cultivated it were obliged to
pay rent to him in the form of crops. As a rule they had to give
to him one-fifth of what they produced. In addition to those payments, the tenants were also obliged to render personal services,
some military service, work of a public nature such as irrigation
labor, and other duties.

The Coming of the Hyksos. For centuries peace was maintained in all parts of Egypt, but the time came at last when the king was weakened by the rivalry of his leading ministers. He had to depend upon a large number of officials placed under the charge of the chief minister, or vizier. In the various provinces ruled governors whose titles eventually became hereditary. Thus a new class of nobles was born who shared with the king his royal prerogatives. A feudal aristocracy was also developed and among the priests a similar process took place. The priests finally usurped a great many of the civil offices. Since they also were in charge of religious functions of the state government and wielded great power over the people in that capacity as religious leaders and healers, they acquired great wealth in the form of land and other possessions. Between 2000 and 1800 B. C. the high priests of the god Amon of the city of Thebes in southern Egypt ruled there as real pharaohs. Thus it became a relatively easy matter for invaders to overthrow the Egyptian government, which overthrow actually occurred about the year 1750 B. C., when an Asiatic people by the name of *Hyksos* invaded Egypt and ruled the country for about two hundred years.

The Empire. But the Hyksos were also in time overthrown, and now the Egyptians for the first time exhibited imperialistic ambitions. They staged a national revolt, and expelled the Hyksos from their soil. They then invaded western parts of Asia, conquered Syria, and finally reached the Euphrates River. From about 1550 to 1250 B. C. they maintained this new empire. Although they did not develop an efficient imperial form of government, they were fortunate in having a number of loyal native princes who ruled as governors under Egyptian sovereignty. The Egyptians also maintained strong garrisons at important points.

The Art of Warfare. Under the Old Kingdom the Egyptian army consisted of militia levies that were armed with spears, bows and arrows, daggers, and leather shields. From the peoples of ancient Mesopotamia they borrowed the idea of a horse-drawn chariot. They also improved their spears, and finally began to employ mercenary soldiers.

The Period of Decline. During the thirteenth and twelfth centuries B. C. a long period of decline set in which finally cul-

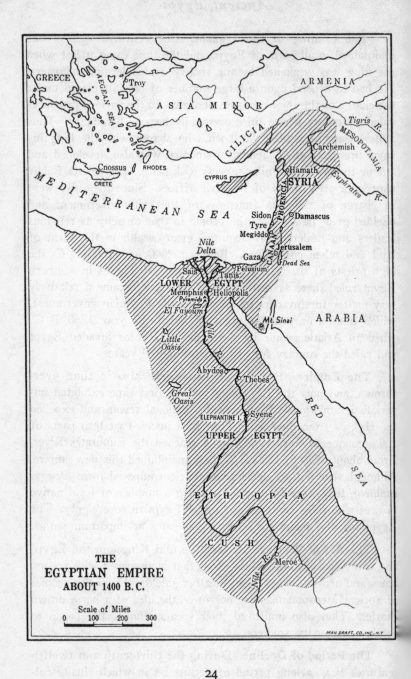

GREECE

AEGEAN SEA

Troy

ASIA MINOR

ARMENIA

Tigris R.

CILICIA

MESOPOTAMIA

Carchemish

Cnossus

RHODES

CRETE

CYPRUS

Hamath

SYRIA

Euphrates R.

MEDITERRANEAN SEA

Sidon
Tyre
Megiddo

Damascus

PHOENICIA

CANAAN

Nile
Delta

Gaza

Jerusalem

Dead Sea

Sais

Pelusium

Tanis

LOWER EGYPT

Memphis

Heliopolis

Pyramids

El Fayoum

Mt. Sinai

ARABIA

Nile R.

Little
Oasis

Abydos

Thebes

Great
Oasis

ELEPHANTINE I.

Syene

UPPER EGYPT

RED SEA

ETHIOPIA

CUSH

Meroë

Nile R.

THE
EGYPTIAN EMPIRE
ABOUT 1400 B.C.

Scale of Miles

0   100   200   300

MAN DRAFT. CO., INC. N.Y.

24

minated in the permanent annexation of Egypt by the Persians. In 730 B. C. Egypt was conquered by Ethiopia, while in 672 B. C. Assyria invaded and conquered the land. Then followed a short period of independence which was terminated by the Persian annexation in the year 525 B. C. About two hundred years later Alexander the Great conquered Egypt, while the Romans annexed Egypt during the first century B. C. At no time since the Persian conquest of 525 B. C. has Egypt led the world in important branches of human thought or enterprise.

AGRICULTURE, COMMERCE, AND INDUSTRY

The Development of Agriculture. For many centuries the annual floods of the Nile River determined the economic life of the Egyptians. Egypt was at all times an agrarian country, for the vast majority of Egyptians were employed in agriculture, either directly or indirectly. Agriculture was indeed the chief basis of prosperity. The fields were cultivated from November until May. The crops rapidly grew to maturity and were harvested. Principal grain crops were wheat and barley, and vegetables grown were the radish, bean, pea, lettuce, cucumber, and leek. There were also numerous vineyards and olive trees as well as date palms. Flax and cotton made possible the manufacture of linen and cotton goods. Oxen and donkeys were used as domestic animals. Rather primitive was the plough since it was a wooden implement, drawn by oxen and occasionally, when the soil was easily broken up, by the peasants. There were also sheep and goats, together with ducks, geese, swans, and doves. In a later period the chicken was introduced from India. Not long before the opening of our era the camel likewise was introduced, but before that time the donkey had been used for carrying burdens.

Industry. Since the Egyptians were able to grow more crops than they used themselves, they were in a position to exchange the surplus for copper mined in northern Arabia and on the island of Cyprus. They also imported wood from Syria, spices and incense from India and adjoining countries, and afterwards iron from Asia Minor. Both stone and brick were used for building purposes. Wooden boats were constructed at a relatively early date, as soon as the Egyptians found it desirable to extend their shipping from local areas to the coast of the northern Mediterranean and Indian Ocean. They ventured also into the Aegean Sea, where they taught the natives many elements of their superior culture. Frequently they exchanged raw materials for beautiful metalwork. The Egyptian craftsmen showed great artistic skill in dyeing linen cloth and in manufacturing glassware and pottery. They also produced exquisite figures in copper and bronze, while their furniture likewise testified to their extraordinary skill.

ARTS AND LITERATURE

Painting and Sculpture. The paintings of the Egyptians are remarkable for their accuracy. Although little distinction was drawn between light and shadow, and although very little or no attention was paid to perspective, the decorations upon the walls of the temples and other large buildings, portraying human and animal life, as well as lovely landscape scenery, show that the artists were endowed with a fertile imagination and were skillful in the employment of symbolism. They seem to have known a great deal about psychology and were given to religious and philosophical speculation. Lovely statues of kings and sacred animals were carved out of stone and wood, while bronze figures were also produced in abundance. Some of the stone figures were so huge as to weigh more than two million pounds each. Among the wonders of the ancient world may be reckoned the obelisks and the sphinxes.

Architecture. Even more impressive than the sculpture and the painting is the architecture of ancient Egypt. Constructed at Karnak is the magnificent temple of Amon, which contains huge stone blocks weighing eleven thousand pounds each. They were beautifully carved in the form of round cylinders and carefully piled on top of one another to form pillars. How the Egyptian architects and artists were able to transport such huge blocks of stone is still a mystery. They must have possessed engineering methods which perished with them.

The Pyramids. The greatest of the pyramids is the Great Pyramid of Cheops of Khufu, at Gizeh near Cairo. It was built in the reign of the pharaoh called Khufu, or Cheops, and the date is about 2500 B. C. It is the greatest monument of ancient Egypt.

Each side at the bottom is 755 feet long, while the height of the monument is 481 feet. It contains about two and a half million blocks of stone so carefully put together that perfection in measurements was reached within one ten-thousandth part of the length of each side. The joints between the blocks had a width of only one-thousandth part of an inch. Such was the skill of the ancient engineers of Egypt in 2500 B. C. that they could place blocks of five thousand pounds each having the sides cut with such minute care as to "equal the opticians' work of today," as one scholar has recently stated.

Literature and Writing. The Egyptians developed two chief forms of writing, the first of which is called *hieroglyphics,* meaning that they inscribed sacred characters upon stone, while the second form was called *hieratic,* or *demotic* (running script) for that was written with a pen made of reed on a piece of papyrus made out of the pith of a plant called papyrus. From this word "papyrus" our word "paper" is derived. The Egyptians did not at first use an alphabet such as we know today, but employed pictures, each of which had a definite meaning and also a definite sound. These sounds were only consonant sounds, for vowel sounds were not yet written down by them. For example, the picture of two arms raised up represented a soul or spirit, and also the sound *ka.* Egyptian literature consisted in historical novels, public records and annals, collections of fables and proverbs, love songs, that is, lyric poetry, and religious and philosophical treatises. The most important religious work is entitled *The Book of the Dead.*

SOCIAL CLASSES AND RELIGION

The Social Classes. In the opinion of the pharaoh, all persons were so far below him that they seemed to be equal. But naturally in a society which depended upon agriculture, commerce, and industry, it was impossible to maintain political and social equality. The nobles and the priests, as we saw, tended to increase both in number and in power. Three classes of people could easily be distinguished from one another. The upper classes were formed by the nobles and the priests. The middle class, as in ancient Sumeria and Babylonia, was made up of members of the professions, businessmen, and owners of industrial establishments. The masses constituted the serfs, that is, those bound to the soil and restricted in their liberties, but not as low as slaves. Nevertheless, the burdens of the serfs were so heavy and their liberties so restricted that many scholars have classified them among the slaves of antiquity. The important fact remains that their labor made possible the existence of a class of people having the necessary leisure to devote to the arts and the sciences. A real caste system did not exist in Egypt, for it was possible at all times to rise from one class to the other. It seems that the serfs as a special class belonged, as a rule, to the pharaoh. Slaves may have been employed at all times, but it is apparent that during the course of three or four thousand years one class would merge from time to time into the other.

The Position of Women. Women occupied an unusually favorable position in Egypt, enjoying unique privileges that were not known elsewhere until very recent times. Not only did women own property in their own name and right, but also only through the mother could property be inherited. It was also a common custom for queens to rule the country. Queens could even transmit to their children the right of kingship. One of the most important queens was Hatsheput.

Egyptian Religion. The religion of ancient Egypt was a mixture of other religions, some based largely upon those of native growth, while others upon those of foreign origin. The Egyptians believed in spirits, including those of human beings who had entered the realm of the dead. For the benefit of the spirit of a deceased person his body was carefully preserved (mummification). This would permit his spirit (*Ka*) to remain in the body for a long period of time. Somehow this art of mummification was lost to posterity. As a rule the mummy was placed in a beautiful tomb, where the *Ka* could be provided with various articles, including furniture and even the use of servants. As a matter of fact, the pyramids were no more and no less than huge tombs erected for the pharaohs. The Egyptians were of the opinion that a good life upon earth would be rewarded with happiness in the life hereafter. The souls of the deceased persons would enter the hall of the god Osiris, who was the ruler of the dead,

Other gods were Ra, the Sun God, and Isis (a goddess). The Egyptians worshipped natural forces and also showed respect and reverence for sacred animals, such as the crocodile, the cat, and the bull. Such animals were kept in the temples where they were given almost as much reverence as the god himself. Various local districts had their own special gods. But some gods began to acquire national importance, which was the case, for example, with Amon of Thebes. For a short time Egypt was ruled by a remarkable pharaoh, called Ikhnaton, who believed in monotheism, and endeavored fanatically to enforce his religion upon his country. But monotheism was not supported by the masses.

EGYPTIAN CONTRIBUTIONS TO THE MAKING OF WESTERN CIVILIZATION

The Beginnings of the Alphabet. Reference has already been made to the system of writing developed by the Egyptians. Now it remains to show how their system affected later peoples. Originally, Egyptian writing was only pictorial, and as such it was of no great historical importance. About 600 pictures were used, and many of them could be employed to represent more than one object. But in the course of some centuries each picture came to stand for some definite object and idea. A sign was used for a syllable, and the syllables were combined to represent words. Eventually the picture signs were intended no longer to convey to the reader the original object shown by the picture, but merely the syllable or the sound. In this manner the phonetic writing was created. Somewhere between 3000 and 2700 B. C. twenty-four definite signs were developed, each of which typified a real sound, though it was only a consonant. These twenty-four consonant sounds represent the earliest alphabet developed in the ancient world. Although most of the Egyptian writers refused to make use of this convenient script, and clung to the pictures of former ages, the original alphabet had been made and was imitated subsequently by other peoples.

Writing Materials. In addition to the invention of paper and pen, the Egyptians made use of ink that was manufactured from water, carbon, and gums.

Decipherment of Ancient Egyptian Writings. Until the end of the eighteenth century European scholars were unable to decipher the hieroglyphics of ancient Egypt. In Egypt itself the ability to read those hieroglyphics was no longer possible after 300 B. C. But it seems that a number of priests who possessed many secrets concerning mummification, the art of healing, and the mysteries of the spirit world, still knew how to decipher this ancestral script. The public at large no longer understood the symbols of old. But it so happened that a slab of black basalt, bearing a trilingual inscription, was found in 1799 by one of Napoleon's soldiers and supplied Champollion with the first clue for deciphering hieroglyphics. The Rosetta stone, so-called after the town Rosetta in Egypt where it was found, is now in the British Museum in London. On this stone there had been inscribed in three different languages—Greek, hieroglyphics, and hieratic—the decree of a ruler, dated 196 B. C. Thus scholars were able to decipher and translate the ancient symbols of Egyptian writing. Unfortunately, however, the scholars that Napoleon had taken to Egypt with him were not able to do this work, since most of them were interested chiefly in the natural sciences. But in 1822 a French historian named Champollion made a careful study of an obelisk upon which were inscribed royal names in both Greek and Egyptian letters. He saw that the Egyptians had made use of a real alphabet and of the twenty-four consonant sounds he learned twelve. Thus, with the use of the Rosetta Stone other scholars began to decipher the writings upon the walls of the temples and upon obelisks.

Influence of the Egyptian Alphabet. In recent years archeologists have demonstrated that on the Sinai Peninsula and in southern Palestine alphabetic writing was known during the nineteenth century B. C. This was an imitation of the Egyptian alphabet. The Hebrews appear to have used an alphabet of twenty-one consonant sounds before the fifteenth century B. C. They probably passed their knowledge of the alphabet on to the Phoenicians, who in turn transmitted it to the Greeks. It was the Greeks who added the sounds of vowels to make the complete alphabet, as will appear.

Reform of the Calendar. In 2776 B. C. the Egyptians perfected the solar calendar, establishing the calendar year of 365 days. This year consisted of twelve months of thirty days each, to which five days were added at the end of the twelfth month. This was a much more satisfactory calendar than that employed by the inhabitants of ancient Mesopotamia. Since the calendar year of the Egyptians was one-fourth of a day too short, scholars afterwards found it necessary to improve this calendar, but nothing definite was done in this direction until the time of Julius Caesar about 50 B. C. But even this reform was not entirely satisfactory to European scholars, so that in the year 1582, the final form was introduced, the one which has been accepted since that time by all European peoples. The Egyptians, in measuring the time of day and night, invented the sun dial and water clock. Unlike the ancient Babylonians and their descendants, the Egyptians were not interested in astrology.

Mathematical Discoveries. Since Egyptian engineers had to measure the irrigated lands and the courses of ditches and canals at a very early time they became interested in geometry. They calculated the cubic contents of silos that were erected on a circular base and made other mathematical computations for practical purposes. Their unit for numbers was ten (decimal system).

Medicine. During the Old Kingdom great progress was made in medicine. Much was known about anatomy and mummification. In the temples great medical schools were maintained. A careful study was made of all the diseases known in the ancient Near East, and these were catalogued, differentiated, and classified according to their symptoms. But, unfortunately, too much attention was paid to magic instead of to scientific diagnosis. Excellent work was done in bone surgery and in the study of the blood. It was well known that the heart was the center of the circulatory system of the blood. In the treatment of wounds much progress was also made. Salt solutions were used for disinfecting, and alkaline appliations were employed in treating physical injuries. Many of the discoveries in mathematics and medicine were passed on by the Egyptians to the Greeks. The same may be said, as the famous Greek historian Herodotus testified, for the religion of the Egyptians.

Influence Exerted Through the Hebrews. As is well known, a number of Hebrew tribes lived in Egypt during the course of several centuries. Among them lived the learned Moses, who had been instructed at the court of an Egyptian princess during the fifteenth century B. C. From time to time a number of Israelites left Egypt and moved to Palestine. The greatest migration occurred under the leadership of Moses, as is carefully discussed in the opening books of the Bible. The language of the ancient Hebrews was undoubtedly affected to a great extent by that of the ancient Egyptians. Furthermore, the conception of God as a dual personality, and of heaven as a double heaven, the Hebrews must have derived from the Egyptians. Although the Egyptian laws are not known to scholars at the present time, there can be no doubt that the famous law of Moses owed more to the Egyptian laws than to those of Hammurapi. During the Middle Ages and in early modern times it was customary for leaders in the Christian Church to refer to the experiences of the Hebrews in Egypt. Martin Luther, for example, first great leader among the Protestants, said in some of his writings that political and social institutions should be modeled after conditions that prevailed in Egypt during the stay there of the Hebrews. He thought that an excellent way of paying taxes, rents, and interest on borrowed money was to give from one-tenth to one-fifth of the proceeds from land and business to the state in the form of taxes. He referred specifically to the experience of Joseph and the Israelites and the Egyptians who were ruled by him.

Influence Exerted Through the Cretans and the Greeks. The superb architecture, sculpture, and painting of the Egyptians; their highly developed commerce, which extended far into the Aegean Sea; the marvelous manner in which they controlled the course of the Nile, which called forth the admiration of Herodotus and other Greek writers; the conception of a number of gods worshipped by the Egyptians and taken over bodily by the

Greeks; the rôle played by the priesthood in Egypt and the wealth of religious and philosophical and scientific knowledge possessed by the priests and maintained by them for three or four thousand years; the extraordinary knowledge of the human body, which could not fail to attract the attention of Greek scholars; and the numerous discoveries made by the Egyptians in the fields of mathematics and the natural sciences, many of which were not recorded by history—these gifts bequeathed by Egyptian civilization to the lands immediately to the north of them, that is, to the island of Crete, the islands of the Aegean Sea, and the mainland of Asia Minor and the Balkan peninsula, were passed on by the highly civilized Cretans and Greeks to the Romans, and by the Romans in turn to the peoples of the medieval and modern world.

The Object Lesson of Ancient Egypt. Ancient Egypt witnessed a phenomenon which exactly duplicated that seen in ancient Mesopotamia. In the latter region the Sumerians from 4000 to 3000 B. C. developed a higher type of civilization than the countries of Mesopotamia knew perhaps until the seventh or sixth century B. C. The same thing happened in ancient Egypt, for almost all the important discoveries made in the fields of science and the arts were achieved during the period of the Old Kingdom, that is, before 2700 B. C. All that later generations of Egyptians could do apparently was to hand down the great gifts of their highly skilled ancestors. These two remarkable phenomena displayed in Mesopotamia and Egypt seem to prove that at one time, that is, between 4000 and 2700 B. C., human beings developed an extraordinarily high level of culture. Much of this knowledge was of a mysterious type and was not recorded upon stone or papyrus or tablet. Even that which is now known to scholars is of such a nature that everybody recognizes a marked superiority of the Egyptians of the Old Kingdom and of the ancient Sumerians over their successors for a period of more than two thousand years.* There can be no question that from 4000 to 3000 B. C. unique contributions were made by the Sumerians and the

* All this appears to negate the application of the evolutionary theory of mankind. For the historian, consequently, the safest course is to observe the laws of growth and of decay.

Egyptians, some of which were entirely lost by posterity, while
others were with great difficulty preserved. It was not until the
Golden Age of Greek civilization in the fifth century B. C. that
another people arose to equal and, in some respects, to surpass
the Sumerians and Egyptians of old. But even these Greeks of
the fifth century B. C. received and frankly acknowledged a great
many gifts from both Egypt and Mesopotamia.

CHAPTER IV.

THE HEBREWS, THE ARAMAEANS, AND THE PHOENICIANS

Among the peoples of the ancient world the Hebrews did not occupy a prominent position, for they were but a small nation. They possessed few great cities with magnificent temples and palaces in their little country. Nevertheless, they contributed a large share of the making of western civilization. Their religion and their literature, as well as their code of laws, were so superior to all similar gifts bequeathed by the ancient Near East that they certainly deserve detailed study.

EARLY HISTORY OF THE HEBREWS

Abraham in the City of Ur. According to the Bible story, Abraham was the progenitor of the Hebrew race, which is the only race dating back to the ancient world that has retained its existence and characteristics until this day. There was a time, not long ago, that Abraham was looked upon by scholars as a legendary character, while his native city, Ur, seemed but an empty name. Its location was unknown until 1924. For was it not assumed for decades that civilization gradually blossomed forth until about 2000 B. C. when Mesopotamia had a culture worth

35

noting? Now we know that when Abraham lived in Ur, the city was but a ghost of its former self. On the site of Ur there has recently been unearthed lovely painted pottery which dates from about 3000 B. C., that is, 800 years before Abraham was born.

Abraham's Position in Society. Another remarkable fact is Abraham's position as the owner of flocks. He was once supposed to be but a mere nomad, wandering from place to place in search of food for his cattle. The spades of the industrious excavators have revealed, however, that when Abraham issued forth from Ur about 2150 B. C., in order to settle in Palestine, persons in his position were highly honored by kings and princes. As one authority observes, such persons as Abraham "were princely rulers, who hired out their flocks and their shepherds, and ruled over their properties."

The Geography of Canaan. Canaan was the name of the country which Abraham visited. Later it was called Palestine, after the Philistines, who are mentioned so often in the Bible. In Abraham's time Canaan was but thinly populated, and, as in the time of Jacob, it was not always able to provide its inhabitants with sufficient food. Abraham was obliged at one time to go to Egypt to buy food. There is no doubt that Canaan was in touch with both Mesopotamia and Egypt. But the country differed considerably from the lowlands of Egypt and Babylonia. The climate was not so hot and dry. Unfortunately, much of the soil was mountainous and rocky, and only in the spring and late summer were the rains abundant. However, valleys were to be found in various parts, and pasture lands were upon the whole excellent.

The Ancient Hebrews. Here Abraham and his descendants lived with their flocks. They learned also to cultivate the soil. As the population increased, some of Abraham's descendants became actively interested in commerce and industry, but it may be said that throughout the long history of the Hebrew nation only a small proportion of the people lived in the towns. As long as the Hebrews remained in their native land, they were noted as a pastoral people. Many of them, however, cultivated the fields, grew olive and fig trees, and produced grain crops.

THE RISE AND FALL OF THE HEBREW KINGDOM

The Government. Until about the year 1025 B. C. the government of the Hebrews may be described as a theocracy, that is, a rule of a people by the church or a priesthood. First under Moses, then under the judges, and finally under the prophets, the Israelites or Hebrews were firmly held together, though they were divided into twelve tribes. Under King Saul, who ruled about the year 1020 B. C., the Hebrews became a united nation. Saul, however, was barely able to defend the country against the Philistines to the southwest.

David and Solomon. But it was his successor, King David, who enlarged the nation far beyond its earlier borders, so that it now included a comparatively large district east of the Jordan River, and the region stretching to the north of the Sea of Galilee. David conquered the city of Jerusalem and made it the national capital. Under David's son, Solomon, the country reached its greatest prosperity, but, owing to the heavy taxation and other burdens levied upon the people by their ambitious king, many of his subjects became disappointed with his rule, and several leaders wished that they had never asked for a monarch but had remained under the rule of God and his priesthood. On the death of Solomon about the year 940 B. C., the kingdom was divided into two parts: the north was called Israel, and the south Judah.

Fall of the Kingdoms of Israel and Judah. These two kingdoms were ruled by separate monarchs, until in 722 B. C. the Assyrians conquered the northern kingdom with its capital, Samaria, and carried off a large proportion of the inhabitants to Mesopotamia. Those who are familiar with the record of the history of Israel as presented in the Bible will understand why the kingdom was destroyed so soon. They also will recall the wretched fate of the southern kingdom, which, after having been ruled by several wicked kings, fell in 586 B. C. before the army of Nebuchadnezzar, the king of Babylonia. Once more a large number of Hebrews were deported to Mesopotamia, but fifty years later, in 536 B. C., when a Persian king ruled over Babylonia, the Hebrews living there were permitted to return to Palestine. Some did so forthwith, but a large number of them chose to remain, and their descendants spread over various lands of the ancient world, including Egypt. After the destruction of the two Hebrew kingdoms just mentioned, the Hebrews were generally called the Jews.

The Lost Tribes of Israel. Since so many of them remained outside of Palestine, the sources in several countries speak of the "lost tribes of Israel." And one day when Jesus of Nazareth had preached a powerful sermon and had talked about taking His departure, some people wondered whether He was going to preach to the lost tribes of Israel.

Many Jews Become Businessmen. Not all the Jews remained herdsmen or farmers. Many of them became talented businessmen, bankers, or scholars. Since their laws did not permit them to make loans at interest to their own people but allowed them to charge interest to Gentiles, they were encouraged to transact business with foreigners and to lend their money freely to them. Furthermore, the Christian nations of the Middle Ages did not favor the loaning of money at interest by Christians, because of the laws of the Hebrews, which they had accepted as binding upon themselves. Consequently, it became customary for Christians to borrow money from the Jews, and so it happened naturally that the Jews became the leading bankers in some European countries. Since they were often persecuted and excluded from many crafts and professions, they tended to band together and support each other.

The Hebrews Who Remained in Palestine. The Hebrews who continued to live in Palestine never acquired great material wealth. For one thing, the country was very small, only about ten thousand square miles in area. And, as we observed, much of the soil was very poor. During the long summers there was seldom enough rain. Minerals and forests were also lacking. When King Solomon desired to build a great temple in honor of Jehova, he was obliged to fetch the lumber from regions to the north and metal from countries to the south. He even had to employ foreign architects and workmen, and when he had finished the structure, it was but a mediocre building compared with the huge temples of Mesopotamia and the vast structures of Egypt.

THE HERITAGE OF ISRAEL

Literary Contributions. The Hebrews made greater contributions to the development of western civilization than did some of the large empires, such as Assyria, for example. Though they failed to produce great mathematicians, sculptors, painters, and scientists, they more than made up for this apparent neglect by giving to the western world their superb literature, their enlightened code of laws, and their unique religion. The Old Testament contains possibly the oldest history of the human race up to the time of Abraham. Moreover, the prophetic and the poetical books show an overwhelming superiority over all similar productions of the ancient world, including India and China. There is certainly nothing in the literature of Egypt and Babylonia that can at all be compared with the book of Psalms and the prophetical books by Isaiah, Jeremiah, Ezekiel, and Daniel.

The Code of Moses. Even the celebrated code of Hammurapi is but a simple and crude document when studied side by side with the much more extensive code of Moses found in the first five books of the Old Testament. Although Hammurapi's code is about six hundred years older than that of Moses, there is no need of drawing the conclusion that for this reason Moses must have copied the older code, but there are many parallels. Possibly both codes had a common Semitic source, for they repeat certain older laws and theories, such as that of "an eye for an eye and a tooth for a tooth." If a person knocked out a tooth in the mouth of another person, he would have to forfeit one of his teeth, as we have already seen. But the peculiarity of Hammurapi's code is that this was required only if a person of prestige had lost his tooth. In case a wealthy man knocked out several teeth of a poorer person, he merely paid a small fine.

Hebrew Laws Are Superior. The code of Moses places a comparatively high value on human life and requires kind treatment of slaves. It demands proper care of the poor and of strangers, something neglected by the Babylonians. The code of Moses required that witchcraft and idolatrous sacrifices be punishable by death, but the Babylonian lawgivers thought such practices were not wrong. The reason for the difference is simple. The Hebrews were expected to trust in God and His prophets, who would tell them all they had to know. There was no need to resort to mediums and ask questions of spirits of departed persons. Thus we read in the first book of Samuel that when King Saul refused to listen to Samuel any longer and God would not tell him anything worth his while in dreams, and when he went to see a "witch," that is, in this case a medium, he committed a serious crime.

The Hebrew Religion. The Hebrews had a unique religion in that they as a whole nation were obliged to worship only one God. There were other peoples in antiquity among whom monotheism was practiced by a few individuals, and in Egypt Ikhnaton had tried to enforce monotheism in the country, but such cases were exceptional. The Hebrews alone had a God who was not like human beings, but a spiritual force. True, Moses was once asked by God to view His glory in physical form, but we are not informed that God had a body like that of human beings. The Hebrews alone were prohibited from considering their kings as more than purely mortal beings in their capacity as rulers, and as descendants of the gods. Even the Romans, as we shall see, came to worship their emperors. At the beginning, before the Flood, monotheism was not often practised in the ancient world.

The Influence of This Religion. Through the influence of the Christian religion the thoughts of the Hebrew prophets, judges, and singers were made known to all the western nations of modern times. The literature of England, Germany, France, Spain, and Italy cannot always be understood without a knowledge of the Old Testament. Indeed, more than that, the whole history of the western world bears the imprint of the Hebrew mind. Every Sunday our great department stores remain closed all day. No great university would require class attendance on the Christian sabbath. Not even the atheistic leaders of the French Revolution were able to destroy this hallowed custom of "six days shalt thou labor" out of each week. Calendars have changed, but the week of seven days has survived all revolutions and all inventions. These are but a few instances out of thousands to show how vast is the power of the Hebrew religion. Surpassing by far that of Greek mythology, it has continued to shed its light upon the West wherever Christians have trod. There was a time when New England was dominated by the code of Moses, and surely the student of history in America can no longer shut his eyes to the influence of the Hebrews.

The Hebrew Alphabet. Until very recently the credit for the origin of our alphabet was given to the Phoenicians, a Semitic people living immediately to the north of Palestine. They were interested primarily in commerce and industry, and from their famous ports they sent out their many ships to trade in all parts of the Mediterranean Sea. Many scholars did not ask whether a people like the Phoenicians, so devoid of literary talents and so little interested in philosophy and religion, could really have originated the alphabet.

The Hebrews Pass on Their Alphabet to the Phoenicians. Recent excavations upon the site of Lachish, the chief walled city of Judah, have revealed that the Hebrews contributed much to the invention of the alphabet and probably passed on their knowledge to the Phoenicians, while the latter instructed the Greeks. From the Greeks in turn the Romans derived their alphabet, but the common source of all may be that devised by the Hebrews about the fourteenth century B. C. During the wanderings of the Hebrews on the Sinai Peninsula they had learned to develop the rudiments of their alphabet, which was fully completed by the middle of the fourteenth century B. C.

THE PHOENICIANS

The Land and the People. North of Palestine lived the Phoenicians, who, like the Hebrews, belonged to the Semitic race. Their country was too mountainous to make possible a flourishing agriculture on any large scale, with the result that the Phoenicians turned toward the sea for a living. They became the most enterprising merchants in the period from 1200 to 350 B. C.

Their Chief Ports and Colonies. As early as 2700 B. C. the Egyptians began to trade with the Phoenician port of Byblos, or Gebal. From about 1550 to 1200 B. C. Palestine (Canaan) and Phoenicia formed a province of Egypt. But after 1200 B. C.

the Phoenicians surpassed the Egyptians as traders. First Sidon, then Tyre, became a world-famed port, from which the Phoenicians carried on their commerce with Egypt, the coasts of Asia Minor, the Balkan Peninsula, Italy, and the western Mediterranean. Their chief colony was the mighty port of Carthage, which in the sixth century B. C. was the largest city in northern Africa, with a population of about 750,000. They also founded flourishing industries, such as the manufacture of metalwork, glassware, objects made of ivory, and a beautiful purple dye extracted from a shellfish. Their purple textiles were indeed highly prized in many lands. Moreover, the Phoenicians possessed valuable forests of cedar, which grew upon the slopes of the Lebanon Mountains.

Their Religion and Literary Attainments. They worshipped many gods, the best-known of which was Baal. Their religious literature was very much inferior to that of the Hebrews. Greatly overestimated, moreover, was their contribution to the shaping of our alphabet, although from them the Greeks did obtain the names of most of the letters, *aleph* becoming *alpha,* and *beth, beta;* hence the word *alphabet,* named after the first two letters of the Greek alphabet.

THE ARAMAEANS

The People. Both the Hebrews and the Phoenicians were closely related to and strongly affected by another people called the Aramaeans. They lived in the region to the east, much of which was a part of the Syrian desert. With the decline of the Hittite rule in northern Syria, the Aramaeans constructed important cities of their own, including Damascus, where they set up a monarchic form of government. From about 850 to 732 B. C. they protected the Hebrews against the Assyrians, although they were usually unfriendly to the kingdom of Israel. In 732 B. C. their state fell before the hosts of Assyria.

History after 732 B. C. From Damascus the Aramaeans traded with all their neighbors, gradually extending their lucrative commerce to distant lands. They adopted the Phoenician alphabetic writing and spread it into India. Such was their influence that from 750 to 606 B. C. the weights employed in commercial transactions throughout Syria and Assyria carried in practically all instances Aramaic names.

The Aramaic Language. Even in Palestine the Aramaic language became very popular, so that by the time of Jesus of Nazareth it had supplanted the old Hebrew tongue. Jesus Himself used the Aramaic tongue, and some of the books of the Old Testament were written in that language. In Mesopotamia the Aramaeans were able to introduce their script, with the result that cuneiform writing ceased altogether. In this instance "the pen was mightier than the sword."

Significant Dates

Establishment of Assyrian Empire	745 B.C.
Fall of Assyria	606 B.C.
Fall of Babylon	538 B.C.
Egypt Annexed by Persia	525 B.C.

CHAPTER V.

THE ASSYRIAN AND PERSIAN EMPIRES

During the twelfth century B. C., when Babylon was rapidly declining, when the Egyptians lost their hold upon Syria and parts of Arabia, and when the Hittites also became subject to decay and deterioration, the Assyrians grasped the opportunity presented by their weakened neighbors and founded a kingdom of considerable power that afterward grew into a real empire. The Assyrians conquered Babylonia, Syria, and Egypt. But, in spite of great political power, they were unable to emulate either the Sumerians or the Egyptians of old in the arts or sciences. In literature and religion they also were merely imitators. When their turn came to decline at last, they were conquered by the Persians, an Indo-European people who had come out of the eastern plateaus of Iran. Sometimes these people were also called Aryan, an adjective derived from the noun "Iran." The Persians constructed the greatest empire that the world had ever known, but it was to be of relatively short duration, lasting less than three hundred years. It was overthrown during the fourth century B. C. by Alexander the Great. The Persians not only were successful upon the battlefield, but they also mastered the art of governing

44

subject peoples. They made great contributions, as we shall see, to the system of imperial government. Furthermore, they likewise surpassed the Assyrians in developing a remarkable and influential religion of their own. Interesting also is the interlude between the fall of Assyria and the establishment of Persia as a great empire. This is the period of the New Babylonia. From 606 to 538 B. C. Babylonia was the most magnificent city in the world, but sudden and great was its fall.

THE ASSYRIAN EMPIRE

Political History of Assyria after 1000 B. C. Shortly before the year 900 B. C. the Assyrians began their expansion in all directions. At first they tried in vain to subjugate Babylonia. But they succeeded in checking the invaders to the north of Syria, part of which they were able to annex. Under Shalmaneser III (860-825 B. C.) the Assyrians defeated an alliance of Israel, Syria, and Phoenicia. In 842 B. C. the king of Assyria compelled the Israelites to pay a tribute to him. The next-king extended the frontiers of Assyria to the Persian Gulf. Then followed the annexation of the Aramaean kingdom in 732 B. C. and the conquest of Israel in 722 B. C. Under Sargon II (722-705 B. C.) the empire of the Assyrians attained its zenith. During his reign about 200,000 persons were deported from conquered lands to Mesopotamia. Among these were many thousands of Hebrews. Babylon, which had been conquered by his predecessor, and which had risen in rebellion, was subdued once more in 709 B. C. Asia Minor was also conquered as far to the west as the Halys River. But during the second half of the seventh century B. C. the Assyrians suddenly underwent a swift decline, terminated by the fall of their great capital, Nineveh, in 612 B. C. and the total destruction of the state in 606 B. C.

The Government of the Assyrian Empire. Unlike the ancient Babylonians and Egyptians, the Assyrians were able to establish a highly efficient government of the conquered lands. The administration of the provinces was excellent. The king established a royal postal service, and was kept in constant touch with the conquered territories through the official letters and reports. The king of Assyria established an absolute form of government

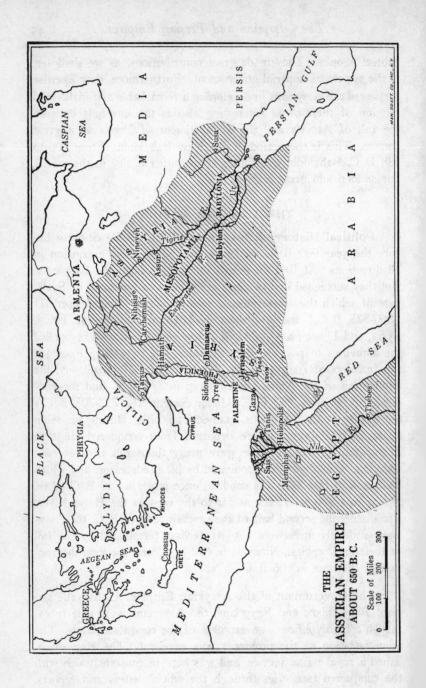

THE
ASSYRIAN EMPIRE
ABOUT 650 B.C.

Scale of Miles
0   100   200   300

with a hereditary kingship. His officials were responsible to him alone, while he as civil ruler and as head of the priesthood was not responsible to the people at large but only to the national god Ashur. Although many of the cities enjoyed a large amount of local independence (*autonomy*), they were nevertheless firmly ruled by the national administration.

Economic Developments. Since Assyria was a large state in which a relatively small amount of land could be cultivated, most of the wealth of Assyria was concentrated in and near the city of Nineveh, the great capital. Commerce was extensive, but was carried on for the most part by foreigners. The Assyrians preferred to attend to agricultural duties. Like the Spaniards of a later age, they preferred that commerce and industry be administered by despised industrial workers. As we have seen, the Aramaeans were the traders of the empire. Most of the land was held by the king who passed on much of it to his officers and the temples, as well as to some of the city-states, where a large number of free farmers or peasants also held land of their own. Moreover, there were serfs, as in Egypt, who received the use of lands partly in return for labor and partly in return for one-third of the crops produced on these lands.

Assyrian Art of Warfare. One reason why the Assyrians paid so little attention to commerce was that as a rule they were preoccupied with the arts of warfare. From the Hittites they learned how to use iron in improving their arms. They employed both infantry and cavalry, but no longer used the old unwieldly chariot. Their soldiers were armed with lances, swords, bows and arrows, breastplates, helmets, and shields. They developed an excellent technique in attacking fortified cities. Since such cities as a rule were surrounded by walls made of brick, they were easily torn down. Unspeakable cruelties attended the seizure of cities and rural districts. The Assyrian Empire was truly built on military despotism.

Learning and Art. In keeping with the huge size of the Assyrian Empire, the rulers saw fit to have enormous palaces and temples constructed. These were built upon a stone foundation, but the structure itself was made of brick, although the columns were of stone. From the Babylonians they learned the use of the arch, but used it much more extensively than the Babylonians themselves had done. The palaces comprised a number of courts, each of which was surrounded by a large number of rooms. Within the central enclosure there was built a great tower temple. The building as a whole was fortified with heavy walls and the customary towers and gates. Assyrian sculpture is not impressive, for the figures of human beings seem inanimate. On the other hand, great skill was displayed in depicting animals, particularly lions. Even so, this work was no more than an imitation of what had been done in Babylonia two thousand years before. Their writing was also an imitation of the Babylonian, while afterwards the Assyrians imitated the Aramaeans. But they surpassed the Babylonians in the size of libraries built by kings. From the library of King Assur-bani-pal 22,000 tablets have been recovered, some of which contain interesting work on science, history, mathematics, and the royal administration. But it can not be said that important contributions were made either in these literary types or fields of thought.

Assyrian Religion. In the field of religion also the Assyrians failed to make notable contributions.* They adopted the Babylonian god Marduk, but retained their own god Ashur. Since they were much less polytheistically inclined than the Babylonians, they seemed to reflect some degree of independence. The priests in Assyria had much less power than those in Babylonia, because the king for the most part concentrated religious functions in his own hands. Like the Babylonians and the Egyptians, the Assyrians believed that the spirits of the dead remained for a long time near the corpses. Nevertheless, they made use of cremation.

THE NEW BABYLONIA

Political History. The peoples who overthrew the Assyrian Empire between 612 and 606 B. C. were the Medes, the Persians, and the inhabitants of ancient Babylonia. The Medes about

---

* It is probably inadvisable to credit the theory that between 722 and 612 B. C. the Assyrians exerted great influence upon the Hebrew prophets—when the latter, for example, are said to have written a number of legends which make up the book of Genesis.

1000 B. C. had constructed a state of their own to the east of Mesopotamia. They established a kingdom during the eighth century B. C., and during the second half of the seventh century B. C. they allied themselves with the Babylonians to overthrow the Assyrian Empire. In 625 B. C. the Babylonians had established their independence under a king of their own, who was succeeded by his famous son Nebuchadnezzar (604-561 B. C.). This ruler proceeded to extend the boundaries of the new kingdom until in 587 B. C. he appeared with a huge army before the city of Jerusalem in the kingdom of Judah. After a siege of eight months the city fell, its temple was burned, and thousands of Jews were exiled to Babylonia. However, he was not able to subjugate the whole of Phoenicia, since its port, Tyre, was impregnable. But when in 561 B. C. Nebuchadnezzar died, the new state began a rapid decline. In 538 B. C. Babylonia was captured by the Persians.

Babylon under Nebuchadnezzar. So large was Babylon during the sixth century B. C. that its walls had a circumference of thirteen miles. The outer wall was constructed of brick and was about eighty-five feet thick. No other city of the ancient world had walls that thick. The principal streets were beautifully laid out and crossed each other at right angles. Imposing in particular was the huge palace of Nebuchadnezzar, the courtyard of which alone measured 193 by 180 feet. One of the rooms measured 171 by 56 feet. The building was constructed of glazed (or enameled) brick, but even more impressive in the eyes of visitors from foreign lands were the so-called Hanging Gardens, which were roof gardens in the form of terraces where grew magnificent plants and tropical flowers. Another great structure was the Temple of Marduk, near which was constructed a temple tower upon a platform three hundred feet square. Some writers are of the opinion that this temple tower of Nebuchadnezzar induced a certain Hebrew writer to contribute to the book of Genesis his account of the Tower of Babel. Such seems an unnecessary conclusion, inasmuch as temple towers of this type—the so-called *ziggurat*—were constructed in ancient Mesopotamia long before the book of Genesis was written by Moses during the fifteenth century B. C.

Babylonian Civilization during the Sixth Century B. C.
At this time Babylon was the largest and most prosperous city in the world, with a population estimated at half a million. Commerce unquestionably reached a height never before seen in Mesopotamia. All the luxuries of the ancient Near East were brought together in this one city. Side by side with the thousands upon thousands of slaves and down-trodden free laborers, there existed a class of society bitterly criticized by some of the Hebrew prophets. The latter claimed that the city was doomed because of its luxurious and wicked mode of living. Contributions made by the city during the brief reign of splendor under Nebuchadnezzar to the making of western civilization are very meager indeed. Only in the field of astrology did the Babylonians excel. Inasmuch as the state often was called Chaldea and its inhabitants of the sixth century B. C. the Chaldeans, one speaks usually of Chaldean astrology in designating that which was in vogue during the sixth century B. C. Even in the time of the Romans, eight hundred years later, it was still customary to speak of Chaldeans as experts in the field of astrology. It is generally assumed that the wise men from the East who are mentioned in the Gospel of Luke, and who are said to have seen the star of Jesus Christ in the East, were Chaldean astrologers. Of such importance in the eyes of the Babylonians were the planets that the astrological beliefs passed on from Chaldea to the Romans later affected the West, and three days out of the week in the English language pay reference to them, that is, the day of the sun (Sunday), the day of the moon (Monday) and the day of Saturn (Saturday).

THE PERSIAN EMPIRE

Political History. The Persians originally lived on the plateau called Iran. About the year 550 B. C. they were led by an important ruler called Cyrus the Great. But as yet they were allied with and dominated by the Medes. In 549 B. C. Cyrus overthrew the Medean government and seized its capital. Now the Persians became the masters of the Medes. In 539 B. C. Cyrus attacked Babylon, which fell in the next year. Upon his death in 529 B. C. his son Cambyses succeeded him. The latter made a permanent conquest of Egypt in 525 B. C., something which the

Assyrians had never been able to achieve. Cambyses was succeeded in turn by Darius (521-485 B. C.), who is chiefly known for his attempted conquest of the Greek city-states.

The Rise and Fall of Lydia. When in 546 B. C. King Cyrus conquered the kingdom of Lydia in Asia Minor, he found there one of the most remarkable states of antiquity. Here lived a king of fabulous wealth called Croesus, whose name is still used when reference is made to persons of exceedingly great wealth. It was one of the first countries to establish the use of a coinage. The Lydians, like the Persians, belonged to an Indo-European race, and not to the Semitic race. They had succeeded the Hittites as the dominating power in Asia Minor. It was during the eighth century B. C. that the Lydians invented the use of metallic coinage, which differed from the gold and silver bars used by the Assyrians and other merchants in that they were stamped with a statement saying that the government guaranteed the correct weight and purity of the metal used in making the coins. The first coins seem to have been made from gold and silver smelted with some alloy. The standard gold coin of Lydia was called the *stater*. Being engrossed in the making of money and the extension of commerce, the Lydians had failed to prepare adequate defense against the coming Persians, and so it naturally happened that their kingdom was quickly destroyed by King Cyrus.

The Government of the Persian Empire. Establishing peace and order in the unwieldy state stretching from the borders of India to the waters of the Aegean Sea and the lands beyond the river Nile, was a difficult task. But the Assyrians had led the way in empire building and in excellent administration of conquered provinces. The Persians improved on the system of the Assyrians, with the result that for more than two hundred years all the dominions were firmly held together by the Persian ruler in his capital Susa or Persepolis. One reason for the success of the Persian administration was that the conquered peoples enjoyed religious toleration. Moreover, taxes were carefully levied and commerce and industry were promoted by the central government. The king was a hereditary monarch, who said that he was responsible only to the chief god, Ahura-Mazda. This was not unusual, since even Hammurapi had followed this course, as we

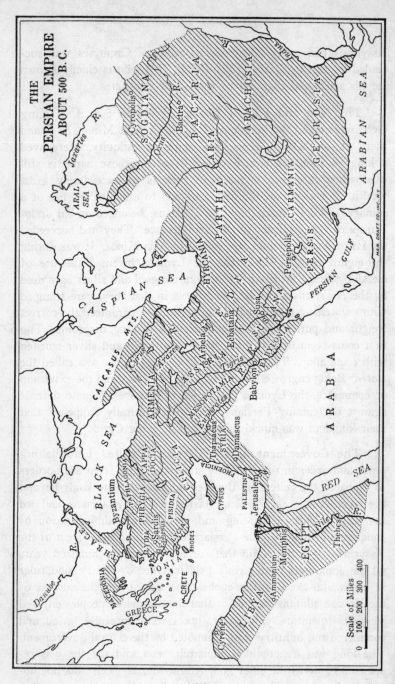

THE
PERSIAN EMPIRE
ABOUT 500 B.C.

MAP DRAFT CO. INC. N.Y.

ARAL
SEA

Jaxartes R.

Cyropolis

SOGDIANA

Oxus

Bactra

BACTRIA

ARIA

ARACHOSIA

Indus R.

GEDROSIA

ARABIAN SEA

CASPIAN SEA

CAUCASUS MTS.

PARTHIA

MEDIA

Cyrus R.

Araxes R.

ARMENIA

ASSYRIA

Arbela

HYRCANIA

CARMANIA

Persepolis

PERSIS

PERSIAN GULF

BLACK SEA

Ecbatana

Susa

SUSIANA

Tigris R.

MESOPOTAMIA

Euphrates R.

BABYLONIA

Babylon

ARABIA

THRACE

Danube R.

PAPHLAGONIA

Byzantium

CAPPADOCIA

PHRYGIA

LYDIA

Sardis

Ephesus

PISIDIA

CILICIA

Thapsacus

SYRIA

Damascus

PHOENICIA

Tyre

PALESTINE

Jerusalem

CYPRUS

IONIA

RHODES

CRETE

MACEDONIA

GREECE

RED SEA

EGYPT

Memphis

Thebes

Nile R.

LIBYA

Ammonium

Cyrene

Scale of Miles
0 100 200 300 400

52

saw. But the king was careful to consult his chief ministers, and he paid careful attention to local customs everywhere. The administration of justice and the collection of taxes were humane and just. This can not be said of the Assyrian rule, which therefore did not last as long as that of the Persians. The empire was divided into 21 provinces, called satrapies, each of which was ruled by a governor or satrap. This governor had military powers only in case of war, for it was held that the civil administration and the military administration could not be combined in the hands of one governor. The central administration sent regular inspectors to the different provinces, and it also maintained a secretary in each of them.

The Persian Army. The success of the Persian government lay more in its efficient administration than in the strength of its army. The armed forces were collected from the various subject races throughout the empire, and formed units of ten thousand each, which in turn were divided into units of one thousand each. The officers naturally were Persians and Medes, so that they would be able to prevent rebellion of the soldiers.

The Persian Navy. After the conquest of the western shores of Asia Minor and Syria and a part of the eastern shores of the Balkan Peninsula, the Persians developed a huge navy, made up of one thousand Greek and Phoenician ships. A merchant marine was also developed, and explorers were induced to venture forth along the coasts of India. In Egypt navigation was restored between the Nile and the city at the head of the Red Sea, the present Suez. The military and naval strength of the empire was considerably enhanced by a magnificent system of roads and bridges. Along the roads were constructed relay stations and inns for the use of the garrisons that had to be stationed at various strategic points.

Persian Civilization. The Persians resembled the Assyrians in that they were too intent on imperial administration to foster the fine arts and sciences. Their architecture and sculpture were largely an imitation of Babylonian and Assyrian patterns. From the Egyptians the Persians learned the use of colonnades. They also received from Egypt the solar calendar. Perhaps their greatest palace was that constructed in the city of Persepolis, which was built on a platform introduced by a huge stairway. This stairway, almost three hundred feet in length, was the most imposing one in the ancient Orient. Impressive also were the beautiful gateway and the fine colonnade.

The Persian Religion. The Persians exhibited great originality in the development of their religion. Although at first the Persians resembled the ancient Babylonians in their polytheistic mode of worship, in the seventh or sixth century B. C. a great religious reformer appeared in their midst, who was known as Zoroaster or Zarathustra. He explained to his followers in Persia that the worship of the sun, which had been common among them, was just as bad as the worship of the moon, which had been prevalent in such cities as Ur. Zoroaster accepted the wide belief in the existence of the evil and good spirits, a belief supported not only in Egypt but also in Babylonia. According to Zoroaster, God had created the world for the purpose of providing for human beings a stage upon which powers of good and evil would oppose each other. In other words, human beings would be put through a school of training upon this earth, and they would be free to listen to either the good or the evil spirits, both guided by a high power, which in the case of the good spirits was the god called Ahura-Mazda or Ormuzd, who was assisted in his work by a savior called Mithra. The god of the evil spirits was named Angra Mainyu or Ahriman. Good was symbolized by light, while evil was symbolized by darkness.

The Promise of Eternal Life. It is interesting to observe that human beings who decided to be good upon this earth, were expected to be rewarded with eternal life, while, on the other hand, the others would be subject to darkness and misery in the realm beyond the gates of death. Some day in the remote future, good would triumph over evil, and Ahriman with his evil spirits would be defeated and destroyed. After this contest was over, the earth as physically constituted would vanish, since it had completed its task.

Influence of the Persian Religion. Many scholars have concluded that, since there is such a close parallel between the

Persian and Christian doctrines concerning the forces of good
and evil, the Christians must have copied their beliefs from the
Persians. They noted that the Hebrews had failed to give definite
expression to the doctrine concerning eternal life. The Hebrews
merely believed that the dead gathered together in a realm called
Sheol, or Hades. It was the Greeks who used the word "Hades,"
but their conception was very similar to the "Sheol" of the Hebrews. The Persians, on the other hand, were much more definite
in their opinion concerning future life, and, apparently under the
influence of the Persians, the later Hebrew writings, such as the
book of Enoch, developed the same doctrine of the victorious
struggle of good over evil and a future life of eternal happiness,
called heaven. Afterward the Persians and the Jews came to the
conclusion that destruction for the evil-minded persons was not
sufficient, and so opined that such people should be tortured for-
ever and ever. Many scholars are now of the belief that the Christians took over the Persian view of the purpose of the earthly
life and of the nature of the future life. Christians are said to
owe their faith partly to the Jews and partly to the later Persians,
who had developed the doctrines called Mithraism and Mani-
chaeism.

Zoroaster and the Jews. There was once a time when
historians believed that Zoroaster flourished in the fifteenth century B. C., and was a contemporary of Moses. After years of
research and excavations, it was seen that he must have lived
more recently. Today certain authorities are convinced that Zoroaster probably lived in the sixth century B. C., or perhaps even
later. It would seem, therefore, that the Persians and the Hebrews affected each other considerably. The exiled Jews who were
living in Mesopotamia, where they had been brought by their conquerors, must have learned much from the Persians, and the latter
also must have been influenced by the Hebrews. Since the kingdom of Israel was overthrown as early as 722 B. C., and many
thousands of the inhabitants of that ancient kingdom were taken
to Assyria, it is obvious that they carried with them the teachings
of their prophets. In 586 B. C. the kingdom of Judah was destroyed, and once more a large number of Hebrews, hereafter
called Jews, were removed to Mesopotamia by their conquerors.

There can be no question about the remarkable change that came over the Hebrews in their new environment. That the Persians had something to do with the change is undoubted. Unlike the Medes and Chaldeans, who had conquered the kingdom of Judea, the Persians, who in turn overthrew the empires of the Medes and the Chaldeans, were much kinder to the Jews than their predecessors had been. In 536 B. C. the Persian ruler gave the Jews permission to return to their own country. Although some of them did so forthwith, the great majority remained in ancient Mesopotamia.

The Avesta. One of the recent books published that deal with the history of the ancient Near East indicates that Zoroaster probably lived at the beginning of the sixth century B. C., that is, at the very time that the kingdom of Judah was destroyed by the Babylonians and many of its inhabitants were taken captive to Mesopotamia. He must have been familiar with the Hebrews who were in his time living under New Babylonian rule in ancient Mesopotamia. This book indicates that Zoroaster completely broke with the old Iranian religion, with its polytheism, animal sacrifices, and priests. It also explains how a large collection of Zoroastrian religious writings which had been composed during the sixth and fifth centuries B. C. were put together in the famous work entitled the *Avesta*. We observe here that the ethical tendency of the Persian religion is reflected in the moral, just, and humane spirit of the Persian government, and is expressed in many inscriptions of the Persian kings, such as that of the great Darius and Behistun inscription, "On this account Ahura-Mazda brought me health . . . Because I was not wicked, nor was I a liar, nor was I a tyrant, neither I nor any of my line. We have ruled according to righteousness."[1]

Influence of the Hebrew Religion upon the Persian Religion. The present writer is of the opinion that there is nothing in the ancient Persian religion to have suddenly developed so extraordinary a point of view as that expressed by the more or

---

1 See A. A. Trever, *History of Ancient Civilization*, Vol. I (New York, 1936), pp. 116-117.

less legendary character called Zarathustra, or Zoroaster. Almost nothing is known about his life, and no one can tell in what century he lived. Nevertheless, in a relatively short time the religion of the Persians was completely transformed. It must be concluded that the influence exerted by the Hebrews upon the Persians was much greater than that exerted by the Persians upon the Hebrews.

CHAPTER VI.

THE BACKGROUND OF GREEK HISTORY

The man of the late stone age in Crete and the Aegean area (now generally called the Early Minoan period) had made considerable progress by 3000 B. C. Owing to the abundance of ores, he had reached the age of metals in southeastern Europe and Asia Minor, and was doing considerable trading with other peoples. Such articles as pottery, beads, copper trinkets, and metal daggers or axes formed objects of bargaining, both with Western Asia and with Egypt. In some respects, though, this man was backward: he had not learned to write, he had no ships worthy of the name, and he had developed no hewn or stone masonry.

THE AEGEAN WORLD

The Land. Lying almost hemmed in by the shores of the Greek peninsula, Asia Minor, and southern Europe, is the Aegean Sea. It is small in size and is dotted with many islands, some of which are too tiny to show on an ordinary map. The closeness of these islands made them accessible to the small boats of people not used to the sea. The climate was mild and sufficiently rainy to produce wheat, barley, grapes, and olives. It was near to Egypt and Western Asia, while to the east and west lay the less developed regions of Asia Minor and the Greek peninsula. This peninsula had an extremely irregular sea coast, many ports and bays, and short mountain ranges, but no river worthy of the name. The climate and products of Asia Minor and the Greek peninsula resembled those of the islands, except that Asia Minor produced iron. The physical features of these regions encouraged a diversity of occupations, made seafaring easy and commerce natural, and hindered political unity.

Asia Minor and the Hittites. Asia Minor is a vast peninsula, bounded by seas, bordered by mountain ranges and fertile valleys, and containing a desert core. Here lived, as we saw, the Hittites, many of whom migrated to the Aegean World. They influenced the Greeks in commerce, coinage, religion, and architecture. With their horses, chariots, and large armies they conquered much of the surrounding country, and made their walled capital, Khatti, a city of imposing palaces and temples.

Influence of Egypt. It appears that the first fruits of civilization were brought to Europe from the south, that is, from Egypt. For reasons still unknown some Egyptians removed from their native land to the island of Crete, located about 400 miles northwest of Egypt. Before 2500 B. C. the earliest settlers built homes in the southern valleys of Crete, where they transplanted Egyptian culture. They learned to cultivate the soil and to grow the olive tree. Presently a relatively small number of people arrived from Asia Minor, as is indicated by the presence of broad skulls buried in Cretan soil, very similar to those of the earliest inhabitants of western Asia Minor.

Metalwork and Pottery. As early as 2500 B. C. the Cretans were using implements made out of bronze, the earliest of which they may have imported from Egypt. But they soon discovered rich deposits of bronze on their own island, and they also found suitable clay for the making of pottery, which, unlike Egyptian and Sumerian pottery of the period between 3000 and 2000 B. C., was not made with the use of the potter's wheel.

Architecture. For building materials they contented themselves with sun-dried bricks which were set in a framework of wood. Numerous houses, however, were built out of stone, presumably before the people had learned to manufacture brick. Large palaces were constructed of brick superimposed upon stone foundations. Especially grand were those at Cnossos and Phaestos in Crete.

Painting and Sculpture. The interior walls were decorated with *frescoes* painted about 1500 B. C. (that is, paintings produced on a wall surface), which reveal the mode of life of the Cretans. We also obtain views of their environment by studying the painted surfaces of the pottery. We learn from them that the Cretans loved sports, such as wrestling and exciting contests with bulls. Most attractive are the elegant figures carved out of ivory, or made out of gold, silver, or bronze. They show that sculpture developed hand in hand with architecture, painting, and writing. They also testify to the powerful influence of Egypt, and later that of Babylonia.

Writing. A graceful form of script was used by the earliest inhabitants, who undoubtedly took with them from Egypt the knowledge of hieroglyphic writing. Afterward the use of pictures in their script was replaced by a form of script which clearly was an imitation of Babylonian writing, for the clay tablets now employed and the characters inscribed upon them resemble the cuneiform writing of Babylonia. Unfortunately, the two forms of script have not yet been deciphered.

Crete's Golden Age (Late Minoan Age). The golden age of Cretan (Minoan) civilization lasted from about 1700 to 1400 B. C., when huge palaces were constructed for the kings and when Cretan ships extended the sway of Cretan political power over the islands of the Aegean Sea and the west coast of Asia Minor. In some respects the Cretans surpassed both the Egyptians and the Babylonians, for they invented an ingenious system of water supply and drainage.

Form of Government. Little is known about their form of government, but we are reasonably certain that they maintained several city-states, each with a king at the head. Very likely the environment in which the Cretans lived—the varied scenery combined with a more moderate climate—impelled them to introduce into their government a distinctly democratic note. The arts show at least that the people were more free from conventional styles, more realistic in their painting, more natural in their actions, more refined than the inhabitants of Egypt and Babylonia. They had as well a finer sense of beauty.

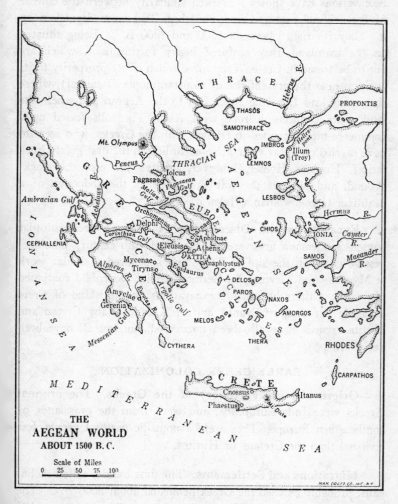

THE
AEGEAN WORLD
ABOUT 1500 B.C.

Scale of Miles
0   25   50   75   100

Religion. However, in their religion we see little progress, for they worshipped a mother-goddess, perhaps in imitation of the people in Asia Minor, with whom they were in intimate contact, and from whom many of their people had come to live in the island.

Troy and Mycenae. Among other centers of Cretan civilization may be mentioned the celebrated city of Troy in the northwestern corner of Asia Minor, and Mycenae in southern Greece. Excavations have shown a marked similarity between the culture of the original center, Crete, and those that were dependent on it. They flourished between 1500 and 1200 B. C. Being situated on the mainland, they required heavy fortifications, which are not to be found in Crete. Troy owed much of its prosperity to its position near the present site of Constantinople (Istanbul), where the straits lead from the Black Sea to the Aegean and where the land route connects Europe with Asia. The tolls levied upon commerce must have led to friction with the Greeks, who seem to have carried on a war with Troy, according to the first great Greek writer, Homer. Homer, however, ignores the economic background, and pictures the war as caused by the abduction of a beautiful Greek woman (Helen of Troy.)

Excavations and Discoveries. A German archaeologist named Schliemann uncovered in the nineteenth century nine successive cities on the site of Troy, and sponsored a similar work at Mycenae and Tiryns. The German scholar Doerpfeld continued his work. Others have made excavations on the island of Crete (notably Sir Arthur Evans) and at Khatti. Many Cretan and Hittite records have also been uncovered, but not all have been deciphered.

EARLY GREEK COLONIZATION

Origin and Early History of the Greeks. The original Greeks were Indo-Europeans, and were from the grasslands of southeastern Europe. They were a nomadic pastoral people, less civilized than the Cretans or Hittites.

Migrations and Settlements. The first bands, called Achaeans, probably reached the Greek peninsula about 2000 B. C. The next group, the Dorians, reached southern Greece about 1100 B. C., conquered the Achaeans and Aegeans and took possession of the country, including Crete, Troy, and the coast of Asia Minor. Sparta became their leading city. The Ionians settled around Athens, while the Aeolians dwelt farther north. By 1000 B. C., these people had conquered the Aegean world. Armenian and Phrygian invaders also invaded Asia Minor in two waves and conquered the Hittites.

Fusion of Greeks and Aegeans. The invaders kept their own language, but adopted much of the civilization of their foes. The arts almost disappeared. (Hesiod calls this period the Age of Iron.) The two peoples intermarried and thus produced the later Greek.

The Transition to Settled Life. The invaders had a tribal government, with a chief to lead the tribe. The smallest unit, the clan, consisted of several families related by blood. Several clans in a tribe often united into a Phratry to supercede the tribe. The chief held his place so long as he could win victories in war. An assembly of the armed men, meeting infrequently, discussed only important questions. A smaller group, the Council of Elders, met oftener and aided the chief in governing. Influenced by the Aegeans, the invaders made kings of their chiefs, quit wandering, took to seafaring and farming, began to live in cities, and adopted city-state government.

THE AGE OF THE KINGS (1000-750 B. C.)

The Greeks and Their Neighbors. Both the Aegeans and the Phoenicians influenced Greek life. The Phoenicians brought them the. products of the civilized world, such as the alphabet. This gift the Greeks perfected to meet their needs.

Greek Civilization before 800 B. C. The noble, with his chariot and weapons of iron or bronze, was a heroic figure, as he is pictured in the Homeric poems, notably the *Odyssey* and the *Iliad*. The bard Homer has been credited with their authorship, but a number of singers doubtless composed them. Because they tell also of the deeds of the gods, these songs became the sacred book of the Greeks.

The Early Greek Religion. Before the Homeric songs the Greeks spiritualized nature. To them almost all natural objects had spirits, and might be worshipped with gifts of food or sacrifices. Gradually the Greeks added many gods and goddesses. A partial list follows: Zeus was the supreme god; Poseidon was god of the sea; Hera, wife of Zeus; Ares, god of war; Apollo, god of light, agriculture, and destruction; Demeter, earth mother; Dionysius, god of suffering and wine; Athena, protectress of cities; Aphrodite, goddess of love; Artemis, goddess of the moon and hunters; and Hermes, messenger of the gods. These gods showed human defects, but were immortal. Mount Olympus was their home, but they often visited the earth. Hades was a gloomy region ruled by Pluto and Persephone, where almost everyone went after death. Heroes and a favored few, the spirits of the good, went to the Elysian Fields. Tartarus was a region below Hades peopled by the very wicked. The earth was a curved disk, with Olympus as the center. Temples and oracles were built in honor of Zeus, Apollo, and Athena.

Significant Dates

Draco's Code . . . . . . 621 B.C.

The Reforms of Solon . . 594 B.C.

Greco-Persian Wars . 492-479 B.C.

The Athenian Empire . 461-404 B.C.

Spartan Supremacy . . 404-371 B.C.

CHAPTER VII.

THE GREEK CITY-STATES

In the whole history of the civilized world no country as small as Greece and no part of any other country as large as Greece has shown such a profusion of learning, sane standards of living, enlightened experiments in practically every known form of government, industrial and commercial development, successful colonization, and artistic production as did the Greeks in the short period from 600 to 300 B. C.

THE AGE OF THE NOBLES (800-600 B. C.)

Overthrow of the Kings. Four city-states developed: Argos, Sparta, Athens, and Thebes, and kings ruled these. But the Greeks had none of the Oriental reverence for kings, and hence often aided restless nobles to overthrow the rulers.

Continued Colonization. The nobles built ships and encouraged commerce, especially with the Phoenicians and other neighbors. Three leading causes promoted the establishment of colonies: the harshness of the nobles, the poverty of the peasants, and the desire to promote commerce. Under such impulses, Greek colonists went out in every direction, until they fairly dotted the Mediterranean world. These colonists spread Greek civilization and made it supreme in the Mediterranean.

65

Government. The nobles gained leadership of the government and the army. Sometimes they overthrew the king, but often they simply usurped his powers and allowed him to remain.

Economic and Cultural Progress. Commerce developed greatly, and architecture showed some advancement, especially in the erection of temples. The epic poems of Homer and of Hesiod formed the principal literature.

Influences For and Against Unity. The Greeks had many interests in common. The athletic contests, held in honor of the gods, served to dispel suspicion and distrust. Their religion and common management of temples made cooperation necessary. Their common language and inheritance acted as bonds of unity. To counter-balance this was the powerful geographical factor—the separation into isolated valleys that made for strong local feelings. Neither did they have any unity arising out of earlier habits and customs, or even trade, nor did they seem to possess political ability.

THE AGE OF THE TYRANTS (650-500 B. C.)

Nature and Position of a Tyrant. A tyrant was one who seized control by violence and who had no royal ancestry. Some tyrants were good men and able rulers, and for such the Greeks might have gratitude, perhaps, but no love. To kill a bad tyrant was a noble deed.

Cause for the Rise of Tyrants. Many persons were dissatisfied at their losses of political privilege and land. Furthermore, certain military changes deprived the nobles of exclusive control over the army. The foot soldier became more prominent and the chariot less so. Many of the newly rich industrial leaders could equip themselves without noble aid. Factions among the nobles weakened them. The increasing use of money made many independent of the nobles, and caused its possessors to desire the positions that were denied them. The migration of peasants to colonies deprived the nobles of their following.

Examples of Tyrants. Thrasybulus of Miletus kept his city independent of Thebes. Periander of Corinth encouraged commerce and letters. Gelon of Syracuse maintained a great army and navy. Pisistratus of Athens encouraged commerce, manufacturing, art, music, drama, and literature. Many others might be added to this list.

Growth of Commerce and Industry. Corinth and Athens led, but others followed, and the new colonies contributed much. Greek cities exported such articles as metals, woven goods, and pottery, and imported grain, fish, amber, and bronze utensils. Slaves became plentiful. By doing most of the labor, they helped to make possible a life of intellectual attainments for their owners. They increased the output of factories, especially of vases. Ships were improved and money came into general use. A regular monetary system arose, with coins stamped by the state.

THE RISE OF DEMOCRATIC GOVERNMENT AT ATHENS

Causes for the Adoption of Law Codes. Many felt that written law would be easier to follow than mere custom, and that oppression would be less likely. Once the process was begun, reforms were necessary to correct the defects of existing codes.

Draco's Code (621 B. C.). This was a collection of existing customs, especially regarding court procedure. It acquainted the people with the law and limited the power of officials, but was too harsh, forfeiture of mortgages and enslavement for debt being common.

The Reforms of Solon (594 B. C.). He abolished land mortgages and slavery for debt, provided a citizen jury to hear appeals, and made all citizens members of the Public Assembly. He divided the citizens of Athens into four classes, according to income, and created a Council of Four Hundred to prepare laws for the Public Assembly. This code remedied many defects, but did not prove entirely satisfactory.

The Reforms of Cleisthenes (502 B. C.). He re-arranged the citizens along territorial lines into tribes, or demes, and increased the Council to five hundred. To minimize the danger of tyrants, he introduced the practice of ostracism. (The name of an undesirable citizen would be written upon a ballot called *ostrakon,* and if the majority so voted, this citizen would be sent into exile.)

CIVILIZATION OF THE AGE OF THE TYRANTS

Education and the Theater. Open air gymnasium work, writing, and music formed most of the boy's education. Choral dances developed, and from these came tragedy, which the actors presented in state-owned outdoor theaters.

Architecture and Painting. Limestone replaced sun-dried bricks as building material. Temples with Doric columns and relief figures of the gods became common. Sculptors created bronze and marble statues of heroes and athletes. Vases bore scenes depicting stories of the gods, myths, legends, and scenes of life.

Religious Changes. There was a growing feeling of right and wrong in connection with religion, and a tendency to deprive the gods of human traits.

Science and Invention. Thales of Miletus foretold eclipses; Pythagoras discovered important laws of geometry, physics, and geography. Anaximander believed in the evolution of lower animals to higher forms, and was the first Greek to make a map of the then-known world.

THE PERSIAN WARS

The Coming of the Persians. In Italy and Sicily the Greek colonies lay open to invading Carthaginians, while those in Asia Minor were subject to attack from the interior. Moreover, the colonies had no political unity and suffered from jealousy and class struggles.

The Lydian Kingdom in Asia Minor Falls. The Lydians occupied much of Asia Minor and many had drifted into Greek colonies, where they became known as Anatolian Greeks. In 546 B. C. Persian forces defeated King Croesus and captured Sardis, his capital. They allowed the conquered their local freedom, but required tribute and army service.

Causes of the Persian Wars. The Persians, having started to conquer the Greeks, had to retreat or go all the way. Moreover, Persia and Greece were naval and commercial rivals, and represented conflicting racial and cultural standards. The immediate cause was a revolt of Ionian cities against Persian rule, while Athens and Eretrea assisted. In revenge the Persians annexed Macedonia (497 B. C.) and prepared to conquer Greece proper.

The Battle of Marathon. Persian messengers went to all Greek cities to demand submission. In the first attempted invasion, the Persian fleet was wrecked near Mt. Athos, but a second attempt straight across the Aegean was more successful. The rival armies engaged in the battle of Marathon (490 B. C.), which proved to be a decisive Greek victory.

Final Repulse of the Persians. After a delay of several years, the new Persian king, Xerxes, invaded Greece by land and sea from the north. His army overcame the Greeks at Thermopylae (480 B. C.) and even captured Athens, but his navy suffered defeats at Salamis and Mycale. Finally, the Persian army was decisively defeated and almost destroyed at Plataea (479 B. C.). These failures ended the Persian invasions of Greece.

THE RISE OF SPARTA

The Land and the People. Sparta was located in southern Greece, on a level spot, but with mountains nearby. The ruling class, or Spartiates, probably never numbered over 10,000 men. The Perioeci (allied subjects) were remnants of earlier settlers that had been conquered by the Spartiates. The lowest class or *Helots* were state slaves.

Government. Two kings, co-equal in power, led the armies. The Council of Elders and the Public Assembly resembled the original institutions that the Greeks brought with them. Five men called Ephors exercised great power; they were chosen by the Assembly.

Education. Unhealthy children were turned over to Helots or exposed in a mountain glen. From seven to twenty years of age, the boy received military training in camps. Girls also received instruction in physical exercises.

Occupations and Life. From twenty to thirty, Spartan men continued their military life. At thirty a man married, but continued in the army. The Helots worked the land, furnished the food, and paid most of the taxes. The Perioeci had a monopoly of trade and manufacturing. Foreigners were not welcome. Sparta organized and headed the Spartan League, which later opposed Athens.

THE GOLDEN AGE OF ATHENIAN DEMOCRACY

Establishment of the Delian League. Many Greek cities feared another Persian invasion, and sought to resist it by organizing a fleet, through contributions of ships or money. Athens, as the strongest city, led the enterprise. The money was kept at Delos, whence the name of the League.

Conversion of this League into an Empire. More money was collected than ships. When cities grew tired of paying they were forced to continue; even new cities were added by force. The treasury was finally moved to Athens and its contents spent on public works. The League had become an Athenian Empire.

Social Classes in Athens. For a considerable length of time the city of Athens recognized four social classes, the distinction between the respective classes being based on land ownership. In addition to these citizens, there were the *metics,* who were foreigners residing in the state and paying special taxes for permission to remain there.

Officials and Assemblies. Originally only the three higher classes were permitted to vote in the popular assembly, which was called the *ecclesia.* But about the year 594 B. C. Solon had granted permission to the fourth class to vote in the assembly. Solon had also made provision for a council that consisted of four hundred members, whose official name was the *boule.* The members of this council of four hundred were elected by lots from among the higher three classes. Moreover, three political parties had resulted, which were called respectively the *Shore* (the industrialists), the *Plane* (the aristocracy in the rural district), and the *Hill* (the peasants). It was the policy of the industrialists to combine either with the land nobility or with the peasants. Cleisthenes had introduced important changes, among them the division of Athens into ten tribes, which in turn were subdivided into *demes.* He granted increased power to the assembly called the *ecclesia,* which consisted of male citizens who were at least twenty years of age. He also, as we saw above, enlarged the council called *boule* from four hundred to five hundred members, that is, fifty for each tribe. The respective tribes chose their representatives by lot from their citizens who were at least thirty years old. The old institution of *archons,* or chief ministers, continued, but they lost a considerable amount of power to the council called the *boule.* A little later each tribe also elected an official called *strategos* as general of the armed forces.

Reforms in the Fifth Century B. C. In this period the powers of the assembly called *ecclesia* were considerably increased. It met forty times a year, and after the death of Pericles paid the representatives who attended the meetings. The assembly acquired the power to check the accounts of officials upon their retirement, and it also had the right to declare war or peace, to administer the finances, the military defenses, foreign affairs, the distribution of grain, and religion. Although the *archons* retained their offices, they were shorn of political power. The *strategoi* (plural of strategos) remained very important.

Government Revenues. The city of Athens in its Golden Age levied tribute upon its subject states, derived revenue from property owned by the government, collected import and export dues at the harbor, received payments in the form of taxes from the *metics,* and also collected fees paid in the courts. In time of war it also levied an income tax upon its citizens.

Other Developments. After Cleisthenes' day, Athenians overthrew the Council of Elders. They also provided pay for jury service, and added to the jury's powers that of law making. All offices, except those of the military commanders, were filled by lot. The military leaders controlled the army, navy, treasury, and foreign affairs. A combined military leader and orator, such as Pericles, could still be powerful.

Commercial Development of Greek Cities. Almost every city had a harbor, which was dotted with ships. The perils of seafaring were many, but the profits of successful voyages were large. Money was used more and more to pay citizens for state service, to erect temples, theaters, and other public undertakings. To defray the costs of war and military service, Athens worked mines, collected a one per cent tariff, and levied tribute on her subject cities in the Delian League.

THE
AEGEAN WORLD
IN EARLY GREEK HISTORY

Scale of Miles
0   25   50   75   100

Social Developments in the Age of Pericles. Pericles was the outstanding leader and the greatest orator from 461 to 431. So prominent was he that this period was named after him. Few really wealthy people were to be found. Land ownership was the most desirable form of wealth, but service to the state and enjoyment of life were placed above riches. There were many workers and farmers in or near Athens, and all participated in the government. Slaves sometimes outnumbered freemen. They were often honored and trusted, and dressed like freemen.

Family and Home Life. The houses were one-story affairs, built of sun-dried brick or limestone, with few windows, poor heating and ventilation systems, and no plumbing. The man spent most of his waking hours in the city. Little attention was paid to the education of the girl. The woman supervised the household and slaves, and brought her husband a dowry, which he forfeited if divorce occurred. Women were generally treated as inferior to the men.

Education. There were no public schools in Athens during the fifth century B. C., and the majority of the boys from the ages of six to fourteen attended various private schools, where they learned reading, writing, arithmetic, poetry, music, and ethics. Many of the boys also learned a trade by becoming apprentices in one of the industrial establishments. Those whose parents could afford to pay higher tuition than that charged in the ordinary schools, attended establishments conducted by the so-called Sophists. These teachers gave excellent instruction in rhetoric, poetry, political science, geometry, astronomy, and ethics.

When the youth reached eighteen he took an oath of loyalty to the state and the gods, after which he spent a year in military training at the harbor of Piraeus. At nineteen he became a citizen in a public ceremony, after which he sometimes spent another year in the cavalry or on the frontier. The citizen continued to learn in the gymnasium, lyceum, academy, or public theater, and in state service.

Intellectual and Artistic Athens. The Parthenon, built on the Acropolis or great hill in honor of Athena, was unrivalled in architecture. On the south side of the Acropolis was the theater of Dionysius, which seated 30,000 people. Several great play writers appeared: Sophocles, who exalted the gods; Aeschylus, who dramatized legends of old heroes and taught moral lessons; and Euripides, who introduced a note of realism in his versions of the ancient stories. Comedy developed later than tragedy and centered around topics of the day. Aristophanes, supreme in this field, subjected men and events to ridicule and laughter, and though his plays are ribald, his aim was partly that of a reformer. Athenian plays had almost no scenery, but they reached an astonishing degree of literary perfection, and exerted a tremendous influence upon Athenian life and character.

Great Men of Athens, Before and After Pericles. Pericles led Athens for forty years. Three great historians wrote: Herodotus, whose work on the Persian wars is brilliant, but unreliable; Thucydides, whose treatise on the Peloponnesian war is scholarly and reliable; and Xenophon, himself a soldier, who later wrote on the Expedition of the Ten Thousand. Phidias was the greatest sculptor, but Praxiteles, who lived later, was a strong rival. Socrates, Plato, and Aristotle were the greatest philosophers, and Demosthenes was the greatest orator. No city in world history could boast of so pure a democracy, so many great men, or so highly cultured a citizenship, as could Athens. Most of these great men will be discussed in greater detail in the section devoted to the civilization of the Greek city-states.

THE PELOPONNESIAN WARS

The Building of an Empire by Athens. Because Athens was the greatest sea power in Greece, she was chosen as we have indicated, to lead the Delian League. This organization soon drove the Persians out of Asia Minor. Then, spurred on by ambition, Athens converted the League into an empire, composed of unwilling subject-cities, anxious to rebel, with jealous rivals near by ready to aid them.

Jealousy of its Rivals. Other cities not controlled by Athens were jealous of her power. Sparta, her ancient rival, formed a league in opposition. Corinth, Boeotia, and other cities, were also commercial rivals of Athens. This tendency to disunity was due largely to the geography of Greece, with its natural barriers of mountains and rivers, and to early Greek political institutions. It was now promoted greatly by the desire of subject cities to regain their independence.

First Phase of the Struggle (459-446 B. C.). Athens forced Aegina into the Delian League, and likewise gained control over Megara and Boeotia, in spite of Spartan aid to these cities. One Athenian fleet blockaded the harbor of Sparta's ally, Corinth, while another met disaster on the sea. Sparta, on account of trouble at home, could do little. At the end of the struggle Athens retained the islands of Aegina and Euboea, and the warring cities agreed to fight no more for thirty years. But this truce lasted only fifteen years.

Second Phase (431-421 B. C.). Corcyra, a colony of Corinth, became involved in a quarrel with the mother city. She then sought to enter the Delian League, and Athens admitted her. This meant war with the Peloponnesian League, and especially with Corinth, but Corcyra had a great fleet and Athens wanted to use it. War was therefore declared. Sparta and her allies planned to invade Attica; Athens planned to confine the war to the sea or coast alone. During the struggle Athens faced serious difficulties: disease killed many of her citizens, the enemy ravaged her fields, and some of her sea campaigns miscarried. On the other hand, since Sparta and her allies could not control the sea, they could not starve out their rival, and they were unable to secure an open battle. The Peace of Nicias ended the peculiar struggle; each side was to give up all recent conquests and was to maintain peace for fifty years.

Third Phase (421-404 B. C.). Athens was dissatisfied with the previous contest, for she felt that there was a good chance for a complete victory. Moreover, the Persians were again threatening and the subject allies of Athens were very restless. Alcibiades, who had gained the ascendancy after the death of Pericles, planned to force the Greeks in Italy and Sicily into the Athenian Empire. His expedition to Syracuse for this purpose failed, his opponents in Athens deposed him, and he deserted to Sparta. The destruction of an Athenian army and navy, 413 B. C., dampened the ardor of the Athenians and correspondingly encouraged the enemy. Sparta, who had no fleet and little money, sought and secured Persian aid. The Athenians recalled Alcibiades, but his forces suffered defeat at the naval battle of Arginusae, and were finally defeated at Aegospotami. At the end of the war the walls of Athens were levelled and the fleet was destroyed. She was made dependent upon Sparta in foreign affairs, but retained her local independence. The fundamental result was a triumph for decentralization.

THE FAILURE OF THE GREEK POLITICAL SYSTEM

Limitations of the Athenian Democracy. The Athenian law courts began even under Pericles to show themselves susceptible to emotional appeals. The lower classes gained control and according to conservative writers exploited the rich unjustly. (Pericles, however, paints a more favorable picture of the balance of social classes.) The treasury of Athens became drained by the constant expenses incident to free public entertainment, pay to the juries, and wars; a deficit that was made greater through bad methods of collecting taxes and an expensive program of public works. War decimated her farms and caused the disappearance of her peasant farmers, and great estate owners took their places. Her government, therefore, failed to function in a crisis.

Inability of the Greeks to Form a Nation. Had the Greeks united into one nation they might have ruled the world, but they could not do so. Athens, Sparta, and Thebes successively failed to achieve such unity. Failing in this object, they were destined to be ruled by others with less intelligence.

Spartan Supremacy (404-371 B. C.). Athens was by no means crushed; she soon rebuilt her walls, and more slowly possessed herself of another fleet. Her commercial prosperity continued. Sparta was unfitted for the rôle of leadership, for she was almost constantly confronted with a threat of revolt at home, she lacked men and money, and was unable to rule the sea. Moreover, her harsh rule soon aroused opposition in Greece; especially galling were her policies of stationing soldiers and military governors over some of the Greek cities. Also, there was still some danger from Persia. Her strength was declining, as was proved by the Expedition of the Ten Thousand, but she still seemed determined to prevent a national union of the Greek cities, and was also anxious to regain control of Asia Minor. The Persian danger was averted, though, by the King's peace of 386 B. C. This provided that the island of Cyprus and certain cities in Asia Minor were to be under Persian control, that the islands of Lemnos, Imbros, and Scyros were to be ruled by Athens, and that Spartan supremacy on the mainland of Greece was recognized.

The End of Spartan Leadership. This peace hurt Spartan prestige and led to the formation of an anti-Spartan alliance, 395 B. C., consisting of Corinth, Argos, Athens, and Thebes. The Thebans, who were especially resentful because of the Spartan seizure of a citadel in Thebes, took the lead in the overthrow of their Laconian rivals. A Theban leader, Pelopidas, drove the Spartans from his city in 379 B. C., and the next year Thebes induced Athens to join the coalition that was being formed.

Theban Supremacy (371-362 B. C.). Spartan leadership ended and Theban supremacy began with the Theban victory at Leuctra. Thebes pursued the policies of suppressing Sparta and of maintaining her own supremacy on the sea. The war was renewed with another Theban victory, but Epaminondas, commander of the victorious forces, was killed, and with him fell Theban hopes.

THE CIVILIZATION OF THE GREEK CITY-STATES

Agriculture. None of the Greek city-states was what we would consider wealthy. Agriculture was always an important source of wealth, but never could supply the population with surplus capital, as was the case in ancient Egypt or Babylonia. Furthermore, commerce and industry did not give rise to such huge cities as Babylon or Nineveh. The average business establishment in Athens employed but ten slaves, though at the height of its prosperity, the city witnessed certain establishments growing to such proportions as to engage up to forty slaves. One firm, in truth, is known to have employed 120 men in the making of shields. The slaves took the place of our modern machinery. Some had been bought by the merchant class in foreign lands, others had been captured in wars, and still others had in primitive times lost their personal liberty as a result of debts incurred. As a rule the owners of firms which did the same kind of work lived in the same street, such as the street of the potters, or of the masons. It was the custom of the master to work side by side with his slaves or free help. Slavery was not the necessary basis of learning an art in Athens, as has often been erroneously asserted.

Commerce. Merchants often cooperated in chartering vessels for their business ventures. They were sometimes in need of capital and would borrow money from bankers at fixed rates of interest ranging from ten to twenty per cent. But checks and drafts were not used. Transfer of money had to be attested by witnesses. Since manufactured goods were usually sold at or in front of the shops, the merchant class was engaged largely in the export and import trade. Exports included marble, olive oil, figs, furniture, pottery, woven goods, and articles made of bronze or iron. Among the products imported were grain, cheese, dried fish, meat, wine, perfumes, spices, carpets, and tiles. Merchants also brought to the Greek towns such raw materials as iron, lumber, ivory, hides, flax, and wool.

Shipping. The trade on land was handicapped by the lack of good roads, showing that it was not the policy of the government to encourage commerce. Consequently, the foreign trade was carried on most by way of the sea, for which purpose two types of vessels were employed: the small boats for coastwise shipping, measuring about fifteen tons, and larger vessels which could carry burdens of 350 tons. The vessels were propelled by oarsmen seated in rows and these were aided in propitious weather by sails. The trip from Athens to Crete, a distance of 170 miles, required about two and a half days. Seldom did the captain of the ship venture far enough from the shore to be out of sight of land. Primitive sea maps were available, but no compass and no lighthouse existed until about 250 B. C.

Clothing Worn. In examining for a moment the clothes worn by the Greek in classical times (500 to 300 B. C.), we are reminded of the whole environment in which the Greeks as a people were placed. Their men and women were dressed very much as were other civilized persons in the Near East. Each wore a sleeveless undergarment called *chiton,* that was fastened about the shoulders with a clasp, and an outer garment called the *himation.* Often only the *chiton* was worn. It hung loosely and gracefully upon one's body, permitting freedom of action. It might be made of wool or linen, in accordance with the change in the seasons.

Architecture. The Greek arts and sciences evolved under the tutelage of Egyptian and Babylonian masters, but they revealed also unmistakable evidence of genius and independence on the part of the Greeks. Since stone and marble were to be found in abundance, the Greeks freely used them, though private dwellings continued in many cases to be built of sun-dried brick, as was also the case in ancient Mesopotamia. The Greek temples are most impressive, though they were not as large as some of the buildings constructed by the Assyrians or the Persians. The use of the column was also not new. The typical Greek temple was made up of a rectangular hall, at the ends of which were placed one or two rows of columns, while sometimes columns were also placed along the sides of the building. Occasionally porches were provided as well. The hall and porches were covered with a roof made of wooden beams and protected from the elements by tiles. The earliest style is the Doric, and the most famous example the Parthenon, built on the hill at Athens called the Acropolis. The Ionic type was marked by a more slender column which was adorned with spiral volutes at the top (the capital). A superb example is the temple of Erechtheum, also on the Acropolis. An earlier Ionic temple was that of Artemis (Diana) at Ephesus, which was considered one of the Seven Wonders of the World.[1] The third style is the Corinthian, which evolved from the Ionic and is more complex than the two earlier forms. The best-known example of this type may be the choragic monument of Lysicrates in Athens.

Sculpture and Painting. Greek sculpture, even more than its architecture, illustrates the high qualities of the arts developed by the Greeks. They were one of the few peoples in the ancient world who were not dominated by religion, but applied themselves wholeheartedly to the things of "this world." Consequently, they freely portrayed the nude human body, depicted with ardor the beauties of nature, and drew upon their active imagination. Taught by the environment in which they found themselves, they developed the motto of "Nothing in excess, and everything in pro-

---

1 The other six were: (1) the pyramids in Egypt, (2) the Hanging Gardens of Babylon, (3) the lighthouse at Alexandria on the is'and of Pharos, (4) the statue of Zeus by Phidias, (5) the Colossus at Rhodes, a bronze statue of the sun god, 100 feet high, (6) the Mausoleum at Halicarnassus, built for King Mausolus (died 353 B. C.) by his widow.

portion." They combined simple lines with proper proportions. They also were true to nature, patient, and full of joy, free from restraint and void of superstition. For these reasons their statues and other figures carved out of stone and marble, as well as out of bronze, gold, and silver, are superior to nearly all similar productions of other peoples in the ancient or medieval world. Their greatest sculptor, Phidias, perfected the huge statue of the goddess Athena placed before the Parthenon. Since most of the Greek paintings have been destroyed, we can say only that they probably resembled the sculpture in the admirable qualities just mentioned. One of the outstanding painters was Polygnotus.

Literature: Epic and Lyric Poetry before 450 B. C. Very remarkable were the contributions made by the Greeks in the field of literature. They used every form now known, including the satire, but began with epic poetry through the pen of Homer, who no doubt assisted in the composition of the *Iliad* and the *Odyssey*. The two chief writers of lyric poetry were the poet Pindar (about 450 B. C.) and the poetess Sappho (about 600 B. C.).

Drama. The Greek drama, both tragedy and comedy, reached its greatest height in the period from 525 to 400 B. C., when the three famous writers, Aeschylus, Sophocles, and Euripides, flourished. Aeschylus was noted for his description of scenes in the Persian Wars, in which he had fought. He was a serious-minded, philosophical person, given over to a sense of duty and patriotism, as may be seen in his masterpiece, *Prometheus Bound.* Perhaps even better known is his *Agamemnon,* in which he tells of the return of a hero from Troy and his murder by his wife, Clytemnestra, and her lover. Sophocles was more interested in ordinary human activities and relations than in heroic deeds. His finest work is the *Oedipus Tyrannus,* but it is probable that, since only seven out of perhaps over a hundred of his plays are still extant, some of his lost works even surpass that just mentioned. Euripides wrote plays which represented the gods as very human. He directs one's sympathies toward mortals, as may be seen in his beautiful work, *Iphigenia Among the Taurians.* Aristophanes wrote satirical comedies, including the *Frogs,* in which he satirized Euripides, and the *Clouds,* which ridicules Socrates, representing him as one of the less capable Sophists.

History and Oratory. The most famous composer of orations was Demosthenes (385-322 B. C.), whose best work was entitled *On the Crown.* In this and other orations he warned against the power of Philip of Macedon. The two greatest Greek historians were Herodotus and Thucydides, both of whom lived in the fifth century B. C. Herodotus has left a painstaking work dealing with the Persian Wars, and excellent descriptions of society in the many countries he visited, such as Egypt, Babylonia, and Italy. Thucydides wrote about the civil war between Athens and Sparta. He was much more accurate than his predecessor, Herodotus.

General Characteristics of Classical Greek Literature. The classical literature of Greece is noted especially for simplicity of expression, realism (a truthful description of things as they are), appreciation of beauty and grace, both in the theme and the style, and superb literary technique. There has never been a people that was able to surpass the Greeks in these respects.

Mathematics. But in turning to the fields of science, mathematics, philosophy, and religion, we must be on our guard, for fear that we shall repeat the exaggerated praise that has often in the past been bestowed upon the Greeks. The leading authorities on the history of mathematics are of the opinion that in arithmetic, geometry, and algebra the Greeks made very little advance over the Egyptians and the Babylonians, while they did still less with trigonometry. We owe to them, however, the terminology now used in geometry, the methods of proof, and the fundamental principles, as expressed so ably in Euclid's *Elements.* But Euclid lived in a late period (323-285 B. C.).

Astronomy. When Thales, the Greek astronomer, lived (about 585 B. C.), it was known that the earth has the shape of a sphere, while before 300 B. C. it was understood that the earth revolves on its axis once every 24 hours. But this information probably was first known to the scholars to the south and east of

Greece. It is not surprising that the first Greek philosopher and astronomer of importance, Thales, lived near the west coast of Asia Minor.

Medicine. In medicine and the natural sciences the Greeks were exceptionally successful. Ever since 500 B. C. the nature and the symptoms of diseases had been carefully studied by them. Schools of medicine were established, among them that of the famous expert, Hippocrates, who insisted that medicine should be regarded as a serious occupation. His high ideals are perpetuated in the "Oath of Hippocrates," accepted even today by our physicians. The science of biology was practically non-existent until it was founded by Aristotle, whose works on the natural sciences were used as textbooks in the medieval universities. The same is true of his treatises on rhetoric and political science.

Philosophy. Prominent in this field was Socrates (469-399 B. C.), who taught that there is but one God and that the soul is immortal. Socrates argued that one must learn to "know himself," meaning that a person should not waste so much of his time thinking and talking about things that are of no great importance, such as sports, the making of money, amusements, heavy eating and drinking, and the like, but should discuss virtue and seek it. He taught by means of the dialogue (the Socratic method) and left no writings of his own.

Plato's Philosophy. Plato (427-347 B. C.) was the most famous pupil of Socrates and the greatest philosopher of antiquity. He was also the author of works on political science, such as his *Republic,* in which he described an ideal state of society. But he is known principally as a philosopher; even in his *Republic* he speaks more as a philosopher than as an expert in political science, such as was his pupil, Aristotle. According to Plato, God is the creator of the universe, the supreme Spirit, who is present everywhere. The only things that are real and eternal are spiritual forces, or ideas. Ideas, in Plato, are general concepts, which can be known only by the reason. Man was originally perfect and good, but somehow fell from his privileged position. He must learn to return to his original position of righteousness and goodness.

The Position of Aristotle. Aristotle (384-322 B. C.), though a pupil of Plato, differed considerably from his master in that he was immensely interested in the world of material objects, in plants, animals, physics, political institutions, rhetoric, and grammar. He surpassed Plato as a scientist, but was inferior to Plato as a philosopher.

The Sophists. Socrates, Plato, and Aristotle were vastly superior to that host of popular teachers called the Sophists. Some of these were good and capable men, but many were mere quacks. The latter gave rise to the term "sophisticated," for they emphasized elegance of speech and manners at the expense of learning and virtue. Led by the more intelligent ideas of Democritus and Empedocles, but not understanding them, they developed materialistic conceptions of the universe and of human society. They scoffed at popular piety and were in turn despised by such profound thinkers as Socrates and Plato. The latter taught a sort of realism which conflicted with the sheerly materialistic view of evolution held by Empedocles, who stated that air, fire, water, and earth are the four primary and indestructible elements in the universe.

Aristotle as a Scientist. Aristotle, unlike Plato, was more interested in science than in philosophy or religion. He stated, for example, that life is not a separate force but functions only in the operations of organisms like plants and animals. He devoted three works to animals and founded in a sense systematic zoology. However, his knowledge of the human body was mediocre. In his book, entitled *Physics,* he discussed motion, space, the process of becoming a living organism, and the nature of matter. His masterpiece was the *Politics,* which was the result of the study of 158 constitutions of Greek city-states. He recommended popular education for men only, advised the limitations of commerce and industry, in order that men might have more leisure for good living and study, and despised the lower classes.

Plato's Political and Sociological Views. In the *Republic,* Plato stated that slavery should be abolished (Aristotle disagreed with him); all workers should be free, but not all should be citizens, as in Sparta; women and real estate should be held in common, and children be brought up by nurses in the payment of the state. He advocated communism for the sake of better government, not in order to improve the economic conditions among the poor. In his work entitled the *Laws,* he recommended state socialism. It is no wonder that many leaders among the early and the medieval Christians warned their readers or auditors against Platonic politics and social ideals.

Greek Religion. In the period before Plato, that is, before 380 B. C., the Greeks had worshipped or believed in many gods, whom they considered to be endowed with bodies and passions closely resembling those of human beings. As a matter of fact, even the greatest of the gods were supposed to be unspeakably immoral, an idea which clearly reveals the spiritual blindness of the Greeks when they were at the height of their power, that is, in the fifth century B. C. Hesiod, who lived in the seventh century B. C. and who wrote *Theogony,* or the *Genealogy of the Gods,* believed that man originally had been much stronger, wiser, and better than he was now, having descended from the first age (of gold) to the fifth age (of iron). The story of the Flood also was one of the features of early Greek religion. But whatever may have been the sources of the Greek religion, it became a jumble and a confused mixture of myth, legend, and tradition.

The Priests. The Greeks were of the belief that every state, social group, even the family, had some patron god who had to be placated. In each city the priests were appointed for public duties just as were the civil officials. The priests officiated at many functions, including divination, or the art of examining sacrificed animals to see what could be learned from their actions or the appearance of their internal organs. This practice was widely followed in the ancient world and is severely condemned in the Old Testament. More important were the signs and omens presented at temples or shrines of the *oracles,* particularly that of Apollo at Delphi. Both private individuals and state governments consulted with the priests in these sacred places. The thought does not seem to have occurred to the ordinary Greek between 700 and 400 B. C. that human beings might establish a direct spiritual relation with the gods or with God.

Eternal Life. The notion of a future life was almost totally neglected by many of the Greeks. They could conceive only of a drab existence in the realm of the dead, controlled by the god called Hades. Such Greeks as Socrates, however, looked toward communion with the spirits of the great. The demand for a more satisfactory religion led to the growth of the so-called "mystery" religions, which promised a life of future happiness after death to those who would cleanse their souls of impurity and sin, and would pass through certain secret ceremonies. Through the priests the god of each cult gave instructions to the devotees.

Greek Religious Celebrations. Very interesting were the great religious festivals intended to propitiate the deities of the respective states. One of these was of a national character, that is, it made an appeal to the inhabitants of all the Greek states, and it was naturally held in honor of Zeus, chief of all the gods. The place selected for the festival was Olympia and gave rise to the Olympic games—racing with horses and chariots, wrestling, running, jumping, and so forth. Participants arrived each time from many Greek states and colonies. In 1896 the Olympic games were renewed, the first at Athens, the next in Paris (1900), the next in St. Louis. It will be seen that now, as formerly, they are held once in four years. That such games were the accompaniment of a religious festival among the Greeks was only natural, and indicates the peculiar nature of Greek religion.

CHAPTER VIII.

HELLENISTIC CIVILIZATION

The period from 338 to 133 B. C. is usually designated as the Hellenistic Age, because the old Greek city-states had made room for the empire of Alexander the Great and the empires of his successors, with the result that the whole of the Near East became Greek in culture and language, and Greece itself was subjected to intellectual and moral decline.

MACEDONIAN SUPREMACY (338-275 B. C.)

The Land and the People. The land of Macedonia lay north of Greece proper, and skirted the Aegean Sea for some distance. The region was the home of a mixed people. Some of them were Greeks, and many were Thracians in whose veins flowed Greek blood. To the north and west lived the non-Greek Illyrians. The nation was ruled by a king who wielded much power. Macedonia and Greece were friendly; in the Persian wars the Macedonians had objected to the passing of Persian troops through their territory; they also encouraged Greeks to settle in Macedonia, and sent young men to the Olympic contests.

The Ruler, Philip—Training and Ambitions. From boyhood Philip had been sympathetic with the Greeks in their struggle for unity. He learned the art of war under Epaminondas. When he became king he set about consolidating his own power. He conquered the surrounding tribes, unified his kingdom, and acquired control of the sea coast, including a number of Greek towns. Presently he saw an opportunity to enter Greece proper; it came in the shape of an invitation to punish the Phoenicians for looting the temple at Delphi. Once there, he stayed.

Philip as Ruler of Greece. The Greek cities did not all welcome him with open arms. Although many men like Isocrates and Aeschines hailed him as the savior of Greece, a considerable element, led by Demosthenes, opposed him. But Philip defeated the opposition at the battle of Chaeronea, and became master of all Greece (338 B. C.). He called a congress of Greeks at Corinth, to whom he presented his plans of uniting all Greek states into one government and of leading them against the Persians. Death in 336 B. C. cut short his plans.

THE WORK OF ALEXANDER THE GREAT

Preparation for the Throne. It was said that Alexander was so like his father, Philip, that the two could not agree. Be this as it may, Philip neglected no opportunity of giving his son the best training possible. He educated him in his own army, gave him the philosopher Aristotle for his teacher when he was not fighting, and made him thoroughly Greek in sympathy. Alexander was only twenty years old when the death of his father called him to the throne.

The First Invasion of Persia. After subduing rebellions in Greece and Macedonia, he set out to carry out Philip's plan of invading Persia. That country had degenerated from its earlier greatness, and although it was still large, it contained many restless subjects. The king, Darius, was not a brilliant warrior. Alexander, after dividing his army and leaving part of it at home, and adding some Greek soldiers, boldly crossed into Asia Minor. He defeated the Persians at Granicus (334 B. C.), and spent the rest of the year winning Asia Minor.

Invasion of Syria and Egypt. The next year he defeated the Persians at the important battle of Issus and put the Persian king to flight. This battle opened up the way to the conquest of Syria, and from there it was but a step to Egypt. The Egyptians welcomed Alexander with open arms. While there, he founded Alexandria and visited the temple of Zeus-Amon, where he had himself declared a god.

The Second Invasion of Persia. Alexander's protracted stay in Egypt had enabled the enemy to gather another army which he routed at the battle near Arbela at a place called Gaugamela (331 B. C.). He turned aside long enough to seize immense treasures at Babylon, Susa, and Persepolis and to complete the final conquest of Persia.

The Campaign in India. The young Macedonian King now formed the daring plan of invading India. After calling together his army and granting the Greeks permission to go home if they desired to do so, he set out on the campaign (327 B. C.). For four years he was gone, during which time he penetrated India but a short distance, by no means up to the Ganges River. The complaints of his army finally impelled him to turn back, and he made the return to Babylon by land and sea. There, in the midst of revelries celebrating his victories, he died.

Alexander's Plans. It was his ambition to create a world empire, with himself at the head. To this end he had himself declared Oriental god-king, in order to win the allegiance of his Eastern subjects. The extreme servility thus required galled his own soldiers, though, and led to more than one sad episode. He planned to unite into one nation all the conquered peoples. One means of achieving this aim was intermarriage. To this end, he and several thousand of his troops took Eastern wives. To further this same aim he began the practice of establishing cities and Greek colonies throughout the conquered regions, and of spreading Greek civilization everywhere.

Estimate of His Work. He was undoubtedly a supreme military genius, and was unquestionably a ruler with far reaching plans, the first military leader to meditate on world-unity. As a founder of cities he was pre-eminent, over seventy cities having sprung up at his command, many of them bearing his own name.

Moreover, he distributed Greek civilization and made it supreme in the Near East and gained political supremacy for the Greek world.

The Break-up of Alexander's Empire. No one could rule the huge empire that he had built up, so it fell into three distinct pieces shortly after his death: (1) Ptolemy, one of Alexander's generals, founded at Alexandria a far-flung, Oriental, despotic, bureaucratic government, similar to that of the earlier Egyptian Empire. Cleopatra, the last ruler of the line, lost her throne to Augustus. (2) Seleucus made Antioch the capital of Alexander's Asiatic kingdom, but had many self-governing cities (including Seleucia on the Tigris). He insisted, however, on being recognized as a god to whom all should pay tribute. (3) Another of Alexander's generals, Antigonus, became supreme, after a long struggle with enemies in Thrace, Greece, and Macedonia. Moreover, Pergamon, in Asia Minor, constituted another independent state.

The Two Federal States. In Greece, two loose organizations of cities grew up—the Achaean and the Aetolian Leagues. Both met in congresses, had armies, and levied taxes. Macedonia befriended the Achaean League; Rome the Aetolian. Some Greek cities, however, held aloof from both organizations. After the defeat at Leuctra, Spartan leadership and numbers declined. Cleomenes built up her power again, but it could not long withstand the powerful enemies to the north and west. Though Athens was not always politically independent, it continued its commercial and cultural leadership, even after Rome controlled it.

CIVILIZATION OF THE HELLENISTIC AGE

The Cities. There was a great development in cities, both as to number and size. Furthermore, the new cities were systematically planned and built in blocks with long straight streets. State buildings were larger and better than before, and even the residences were greatly improved. With their stone houses and floors, plastered and adorned walls, elaborate furniture, carpets and hangings, and private water supply and drain pipes, they bore scant resemblances to their predecessors. Moreover, the cities were frequently equipped with market squares, indoor theaters, gymnasia, and baths,

Alexandria. The most outstanding of the newer cities was Alexandria, with its prominent harbor, docks and lighthouses, rich palaces, royal library, museum, and other buildings. The most famous lighthouse of the ancient world was constructed at Alexandria in Egypt, which was built of stone, three stories in height with an altitude of 370 feet. A fire of wood was kept burning at night, visible perhaps as far as 30 miles. No city in early modern times could equal in size and wealth the port of Alexandria from 200 to 30 B. C. It had a population of about one million, and saw at its harbor ships from all parts of the Mediterranean Sea, and even from countries as far to the west as the British Isles, and as far to the east as India. Its streets, unlike those of Paris or London before the nineteenth century, were laid out with great care as to the needs of traffic and the beauty of the entire city. The streets intersected each other at right angles, and were crossed here and there by boulevards. Very different was ancient Athens or Sparta, both in size or in the appearance of the streets. The first city in Greece to be laid out in a fashion like that followed in Alexandria was Piraeus, the harbor of Athens, when it was rebuilt.

Shipping. After 300 B. C. vessels became rather large, the largest being the famous ship called *Syracuse,* with the astonishing capacity of 3900 tons for cargo space alone, and luxurious accommodations for passengers and a crew of 600 men. Its total size was 5000 tons, as compared with a tonnage of 125 for the ship that led Columbus' tiny fleet in 1492.

Banking. After centuries of expanding commerce in the Near East, the fifth and fourth centuries B. C. witnessed the rise of banks, which partly took the place of the private moneychangers in or near the harbors. The Greek banks operated on principles that closely resemble those of our modern banks. They received money on deposit and paid interest on it. With this capital they issued loans at higher rates of interest, averaging one per cent a month. There were also finance companies which charged still higher rates, since they took greater risks than the banks. Although the leading philosophers and statesmen frowned upon such practices, arguing that "money is sterile," the businessmen paid little attention to such scruples, exactly as did the leaders of the Middle Ages, when the Church prohibited the loaning of money at interest.

Capitalists and Paupers. In the Hellenistic Age many rich persons existed, while the vast majority of the people lived in extreme poverty. Their labor was hard and required from 50 to 70 hours a week, but their pay was not commensurate with their work. During the fourth century B. C. the gap between the wealthy and the poor became even wider. Thus radical socialism was born to remedy social injustice. The government had to pay unemployment relief and distributed grain to the poor at cheap prices. A form of communism was recommended by Plato, and satirically pictured by Aristophanes ; as a matter of record, the ancient Greeks as well as the Hebrews operated some communistic settlements.

Science. In the third century B. C. lived **Aristarchus,** who developed the theory that the earth moves around the sun ; but Euclid reasoned against it, and so it was dropped as false on his authority. Another Greek scholar who rejected the theory of Aristarchus was the capable astronomer Hipparchus, who lived in the second century B. C. and assisted in founding the science of trigonometry. Eratosthenes, a librarian at Alexandria, computed the length of the equator to be 24,662 miles, only 195 miles fewer than it is. He asserted that one could sail around the world by continually going in the same direction. Perhaps the greatest mathematician of the Hellenistic Age was Archimedes, who founded the science of hydrostatics, combined mathematics with scientific experimentation, and almost created calculus. What he lacked was the necessary algebraic figures and accurate instrument for measuring time.

The Fine Arts. Two famous works of sculpture are "The Gaul Killing Himself" and "The Dying Gaul," both by Epigonus of Pergamon (Pergamum). The following statues are also excellent and well-known: "Venus of Milo," "Laocoön," and "The Winged Victory of Samothrace." One of the outstanding painters was Apelles of Cos. In Alexandria a large number of mosaics were produced during the Hellenistic Age. But upon the whole we may say that the arts were stagnant.

Museums and Libraries. The first of the Egyptian Ptolemies founded at Alexandria the celebrated Museum, an institute for the promotion of research. He and his successors also established a great library, which contained more than 450,000 papyrus rolls—in later days perhaps 650,000. Two other libraries were founded respectively at Antioch and Pergamon. In the period between 330 and 146 B. C., which is commonly referred to as the Hellenistic Age, Alexandria surpassed Athens as a center of learning, and Athens continued merely to be a great center of philosophical studies. It would not be accurate to surmise that the scholarly work done at Alexandria was merely the result of Greek civilization, or that it was only a part of Greek culture, though both the language and the names of the scholars were Greek.

Philosophy. Shortly after the death of Aristotle, two new schools of philosophy made their appearance in Greece. One was called that of the Stoics, a name derived from the porch (*stoa*) where its founder, Zeno, taught. They emphasized the need of reason and virtue, the obligation to perform duties to the state and the family. The other school was that of the Epicureans, founded by and named after Epicurus. It was their belief that man's happiness is a worthy object of study and application, and that one need not wait until the life after death to find it; probably there is no such thing as life after death, they argued. The universe was made as a result of a remarkable course taken by atoms, which flying through the universe happened to make mankind and the planets. Belief in gods was therefore a foolish fancy.

Education. In the period after Plato and Aristotle much progress was made in education. Formerly the state had provided only physical and military instruction or training, but now the children of free parents, sometimes girls as well as boys, received instruction in reading, writing, literature, and music. The pupils made use of wax tablets, corresponding to the clay tablets utilized in former days by Babylonian children. In many cases public endowments provided the means of support for these schools. There were also institutions of higher learning, financed as a rule by private capital, as was the case with Plato's Academy, for which Plato had left funds of his own. The *gymnasium* was a schoo to which only the children of purely Greek descent were admitted; they received physical training here, as well as instruction in reading, writing, and music. Those who were graduated from it were more highly respected than college graduates in this country. In some modern countries, notably Germany, the word *gymnasium* has been perpetuated and applied to secondary schools, which prepare the pupils for work in the universities.

THE INFLUENCE OF THE GREEK RELIGION

Disappointing Features. The various aspects of Greek culture have revealed the versatility of the Greek mind, particularly the remarkable views of Plato, but it is a disappointment to find that Greek religion did not keep pace with Greek art and science. Plato was an exceptional person, and but comparatively few of his countrymen fully understood or followed him, not even his own pupil Aristotle. Consequently, we shall not be surprised to find that the Greeks developed religious views that were decidedly inferior to those of the Hebrews.

Clement of Alexandria. The relation between the Greek religions and the rise of the Christian Church is perhaps best illustrated by the career of that illustrious Church Father, Clement of Alexandria, who was probably born in Athens about the year 150 A. D. Originally he was not a Christian, but appears to have been well versed in the mystery cults. Unquestionably he had been initiated in several of them. He said in his writings that he traveled in many countries. He became an elder in the Christian Church, and he taught in Alexandria for more than twenty years. In one of his works, entitled *Exhortation to the Greeks,* he throws much light upon the real character of the Greek mystery religions. He quoted profusely from almost all the important writers among the Greeks. It is understood by authorities that he mentions by name more than three hundred writers whose works are no longer in existence. He was familiar especially with the writings of Plato and Homer. He felt great admiration for Plato, and referred to him frequently.

His Method. Clement of Alexandria wanted to render a great service to the Christian Church by explaining in learned language all the errors committed by the Greeks. He chose to meet the pagans on their own ground, that is, in the scholarly field. He intended to convince everyone that he himself had been a great scholar and that for reasons well-known to himself he had deliberately left the Greek pagans and had become a Christian. He argued that Greek learning was not to be rejected, but that one ought to study it with the greatest care. Wherever the Greeks had been wrong, that should be admitted. But he felt that even the Greek pagans, no matter how blind they were, had prepared the way for the coming of Christianity. The most exalted thoughts of Plato were a prefiguration of the principles of the Christian religion. The pagan world had prepared the path for Jesus Christ, the Savior of all mankind. There were in Greek writings, glimmerings and forebodings and foreshadowings of the great religion of Jesus Christ. He scorned with unspeakable hatred and contempt the ceremonies of the ancient Greeks. He derided the faith the Greeks had in their immoral gods. He ridiculed the idea that gods resembled human beings in their passions and their sinful lives. He condemned the use of images. He said a god should not be represented in material form.

Clement Condemns the Greek Philosophers. In the fifth chapter, Clement attacks the Greek philosophers, beginning with Thales. He explains that many of them were positively atheists. But some tried to find a higher principle than did the others. He condemns especially the Stoics, who say that the divine nature permeates all matter, even in its lowest form: "These men simply covered philosophy with chains." Clement also disliked Aristotle, who believed that God had no care for the world. In the next chapter he refers to many absurd doctrines that were taught by some of the eminent philosophers of ancient times. He points out that Plato was a better guide. Yet Plato also was disappointing. Plato said that God cannot be found and cannot be described. Moses is much more ancient, since Moses had preceded Plato by about 1000 years.

Explains the Superiority of the Hebrew Writings. Clement next takes up the Hebrew writings and compares them with the books of the Greeks. He says that the prophetic books in the Old Testament are simple in style but great in power. Isaiah stated that idolaters shall be destroyed. Moses wrote of the greatness of God's power. Hosea spoke of the Holy Spirit. Solomon described God as the source of wisdom. Jeremiah prophesied that God would restore the world through His wisdom, which is, His Word. David exhorted us to listen to God's voice. The Apostle Paul in his famous Epistle to the Romans showed that the Greeks have become idolaters and "changed the glory of God to the likeness of an image of corruptible man." No one must think lightly of the Word, for the Scriptures say, "Today if you hear His voice, harden not your hearts." Finally the writer contrasts the mystery religions of Greece with the pure religion of the Christians. Instead of initiation into the unwholesome ceremonies of the Greeks, he suggests that his followers become initiated into the worship of the only true God.

Position of Justin Martyr. Another influential Church Father who pointed out the immense difference between the religions of Greece and that of the Christians was Justin Martyr. In Chapter LIX of his *First Apology,* he asserted that Plato was greatly obligated to Moses. He also ridiculed Hesiod, the author of *Works and Days.* He is of the opinion that it is impossible to learn anything true concerning religion from the Greeks, who by their mutual disagreement have furnished their followers sufficient proof of their own ignorance. For that reason he suggests that he and his auditors or readers will go back with him to the progenitors of the Christian faith. He even assumes that Plato, when he was in Egypt, became acquainted with the books written by Moses. Those who have carefully studied Justin Martyr, know that he did not consider any Greek philosopher before 30 A. D. a Christian, contrary to some textbooks of ancient history. It is also important to note that Heraclitus, who is said to have provided the Christians with the idea of the *logos,* was severely condemned by Clement of Alexandria and by the Church Father Hippolytus, as well as by Plato.

Influence of Neo-Platonism. Much has also been written about the alleged influence of Neo-Platonism on the growth of the Christian Chruch and the Christian religion, but only the heretics in the Church reflected that influence, as will appear.

SUMMARY OF THE CONTRIBUTIONS OF THE GREEKS TO THE MAKING OF WESTERN CIVILIZATION

Reasons Why It Is So Difficult to Evaluate These Contributions. The importance of Greek history is not treated the same way in all textbooks. While in some Greece receives far more attention than all the other nations of the ancient Near East put together, in others it gets about one-half or one-third as many pages as all the others combined. In some textbooks a whole chapter or at least ten pages are devoted to the contributions made by the Greeks, while in others the discussions take only two or three pages. There are also textbooks in which the subject is not treated at all. Furthermore, it is by no means an easy task to determine what was the share of certain nations in the development of an institution or a system of thought or a custom. We have seen, for example, that in the development of the alphabet Egypt, Israel, and Phoenicia all had a share. Nevertheless, some textbooks state that the Egyptians invented the alphabet, others that the Phoenicians did it, and still others that the Hebrews did it. It should be noted also that both the Greeks and the Romans played a rôle of great importance in the completion of the process. Another difficulty is presented by the fact that when a certain code of laws is developed by a people, and another code is perfected by a people several hundred years later, it is taken for granted that the later code must be copied from the earlier code. But even where the codes are very much alike, it is not always possible to prove that the later code is dependent upon the earlier one. Finally, historians have often treated history as a mere science, and have neglected utterly to pay any attention to such phenomena as inspiration, intuition, and telepathy. The question is seldom asked, for example, where a great musician gets his inspiration for one of his most important compositions. Did the brain cells produce a lovely melody in his mind, or did he recall similar melodies, or did he establish contacts with certain forces of the universe that at present are not known to the scientist? The greatest thinker of the ancient world, Plato, believed with the outstanding thinkers of the Middle Ages, especially St. Augustine and St. Thomas Aquinas, that material phenomena are dependent upon spiritual forces. Likewise, the outstanding thinkers of early modern times, such as Erasmus, Luther and Calvin absolutely believed in the possibility of inspiration or intuition. Both Erasmus and Calvin discussed the subject at length, and it can not be said that these men were mediocre thinkers or scholars.

The Influence of the Greek Language. There can be no doubt that this influence was great, for during the whole of the Hellenistic Age, the Balkan Peninsula, Asia Minor, Syria, Mesopotamia, and Egypt were thoroughly Hellenized in speech. For though Jesus of Nazareth and His early followers spoke in an Aramaic language, all of the books in the New Testament with the possible exception of one were written in the Greek language. The language of the early Christian Church was Greek, and its institutions were affected to a considerable extent by those of Ancient Greece. Even in Rome itself it became fashionable to write in Greek. The official language of the eastern half of the Roman Empire in fact was Greek. Although during the Middle Ages the language was somewhat neglected, the Renaissance of the fourteenth and fifteenth centuries restored the knowledge of classical Greek. As a result of the labors of a host of humanists, Greek became an important part of the curricula in the secondary schools of Europe and America until the end of the nineteenth century.

The Importance of Greek Literature. The Greeks perfected almost every branch of literature. They were particularly successful in drama and in the writing of history. In epic and lyric poetry they were also imitated by practically all the peoples of the modern world. Not only Shakespeare, and later Milton, but also the writers of the eighteenth century, deliberately imitated the standards set by the Greeks of old. The Greeks established the system of historical writing. On the other hand, it must not be imagined that we owe all forms of writing to the Greeks alone. As observed previously, the Bible also contains excellent historical treatises and poetry. The Sumerians likewise had their historical writing. But systematic historical writing was not developed until the Greeks did it. In scientific literature the Greeks also made notable contributions, especially through the labors of Aristotle. His works formed the important textbooks in the natural sciences, in physics, and in political science during the thirteenth, fourteenth, and fifteenth centuries. Even in early modern times the leading universities accorded to Aristotle's scientific works considerable importance. The philosophical literature of Plato and others likewise enhanced the value of Greek literature.

Greek Science and Mathematics. As just stated, the Greeks made notable contributions in the fields of science and mathematics. Aristotle established systematic zoology. The Greek experts in medicine were so important that the physicians of today still take the oath of Hippocrates. Moreover, the textbooks of Galen, who flourished in the Hellenistic Age, were used in universities for more than a thousand years, for it must be remembered that long before the universities were established in the West, Constantinople had two universities of its own. The Arabs also studied the scientific works of the Greeks which were translated into the Arabic language. The Renaissance was partly based on the labors of the Arab scientists, who spread the knowledge of Greek science throughout the Mediterranean world, especially in Sicily and in Spain. From the latter two regions, Arabic science, based upon Greek science to a large extent, was introduced into the universities of France, Italy, and Spain. So important was Greek science that today nearly all scientific terms are in Greek or in Latin.

Political Science. The same may be said about Greek contributions to political science. Here the use of the Greek language is even more notable than in science. Every important term used by the political scientists is of Greek origin. Aristotle was quoted by practically all the leading experts in political science during the end of the Middle Ages and in early modern times. Again one must be very careful not to overemphasize the importance of the Greeks in this field. During the sixteenth and seventeenth centuries it was fashionable for the outstanding scholars and writers to quote more often from the Bible than from the Greek sources. Even Hugo Grotius, the father of international law, paid more attention to the Bible and the works of St. Augustine than to the Greek experts. Furthermore, the study of Roman law at the end of the Middle Ages was not a testimony to the importance of Aristotle. On the contrary, the scholars of late medieval and early modern times were well aware that the Romans had superseded the Greeks in the field of political institution and political thought. The Greeks had been a notable failure in maintaining efficiency and order in their social fabric. But it is true that the Romans made few contributions to the rise of modern democracy. The Greeks left a model for the leaders in democracy to follow. They not only experimented with pure democracy in the state of Athens, but they were eminently successful in the formation of federal and representative government, as was shown by the two city leagues that flourished in the Hellenistic Age. The makers of the American constitution during the second half of the eighteenth century paid careful attention to these two federations of city-states.

The Social Order. In this field certain writers in their admiration for the Greeks have placed far too much emphasis upon the contribution made by these people. One must not forget that the Middle Ages were thoroughly Christian, rather than thoroughly Greek or Platonic. Although the early Christian writers had written in Greek almost exclusively, there followed several centuries in which the greatest leaders in the Christian Church used Latin, such as St. Augustine and St. Gregory, or Gregory the Great. Monastic orders of the West also used the Latin language, and Latin became the language of the Christian Church in the West. The Roman Catholic Church became far more important in the development of western civilization than did the Greek, or Orthodox Catholic Church. For that reason it must be remembered that Latin civilization played a greater rôle in this field than Greek civilization. It is in fact entirely impossible to evaluate the Greek contribution made to sociology until one has studied the rise of the Christian Church and the rôle played by this institution in European and American history. Those who have failed to analyze the works of influential writers like St. Augustine, St. Thomas Aquinas, Luther, and Calvin, have no correct conception of the rôle played by the Greeks. It must be remembered, after all, that during the Middle Ages and in early modern times the influence of the Bible surpassed that of all Greek writers in many fields of human endeavor and human thought. In New England, for example, until the middle of the eighteenth century the Bible was the textbook even in the field of political science. During the sixteenth century the English government was regulated by the precepts contained in the Bible, rather than by the teachings of Plato, or Aristotle, or any other Greek writer. The same may be said of other governments, not only during the sixteenth century, but also during three or four centuries preceding it and at least one century after it.

Economics. In the field of economics the Christian Church also has played a rôle that is not commonly understood. But when one weighs the fact that shortly after the fall of the Roman Empire during the third and fourth centuries of our era, the Christian Church became for a subsequent thousand years the most powerful institution of Western Europe, one can understand the ascendancy of the clergy, who were practically the only educated persons of the time, and wielded great influence upon the thought of men and women. The clergy conducted most of the schools from 400 to 1200 A. D. They were used by all the governments in the west as chief ministers. They instructed the kings in how to organize and promulgate their laws. They dominated the social customs of the people. They had much to say about how commerce and industry ought to be organized. For a long time they succeeded in prohibiting the loaning of money at interest. Only the Jews for centuries were permitted to lend money at interest in the Christian world. The question of poverty, of slavery, of social justice and proper relation between employers and employees received consideration on the part of the Church. There was also a practical side to business. When the Church prohibited the taking of interest, even popes ignored their own laws from time to time. Some civil governments also thought themselves not subject to their own laws. Aristotle continued to be read, although his works were not well known between the third and twelfth centuries of our era. While Plato was also carefully considered, his views on private property and family life were severely condemned by ecclesiastical and secular writers.

Philosophy and Art. In these two fields the Greeks made contributions of the greatest importance. The Parthenon was imitated thousands upon thousands of times. Greek sculpture has always been recognized by artists as having reached the highest perfection. The influence of Greek paintings has been slight, for the simple reason that most of these perished at an early time.

In the realm of philosophy the name of Plato still receives the highest recognition. Next to him ranks Aristotle, while Socrates also deserves an important place in the history of philosophy. Even the Christian philosophers of the Middle Ages returned to a great extent to Plato and Aristotle. But it will not do to say that medieval civilization was "thoroughly Platonized."

CHAPTER IX.

THE ROMAN REPUBLIC

While the brilliant civilization of classical Greece was rapidly declining, a new power arose on the peninsula to the west (Italy) that was destined to build an empire surpassing even that of Alexander the Great. The guiding hand of culture and progress now moved once more to the west, deserting Greece, just as in former centuries it had forsaken in turn Egypt, Babylonia, Assyria, and Persia in favor of Greece.

GEOGRAPHY AND EARLY INHABITANTS OF ITALY

Advantages Enjoyed by Italy. It is very easy to see why civilization reached Italy after it had completed part of its work in Greece. Although both Egypt and Babylonia are located to the east of Italy, Italy had at least one advantage over Greece. It was centrally located in the Mediterranean Sea, and, besides, it was larger than Greece. Its temperate climate and the abundant rains in winter combined to make possible the production of grain, olives, vineyards, vegetables, and some tropical fruits. Today one may see orange trees growing in the city of Rome, and especially in the island of Sicily, where oranges can be grown with ease. On the other hand, certain fruit trees like the apple tree, which does not flourish in the southern half of the peninsula, do very well in the northern section.

Geographical Features of Italy. In area, the Italian Peninsula is about four times the size of Greece. It is in the shape of a boot, with its straps in the Alps mountains and its heel and toe extending to southern Italy. It may be divided into four zones: (1) the Apennines mountains, about eight hundred miles in length and occupying the center of the Peninsula, (2) the eastern slope, narrow and steep in the north and wider in the south, (3) the western slope, just the opposite, and (4) the northern plain, which stretches from the Apennines to the Alps. A fifth division might be added—Sicily, a large island almost touching southern Italy.

Natural Resources. Although two-thirds of the peninsula is mountainous, so that the area left for cultivation is not very large, even the mountains used to add to the wealth of Italy. On the lower slopes excellent pastures were to be found, which explains why Italy used to be called "Vetulia" (Calfland). Moreover, the Latin name for money was *pecunia,* which originally signified cattle. The mainland contained rich deposits of copper; Sardinia also possessed copper deposits; and Elba was rich in iron. The sea also contributed to the making of Roman civilization, for it provided employment for numerous fishermen, and gave Italy an inexpensive means of transportation in a time when roads on land were still very poor. Among the numerous rivers of Italy may be mentioned the Po, which waters the largest valley in the peninsula; the Tiber, a stream of only 190 miles in length, but famous because Rome was built upon its banks; and the Arno, which flows through a very beautiful and fertile valley—the heart of modern Tuscany.

The First Settlers. Little is known about the earliest inhabitants of Italy except that about 3000 B. C. they had arrived from northern Africa, and belonged to the Mediterranean white race. They made use of polished stone weapons, as well as the bow and arrow. They raised crops in a rather primitive fashion, and they kept domesticated animals. The clothes worn by them were made of woven material, thus indicating some knowledge of primitive industry; their pottery is further proof of their comparatively good skill in making a suitable living.

The Cretans. About 2000 B. C. merchants from Crete and perhaps also from some of the islands of the Aegean Sea appear to have carried with them to Italy some elements of Cretan culture, as for example, the use of bronze. In this way the transition from the Stone Age culture to the Bronze Age civilization was accomplished in Italy.

The Nordics. About 1800 B. C. settlers arrived from the north, and in northern Italy built lake villages with houses raised on wooden piles; later they constructed homes on piles even on dry land. They had developed a Bronze Age culture in central Europe, and seem to have introduced the horse into Italy.

Their Separate Tribes. Shortly before 1000 B. C. these peoples migrated farther south into central and southern Italy, absorbing the earlier inhabitants and appropriating much of their culture. They now passed from the Bronze Age to the Iron Age type of culture. These peoples came to be called Italians, and they spoke dialects of a common Italian tongue. The Ligurians, in the mountains of the northwest, were comparatively unimportant. The Illyrians dwelt chiefly on the eastern slope and at the head of the Adriatic Sea. The Italians consisted of three groups: the Latins, who lived in the west central lowlands, the Umbrians, whose homes were in the northern mountains; and the Samnites, who dwelt chiefly in the mountain valleys of the center and south.

The Etruscans. In the ninth century B. C. the Etruscans arrived from the East and before long conquered much of central Italy, reaching the height of their power in the sixth century B. C. After that century they were pushed back into what was later named after them: Tuscany; their language disappeared completely so that today their inscriptions, except for proper names, can no longer be read.

The Greeks. In the extreme south of the peninsula and in eastern Sicily, Greek colonies were founded, as we have seen in a preceding chapter. Although they were ultimately annexed by the Latins, they retained their native language for centuries. We shall see presently that the Romans in the period before 100 A. D. were so impressed by the superiority of Greek civilization that they decreed Greek to be one of the two official literary languages of their empire.

Early History of Rome. The city of Rome was founded about the year 1000 B. C., but the settlements on its seven hills were not united until the seventh century B. C. Rome was at first only one out of many cities in the Latin plain, which is usually called Latium. At the beginning of the sixth century B. C. the Etruscans got possession of Rome and part of Latium. From about 600 to 509 B. C. it was ruled by the Etruscans. The city derived its early importance from its valuable location on the banks of the Tiber at the spot where the best crossing of the Tiber was to be found.

Effects of the Land upon the People. Italy's central location gave it a dominant position in the Mediterranean world. The comparative absence of harbors discouraged early shipping, while the presence of rich valleys and pastures led to farming and stock raising. Invaders found the peninsula easy to approach, while defenders found it hard to protect; a situation that made necessary a martial people. The geographic unity of Italy made for one government, while its nearness to other civilizations led to the ready adoption of other arts and cultures.

ESTABLISHMENT OF THE ROMAN REPUBLIC

Overthrow of the Etruscan Kingdom. The Etruscans maintained a kingdom with Rome as its capital for more than a century. This city-state ruled over the Latin people, but also made contact with the nearby Greeks. Legend says that the last Etruscan king was overthrown by force; whether that be true or not, certain it is that the Romans eventually crowded out the Etruscans and gained the ascendancy in Rome and surrounding regions.

The Early Roman Government. *The Comitia Curiata* was a gathering of the people by groups of families, each group of freemen having one vote. As such, they took part in government matters, but soon began to decline. *The Comita Centuriata* (Assembly of Centuries) were the fighters, supposedly in 193 groups of one hundred, but with wealthy men predominant, on account of the cost of arming for war. (This means that a century of wealthy men was small numerically.) It soon overshadowed the *Curiata,* or Brotherhood. The *Comitia Tributa,* or Tribal

Assembly, was presided over by ten Tribunes, all members having an equal voice. It looked after matters of local interest. The Senate, which under the kings was the Council of Elders, was at first composed of three hundred of the most important men of the realm, but later consisted of ex-office holders, and became the most important body. It eventually took over the powers of the Consuls and the Tribunes, gained the initiative in law making, and came to hold practically all government powers. The members were appointed for life by the consuls. After the overthrow of the king, two Consuls, serving one year only, took his place. They commanded the army, and presided over the Senate and *Centuriata*. Only Patricians, or upper class citizens, held this office. Four or more Tribunes came to represent the Plebs, or lower classes, and to exercise the veto power over the acts of any official. The eight Quaestors were assistant judges and treasury officials. The Censors collected taxes, registered the citizens, nominated senators, and acted as moral guardians of the people. The Praetors were judges. The four Aediles were commissioners of public welfare and public works. The Roman constitution was written on twelve tablets and posted at the Forum. Part of the education of every youth was to memorize these laws.

Conquest of Latium. Shortly after 509 B. C. Rome entered an alliance with other cities in Latium, in order to keep the Etruscans and other hostile peoples at bay. The alliance lasted for 150 years, whereupon Rome fought a brief war with its former friends and subjugated them. This was the beginning of Roman expansion, which almost continually progressed until the second century of our era. For a short time around 390 B. C. progress was halted by the advance of a Celtic tribe (Gauls) from the northwest which seems to have captured Rome, but the city revived immediately and continued on its road to empire building.

Subjugation of the Etruscans and the Samnites. The Etruscans gradually fell from their position of supremacy. Syracuse wrested from them the control of the sea, the Gauls weakened them, and the Romans, after a ten-year siege, captured their chief city, Veii. The Samnites proved to be worthy foes; indeed, they defeated more than one Roman army before the Romans turned the tables on them at Sentinum.

Fall of the Greek Colonies on the Italian Mainland. The Greeks were long in control of southern Italy and Sicily, and to them the Romans owed their ideas of ships, coins, weights and measures, and religion. They even adopted the Greek alphabet, modified by the Latin language. At one time it seemed as though the Greeks would occupy the whole peninsula of Italy, for Pyrrhus, leader of Epirus, brought over some war elephants and threatened to wipe out the Roman colonies. The Romans finally defeated him, however, after which they conquered the Greek cities in Italy.

Treatment of Conquered Peoples. Much of Rome's success lay in her treatment of those whom she conquered. She accorded them all the liberties possible and often made citizens of them in the course of time. This was especially true of the inhabitants of Italy, whom she first subdued, then assimilated.

THE STRUGGLE WITH CARTHAGE (PUNIC WARS)

Causes. Now that Rome was the ruling city of Italy, she was responsible for the protection of the Italian coast against invaders, and for the defense of Italy's commerce against any people that might seek to damage it—and Carthage was the chief offender in both instances. Furthermore, there were now certain clashes of interest between Rome and Carthage that had not before existed. This was true on the sea, to a limited extent, but it was especially true of southern Italy. Most of Sicily was under Carthaginian control, and each power was a threat to the other. The immediate cause of the struggle, however, had to do with a quarrel among the natives of Sicily. Because the Samnites were plundering Sicily, Hiero II, king of the principal Sicilian city of Syracuse, laid siege to the Samnite town of Messina, which controlled the entrance to the strait of that name lying between Italy and Sicily. One group in Messina appealed for Roman aid, another for Carthaginian aid, and both cities responded. The war thus began.

Carthage. At this time Carthage was the largest city in the Mediterranean world, with a population of about 750,000. It controlled the commerce in the western Mediterranean and possessed valuable colonies in western Sicily and southeastern Spain. Its merchants carried home from Britain ample supplies of tin, from the Baltic countries the highly prized amber and furs, from Spain some precious metals, notably silver. In northern Africa they obtained gold and tropical products. Their merchant marine and navy established for Carthage a seemingly impregnable position. But the government of this far-flung empire was a *plutocracy*, that is, the rule of certain few wealthy persons who subordinated the welfare of the people to their own private interests, which, as we saw, were largely commercial. Naval power was supplemented neither by an adequate military force nor by a firm and efficient government at home.

Comparison of the Combatants. Rome had the better army; Carthage, the better fleet. Carthage ruled over a larger territory; but the Roman territory was more compact and easily defended. Carthage also outnumbered Rome in population; but the Roman people were the more loyal. The Carthaginians at first had the better military commanders; it was not until the Romans overcame this deficiency that permanent success crowned their efforts.

The First Punic War (264-241 B. C.). Hiero II espoused the cause of Rome, and the two forces gradually conquered Sicily. On the sea, the Romans, by making use of "boarding bridges," won two victories, but subsequently lost four fleets—two by storms and two to the enemy. A Roman fleet was finally triumphant in a battle near the Aegatian Islands, (241 B. C.) after which a successful invasion of Africa forced Carthage to sue for peace. In the resulting treaty, Carthage gave up Sicily and nearby islands, and paid an indemnity of 3,200 talents.

The Second Punic War (220-201 B. C.). In the interval of peace, Carthage subdued a rebellion at home and extended her interests in Spain, while Rome seized Sardinia and Corsica. Hannibal, the Carthaginian leader, deliberately began the struggle by capturing the Roman-protected city of Saguntum, in Spain. He then crossed the Alps and entered Italy from the north, and for about fifteen years defeated every army sent against him, but he did not capture the city of Rome. The enemies made up for their

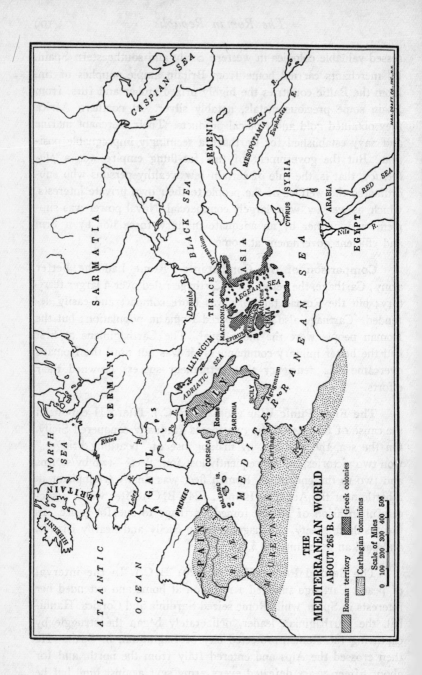

THE
MEDITERRANEAN WORLD
ABOUT 265 B.C.

Scale of Miles
0 100 200 300 400 500

Roman territory
Carthagian dominions
Greek colonies

CASPIAN SEA
ARMENIA
MESOPOTAMIA
Tigris
Euphrates
RED SEA
SYRIA
ARABIA
CYPRUS
EGYPT
Nile R.
BLACK SEA
SARMATIA
ASIA
THRACE
Byzantium
Danube R.
AEGEAN SEA
MACEDONIA
EPIRUS
Athens
ACHAIA
ILLYRICUM
ADRIATIC SEA
ITALY
Rome
SICILY
Agrigentum
SARDINIA
CORSICA
Carthage
A F R I C A
M E D I T E R R A N E A N   S E A
GERMANY
GAUL
Rhine R.
Loire R.
PYRENEES
BALEARIC IS.
SPAIN
BAETICA
MAURETANIA
NORTH SEA
BRITAIN
HIBERNIA
A T L A N T I C   O C E A N
Apennines

defeats in Italy by victories in Spain and by punishing Hannibal's allies. They finally carried the war to Carthage itself, where Hannibal met his first and only defeat at the battle of Zama. At the end of the contest, Carthage paid an indemnity of 10,000 talents, lost most of her fleet, and agreed to make no more war without Roman consent.

The Third Punic War. The continued commercial prosperity of Carthage roused Roman fears of future trouble, and caused the final destruction of the African city, after a three years' siege. (146 B. C.)

CONQUEST OF THE HELLENISTIC EAST

The Situation There. At that time, Syria and Macedonia were allies and were planning to extend their empires. Egypt was weak and friendly to Rome. Some of the lesser states of Greece were vassals of Macedonia and were anxious to secure Roman aid; others were divided into hostile Achaean and Aetolian Leagues.

The Wars with Macedonia. Rome desired to punish Philip, king of Macedonia, for the aid he had extended to Hannibal. Moreover, Macedonia was too close and powerful for safety. Greek influence at Rome also favored war. Rome's first struggle (214-205 B. C.), waged through her Aetolian allies, broke up Philip's league with Hannibal. The second war (200-196 B. C.) forced him to recognize the freedom of all Greek cities. The third contest (190 B. C.) pushed Antiochus of Syria out of Asia Minor and destroyed his fleet. But Rome did not proceed to conquer these regions. At the end of a fourth war against Macedonia and some Greek allies, Rome's patience was exhausted. She therefore made Macedonia and Greece into Roman provinces (148-146 B. C.).

THE ARMY AND GOVERNMENT OF THE REPUBLIC

One Reason Why Rome So Easily Conquered Its Rivals. The Romans were ably served by military leaders, such as Scipio, who had been largely responsible for the downfall of Hannibal. What would the Roman legions have been able to do without adequate leadership? In later days, when such leadership was no longer forthcoming, the army lost its vitality, though all the knowledge bequeathed by Scipio and Caesar was still preserved and had been increased as well.

Importance of the Legions. The legion was the principal unit in the army, and was made up of thirty "centuries," that is, groups of 100 men each. This was the infantry, which used to function in a formation called *phalanx*, in imitation of the famous units formerly employed by the Macedonians. But the Romans had learned that when fighting against armies which were fortified with elephants, the phalanx, being a compact unit operating as a unit only, could not cope with the new situation. So the phalanx was dropped for the more flexible units of infantry in the legion. Gradually cavalry forces were added to the infantry, and the brigade was formed out of thirty centuries of infantry and thirty centuries of cavalry and light-armed troops, or *auxiliaries*. The soldiers were taught to fight in three lines, with the third in the rear held as the reserves.

Arms. The Romans borrowed from the Samnites in the central Apennines the use of the javelin, and from the Gauls the *convex* shield. They learned from the peoples in Spain the use of the two-edged sword. While the front ranks were engaged in fighting with the sword, the troops in the rear would throw the javelins at the enemy over the heads of the front line. For protection the infantry wore armor made of metal or leather, or parts of each; they used helmets and shields besides. Their camps were always fortified in case the men had to stay in them over night. For siege operations the Romans constructed the customary covered terrace, the *testudo*, which enabled a body of men to approach the city without being in danger of attack from above. Battering-rams were also employed with much success.

Provincial Government. The government of the republic kept pace with the increase in territory and the subjugation of other peoples. Governors were appointed to rule over the provinces; their term of office was but one year, and they received no salary, as was also the case with the other officials employed in the republican government. Each governor in his respective province enjoyed complete authority over public and military affairs. He took care that taxes were collected from the inhabitants and that their own language and religion were respected. In many cases the taxes were paid by the subjects to so-called *publicans,* professional tax collectors ("farmers"), who paid a fixed sum to the government and gathered all they could for themselves. Since the governors received no salary, they also were often guilty of extortion, particularly if they had spent large sums of money in obtaining their position.

Struggle Between the Patricians and the Plebeians. Originally the republic had been controlled by certain members of the nobility whom we might style aristocrats, or patricians, and the government had been an aristocracy. But the masses rapidly increased in number, and influence, since their services were much needed in the wars. Led by officials who represented them, called tribunes of the *plebs* (the plebeians, or proletariat), they gradually compelled the patricians to make a number of concessions, so that by 287 B. C. the plebeians were considered the equals of the patricians before the law and in operating the government. Now they could have seats in the senate and were eligible to positions in the national government. They were also permitted to vote in the general assembly. Unlike the aristocracy of many a Greek city-state, the Roman nobles had always yielded on every point rather than foment a civil war. In this manner the Romans had acquired great political power and stability so urgently needed in their many difficult wars.

The New Nobility and Its Opponents. But, as is often the case, the leaders of the masses, after having acquired for the people certain advantages, began to form an aristocracy of their own and to foster friendship and marriage alliances with the members of the original aristocracy. Once more the plebeians asserted themselves. They argued correctly that the senate was a closed body, not a body which represented the people at all. During the wars with Carthage the senate had greatly increased its powers at the expense of the popular assembly, which was too unwieldy to arrive at decisions when such decisions had to be made quickly. The new nobility also was reluctant to give up its hold on the landed estates throughout the peninsula. This time the patricians did not yield, and so civil war followed, in the course of which dictators rose to power and both the nobles and the plebeians resorted to the use of the army.

THE OVERTHROW OF THE REPUBLIC (133-27 B. C.)

The Struggle for the Land. Not only had the Senate become a body of aristocrats, and had usurped most of the powers of the other assemblies, but the senators and their friends had gained control of much of the land, in flagrant disregard of existing land laws. Two brothers, Tiberius and Gaius Gracchus, who were successively elected Tribunes, sponsored land reform laws designed to end this inequality (133-122 B. C.). Tiberius aimed chiefly at aiding the peasants, but he used unconstitutional methods, and was accused of seeking a monarchy; he was murdered by partisans of the Senate. Gaius had more far-reaching plans which included agrarian reform and extension of the franchise. In general, he sought to imitate Greek democracy. The Senate declared him a rioter and made war on him. Overtaken in flight, he committed suicide. The intolerable conditions regarding land and franchise were little improved.

The Social, or Marsic, War. Many of the Italian allies in Italy were not full Roman citizens. Drusus led in an attempt to gain this coveted privilege, but failed. (91 B. C.) These people then resorted to war and defeated the armies sent against them. Rome's tardy concession of citizenship brought peace (88 B. C.).

The Dictatorship of Marius. At this time a new leader appeared—Marius. He won notice by his defeat of the Numidian general, Jugurtha, and came to be known as the Savior of Italy because he defeated the Cimbri and Teutons, Germanic invaders. As a reward, he became dictator, but was a failure as a political leader.

Triumph of the Senate. A military champion of the Senate now appeared—Sulla. After displacing Marius from command of the army, he won popular fame by leading a successful expedition against Mithridates, King of Pontus. He then returned in triumph and had many of his enemies put to death. After having restored the Senate to full power, he voluntarily retired.

Leadership of Pompey. It was evident, though, that the Roman mind was turning to a one-man deliverer, for Pompey next became prominent. As a Consul representing the people, he restored to the Assembly and the Tribunes their lost powers. But his fame rested on military successes—a successful campaign against the Mediterranean pirates, and a brilliant expedition against Mithridates.

Other Prominent Leaders in Rome. Julius Caesar, then a young man, had been a supporter of Marius, was a liberal spender, and possessed the gift of oratory. Catiline, a ruined spendthrift of a noble family, ran for Consul, but Cicero defeated him, and later had him executed on a charge of armed treason. Cicero, Rome's greatest orator, was a member of the Equestrian order. He desired a return of the republic.

The First Triumvirate. Three of the men seeking leadership agreed to combine their interests in an arrangement known as the First Triumvirate. By the terms of this agreement, Caesar was to become Consul, and Pompey was to get land for his troops, have his peace treaty for Asia Minor ratified, and become governor of Spain. Crassus was to furnish money for the undertakings, was to become Consul, and later was to command an army for an invasion of Syria.

The Conquest of Gaul. Caesar was soon made governor of Illyria and Gaul, with command of an army. He conquered Gaul (58-51 B. C.), and also invaded Britain, after which he wrote a history of his conquests.

Caesar, Master of Rome. Caesar's appointment of five years in Gaul was too short a period, so he asked that it be renewed. Crassus was defeated by the Parthians. Pompey, now jealous of Caesar, persuaded the Senate to refuse a re-appointment and to ask him to resign at once. Caesar's refusal to resign meant war; he came southward, crossing the Rubicon in 49 B. C., soon met and defeated Pompey now representing the Senate, and thus became virtual ruler.

His Political and Economic Reforms. Caesar made provincial governors strictly responsible to him, gave them fixed salaries and no other pay, and sent other officials to report as to their behavior. He also extended citizenship to many provincials. He increased the membership of the Senate to six hundred, including many provincials, and dominated that body himself. He became Tribune, Censor, and Dictator for life, and also held the office of Imperator for himself and descendants. He required landlords to employ one free laborer for each two slaves, reclaimed and allotted more public lands, and settled eighty thousand citizens in the provinces. He sponsored agrarian relief laws and aid for insolvent debtors, reformed the calendar and the coinage system, took a census, drained marshes, improved roads, and erected public buildings. A group of political enemies assassinated him (44 B. C.).

The Second Triumvirate. Octavius (later Augustus), a grand nephew of Julius Caesar, upon receiving news of his uncle's death, went to Rome and placed himself at the head of the army to secure the place his uncle had held. He succeeded in obtaining the office of Consul, but found two opponents for power in Antony and Lepidus. The three formed the Second Triumvirate, in which they agreed to a general execution of all enemies, and to an overthrow of the Republicans, headed by Brutus. But Lepidus soon retired with the office of Pontifex Maximus and the other two men fought- for supremacy. Octavius defeated the forces of Antony and Cleopatra at Actium, and made Egypt into a Roman province (31 B. C.). Thus was the Second Triumvirate broken up.

ROMAN CIVILIZATION BEFORE 27 B.C.

The Romans Were Taught by the Greeks. As had been the case with the Greeks when they rose to power and led all the world in learning and art, so the Romans had to learn much from other peoples before they themselves could become teachers and leaders. The Greeks taught the Romans philosophy, literature, rhetoric, art, and science. Since the rise of Rome followed that of Athens within such a short time, the Romans were never able to surpass the Greeks in the fields just mentioned. Only in the shaping of law and of political institutions, in the building of character and patriotic virtues, and in a sense of the practical did they overcome the lead taken by the Greeks. They applied themselves less to philosophy and more to road building and scientific agriculture. They knew less about literature and sculpture, but more about government. They spent less time arguing about social justice but did more for the creation of good law. They said less about individual rights and had less time for civil war, but they built a state that established peace and order for hundreds of years. When the Romans first entered the Near East (about 200 B. C.), they found the Greeks quarreling among themselves and promptly destroyed their respective states. Where the Greeks failed to provide a proper environment for the spread of their culture, the Romans arrived just in time to give it to them.

The Constitution. The Roman constitution was made up of the laws and political institutions existing at any given time. Only when the whole body of free citizens assembled and wished to change the constitution, could it be modified. Nevertheless the government at Rome became increasingly a matter of balance of power between the Senate and some single leader, the latter gradually gaining until, in the time of Augustus, it was accurate enough to call him an emperor. The Romans were strikingly successful in the management of local government by establishing municipal units, which work was brilliantly done. But their government of the empire as a whole was not so good, for they failed to see that an empire cannot be ruled as a huge city-state.

Early Development of Roman Law. Roman law was based upon a code of civil and criminal law perfected about 450 B. C. and published upon twelve painted wooden tablets, called the Twelve Tables. It was rather primitive, being intended for a small state of some four hundred square miles, in which agriculture was the principal mode of making a living. But capable judicial officers called *praetors,* employed by the national government, enlarged and liberalized the code. There were also other experts and lawyers who interpreted the law from time to time, so that Roman law always was adequate for the needs of the people.

The Family. Perhaps the greatest single cause of the power of Rome was the way in which family life was conducted. The *familia,* or household, gave concrete expression to the unusual respect the average Roman had for authority and law. The father was the head of the whole unit, including the various members who were dependent upon it, both slaves and freemen. He wielded unlimited power in his little domain and expected to be obeyed by all members. It was a definite part of Roman "piety" to render such obedience to an authority or superior. The Greeks, on the other hand, were too much interested in individual rights to foster such a spirit, and so their states quickly collapsed as soon as they faced the might of Rome. Another important point of difference was the manner in which the Greeks and the Romans regarded their women. The Romans were like the Spartans, whom we mentioned in the preceding chapter, and in general treated the women with proper respect, while the Athenians in general did the opposite.

Slavery. It cannot be said, however, that the Romans showed a kinder feeling for slaves than did the Greeks. By 30 B. C. there were about 400,000 slaves in and near Rome, and about 1,500,000 in Italy. Slaves were regarded as no better than cattle, having no rights, no permission even to get married as a rule. What a pity that highly educated men and beautiful women from oriental countries were mistreated by barbarous and ignorant masters! Branded with a hot iron, herded like cattle, the wretched creatures often passed the nights in damp cellars and were driven into the fields where once free citizens had labored on their own land. Most of those free farmers and their descendants had lost their lands to more wealthy neighbors, as they could no longer compete with the latter. They had gone to Rome in many cases, where now they were on relief. By 50 B. C. about 300,000 persons, or more than one-third of Rome's population, were dependent on government support.

Economic Developments. Commerce and industry naturally expanded with the continual extension of the Roman frontiers; but never reached such proportions as might be expected of the greatest empire that the world had ever seen. This may have been partly because of aristocratic prejudice; senators and their sons, for example, could not lawfully engage in large commercial enterprise. The Romans under their republican government remained essentially a simple-minded people, attached to their own homes and families, and always happy to find a retreat from the uproar of the city crowds somewhere in the country. It is almost a marvel that the city of Rome never attained a population considerably in excess of half a million souls, at least not until we reach the period after the end of the republic.

Architecture and Engineering. As we have said, the Romans made but mediocre contributions to the arts and the sciences. For building, they followed the Etruscans, but afterwards they imitated the Greeks. Their earliest temples were constructed on a stone foundation, with a porch placed in front. The building was as a rule made of soft sandstone, covered with stucco. The roof was constructed of wood and decorated with sculpture. As the Romans became more familiar with the magnificent Greek structures, they were moved to emulation. About the year 150 B. C. they invented cement, which enabled them to erect huge buildings out of brick, and to construct rounded arches in the building of bridges and triumphal monuments. Among their typical buildings we may mention amphitheaters, aqueducts, and *basilicas* —the latter in the nature of public halls used for the administration of justice, although sometimes also built as private business offices. Essentially, the *basilica* was an oblong hall with side aisles; many of these structures were adapted later for Christian churches, and the type influenced Christian architecture powerfully.

Street and Road Building. The Romans were in the habit of laying out their streets in rectangular fashion, in imitation of the plans followed by the Greeks in building Alexandria. Originally, like the Greeks, the Romans had followed no definite plans, but it was obvious that straight and wide streets were much to be preferred to the narrow and crooked streets of old Rome. But in the matter of road building, the Romans required no instruction from other peoples. Even their first great road, the *Via Appia,* or the Appian Way, built before 300 B. C. from Rome southward to the sea, was so durably constructed that today, more than two thousand years later, it can still be used for heavy traffic.

Home Construction. Private homes varied from beautiful stone structures belonging to the rich, to the many-storied tenement houses of the city poor, built of flimsy wood and stucco. The larger homes were provided with a sort of central courtyard called the *atrium;* originally it had been the living room, but afterward under the influence of the Greeks, it expanded into a much larger room. In many cases a home included an enclosed garden, open, like the *atrium,* to the sky, in imitation of the homes that had been constructed in Oriental countries. This was surrounded by columns, and was called the *peristyle.*

Sculpture. The Romans never developed great skill in the field of sculpture, which was dominated by Greek artists. As a rule the sculpture that was produced in Italy was practically nothing but a copy of Greek models. Roman painting was similarly affected by the Greek and Egyptian artists and patterns. It is interesting to note that the Romans had the habit of carrying large wax images of their ancestors in funeral processions, which created a brisk demand for such examples of sculpture. Moreover, bronze statues of heroes in Roman history were often placed in prominent spots in the leading cities. These, and the portrait-busts, show a realism which was lacking in Greek sculpture. The frequent triumphs achieved by the Roman legions led to the painting of scenes to commemorate these victories. Unfortunately, nearly all of the Roman painting has perished, so that we are not in a position to judge how far the Romans were able to emancipate themselves from Greek art.

Education. Public schools were not maintained in the Roman republic, but instruction was given in private schools, under the influence of Greek teachers. Here the liberal arts (literature, arithmetic, geometry, astronomy, music, and dialectics) were taught. The Roman alphabet was derived from the Greek alphabet; it consisted of 23 letters, every one of which we are using today, having added the following three letters: J, U, and W.

Literature. The Romans were extremely slow in developing a literature of their own. Plautus and Terence wrote versified comedies, but these were imitated from the Greek. Catullus wrote passionate lyric verse; Lucretius, an Epicurean poet, was the author of *On the Nature of Things;* Cicero, the famous orator, also composed philosophic treatises; and Caesar, who left an excellent history of his campaigns in Gaul (The Gallic Wars), and of his Civil Wars also. Sallust was also a capable historian in the period before 30 B. C.

The Development of the Calendar. Even the celebrated Julian Calendar, named after Julius Caesar, was simply an Alexandrian production. It was perfected by an Alexandrian astronomer, who established the length of the year as 365¼ days, with one extra day added at the end of February once in four years. Slowly the use of this calendar spread throughout the Roman Empire, and it remained in use for more than 1600 years before it was reformed by Spanish scholars for Pope Gregory XIII. For that reason the new calendar has ever since been called the Gregorian Calendar. It was established in the year 1582, when eleven days were eliminated from the calendar, because in those 1600 years since the perfection of the Julian Calendar eleven days had been wrongly added to the Solar Calendar. The new calendar made the following change: Centennial years, that is, every last year of a century, such as 1800 or 1900, were regarded as leap years only when they could be divided by four hundred. Consequently, the year 2000 A. D. is a leap year but the year 1900 is not a leap year. England did not change her calendar until 1752, while Russia and Greece did not adopt the new calendar until after the First World War. Other nations had changed theirs much earlier.

Philosophy. In the field of philosophy the Romans made practically no contributions. Both Stoicism and Epicureanism were widely followed, with Epicureanism degenerating into a system of thought which placed undue emphasis upon the pursuit of physical pleasures. However, there were Roman philosophers who remained true to the written principles of the Epicurean philosophy. Most notable among these was the poet Lucretius, whose philosophical ideas, however, are founded upon those of Democritus as well as those of Epicurus.

Religion. Early Roman religion is often designated as animism, that is, the belief that spiritual power resided in natural forces or objects. These powers were thought to affect a human being either for good or for ill. For example, there was Janus, the spirit of the doorway, who could affect anyone entering through the door. Another was Vesta, the spirit of the hearth; a third was the spirit of the storeroom; and still another was the spirit of landed property. These spiritual powers were worshipped in every home, the father taking the place of the priest. As in some Oriental countries, so in the Roman Republic it was widely believed that the spirit of a deceased person remained near his dead body, and that, if not properly buried, he would cause a great deal of trouble to those responsible. Good and evil spirits were present everywhere, and it was desirable to placate the good as well as the bad.

The Gods. As the Roman state expanded, some of the gods assumed a more national aspect. New gods were added to the list of the deities that one was expected to worship, most of them borrowed from the Greeks, as shown below:

Roman Deity	Duties	Similar Greek Deity
Jupiter	supreme god	Zeus
Mars	god of war	Ares
Venus	goddess of love	Aphrodite
Bacchus	god of wine	Dionysius
Juno	goddess of the sky marriage, and birth	Hera
Minerva	goddess of wisdom and commerce	Athena
Ceres	goddess of the fields	Demeter
Neptune	god of the sea	Poseidon
Mercury	messenger of the gods	Hermes

The list could be extended. Another notable feature of the Roman religion was the *Sibyllene Books,* which were supposed to foretell the future of the state.

Tolerance of the Romans. From the Greeks and the Etruscans the Romans borrowed the idea of omens and signs. As soon as they became acquainted with Greek mythology, they also took much of that over. Since they had no important religious dogmas of their own, they were upon the whole a tolerant people. They had no definite notions about salvation or of the immortality of the soul, but were of the opinion that somehow one could improve one's future by seeking the favor of the gods. It can readily be understood why the Romans so freely tolerated the worship of many different gods. When Christianity first made its appearance in the city of Rome many thousands of citizens gladly listened to the preaching of the missionaries. What is more important still, it was the Roman peace that made it possible for the Christian religion in a relatively short time to spread over the whole of the Mediterranean world.

Significant Dates

Reign of Augustus
    (Octavius) . . 27 B.C.-A.D. 14
Reign of Tiberius . . A.D. 14- 37
Reign of Nero . . . A.D. 54- 68
Reign of Trajan . . A.D. 98-117
Reign of Hadrian . . A.D. 117-138
Reign of Marcus
    Aurelius . . . . A.D. 161-180

CHAPTER X.

THE ROMAN EMPIRE UNDER THE PRINCIPATE

For more than 250 years after the founding of the Roman Empire, the whole of the Mediterranean world enjoyed peace and prosperity such as it had never known before. So notable was the efficiency of the imperial government of Rome and the excellent management of its armies that the turbulent barbarians on the northern frontier and the restless Orientals east of Syria were firmly held in check. The government established by Caesar and developed by Augustus was ably maintained by Tiberius, and for the next two centuries such able rulers as Nerva, Trajan, Hadrian, Vespasian, Titus, Antoninus Pius, and Marcus Aurelius administered the Empire sufficiently well to offset the reigns of Terror of such emperors as Caligula, Nero, and Domitian. It was then that Rome extended its sway over all of southern Europe, Great Britain, western and southern Germany, Asia Minor, Syria, and all of northern Africa. It was by far the greatest empire that the world had ever seen. It made it possible for Greek civilization and the Christian Church to spread their principles and teachings over a vast area, thus laying the foundations of western civilization.

POLITICAL DEVELOPMENTS FROM 27 B.C. - A.D. 235

Powers Assumed by Octavian (Augustus). In 27 B.C. Octavian established a new imperial government by setting up for himself the position of *Princeps* (leader). He also acquired the title of Augustus, as we observed in the preceding chapter, while two years previously he had been made Imperator. In his capacity as *Pontifex Maximus* (high priest) he was the head of the religion of the state. Furthermore, he was in control of the military forces in the country. In the provinces he was worshipped as a god, and after his death he was regarded as a god in all parts of the empire. In spite of his great powers, he was responsible to the Senate and the popular Assembly. However, after the first century the emperor was responsible only to the Senate. He held this position for life, though it was not hereditary.

The Imperial Government. The various offices and positions throughout the empire, such as that of governor of the provinces, as well as those of the Senate and the Assembly, were all preserved. Gradually, however, the emperor took over from the Senate and the Assembly most of their respective powers. The Assembly ceased to function, and the Senate was largely deprived of its superiority. We may conclude, therefore, that before long the emperor became an absolute monarch. He retained this position until the year A. D. 235, when a change occurred, but instead of reverting to earlier conditions, the emperor increased his power even more than before. After A. D. 235 he dropped the title of Princeps, but assumed that of *Dominus,* or Lord, while he retained those of Augustus and Imperator. This position was maintained until the end of the empire.

The Armed Forces of the Empire. The army in the time of the Empire differed very little from that employed in the earlier period. The only important difference was that now less depended upon the infantry and more upon the cavalry forces. Moreover, archers were in many cases substituted for the old infantrymen. As long as discipline was maintained the Roman legions remained upon the whole invincible. The army numbered about 350,-000 professional soldiers. One-half of these were Roman citizens from Italy, and the others were from the provinces; the Roman citizens served in the legions, that is, the infantry forces; the provincials constituted the auxiliaries, both cavalry and infantry. The navy was greatly enlarged and remained adequate for the needs of the empire.

The Government of the Provinces. Provincial government under the empire was superior to that of the earlier period, for the governors now served for a longer term than one year and received salaries, thus being relieved of the temptation of exploiting the subjects in their respective provinces. Moreover, the taxes were being collected by government officials instead of tax farmers. Throughout the empire colonies of Roman citizens were founded or enlarged. In A. D. 212 the privileges of citizenship were granted to all males who were free members of municipalities.

How the Barbarians Were Held in Check. Protected from invasion by the magnificent army, which was stationed along the frontiers, the empire was not disturbed from without until the fourth century A. D. It is true that in the time of Augustus some of the Roman legions were annihilated by German troops under Arminius (Hermann) in western Germany (A. D. 9). Also to be remembered was a revolt in Britain during the first century and an uprising of the Jews in A. D. 70. Order was quickly restored in Britain and the Jews were harshly suppressed; Jerusalem was razed to the ground. The emperors aimed to maintain natural frontiers, including the Atlantic Ocean and the North Sea in the West, the Rhine and Danube rivers in the North, the Black Sea and the Syrian Desert in the East, and the Sahara in the South. A wall was constructed in Britain to keep the inhabitants of what is now Scotland out of the province, and a heavily fortified frontier was drawn from the Rhine near Mainz to the upper Danube. Aside from these two relatively short lines, all important borders were fortified by nature.

Size of the Empire. The Roman Empire in the second century A. D. comprised an area of about three and a half million square miles, that is, nearly twice as much as the empire of Alexander the Great. Its population at that time is estimated to have been approximately eighty millions.

THE LEADING EMPERORS AFTER AUGUSTUS

Tiberius (14-37). He proved to be a wise, but unpopular ruler. He alienated the army by his policy of peace, angered the Senate because he spent money on the Asiatic provinces and refused to pension the nobility, and aroused the populace because he cut down the supply of free wheat.

Caligula (37-41) and Claudius (41-54). Caligula was of unsound mind and squandered much money. His own officers finally assassinated him. The Praetorian Guard forced the Senate to select Claudius. Though lacking firmness, he accomplished much. He brought many provincial governors to task, bettered conditions of slave life, constructed aqueducts, and used ministers.

Nero (54-68). His mother pushed him into power. For a while he ruled well, but soon became despotic and developed assassination to a fine art. Rome was burned, an event which was attributed to the Christians, followed by a vicious persecution of them. Finally facing a revolt, Nero killed himself.

Problems Now Facing the Government. The wise reforms instituted in political and economic affairs, plus a succession of able rulers, gave Rome a new lease on life. Although the Augustan rulers had done much, two important matters still faced the government: protection of the frontiers, and the organization of a more efficient government. To correct the first, the emperor stationed troops along the northern boundary, the Danube frontier, and Parthia. Various steps were taken to remedy the second fault: a civil service system was created, tax farmers were largely replaced by government collectors, a uniform system of law was developed, and the government of the provinces was improved.

Vespasian (70-79) and Titus (79-81). Vespasian, proclaimed Emperor by his soldiers, conducted a thrifty and economical administration. Titus, popular on account of his generosity, is, however, remembered for the destruction of Jerusalem and the scattering of the Jews. A volcano destroyed Pompeii and Herculaneum during his reign.

Domitian (81-96) and Nerva (96-98). Domitian fortified the frontiers, conquered Britain and Gaul, quieted the Dacians, and persecuted the Christians as well as any pagans whom his spies labeled disloyal. He fell at the hands of a Republican assassin. Nerva was the first of the so-called "five good emperors." As a member of the Senate, he increased the importance of that body.

Trajan (98-117) and Hadrian (117-139). Trajan was a warlike ruler, who subdued Dacia and established a Roman colony there. He also conquered Arabia, Armenia, and Parthia, and made these regions into Roman provinces. Hadrian gave up some of Trajan's conquests, built a wall across Britain, and established a Federal civil service system. He also reorganized the army by introducing sound discipline, extended citizenship to many provincials, and encouraged learning.

Antoninus Pius (138-161) and Marcus Aurelius (161-180). Antoninus Pius improved the lot of the slaves, and adopted the principle that a man is innocent until proved guilty. He neglected the defense of the frontier. Marcus Aurelius was a Stoic philosopher and writer, his *Meditations* approaching Christianity in spirit; however, he persecuted the Christians. He died while defending the frontier against the barbarians.

Evidences of Internal Disruption after the Reign of Marcus Aurelius. The process of concentrating land into great estates, or villas, which had been noticeable for some time, now went on apace. The small-scale farmers, unable longer to keep their land, became bound to some lord for their holdings, which could not be sold. They were the *coloni*. The supply of slaves decreased with the decline of war. Those remaining had their condition improved by law, some became *coloni,* and others were even set free. Wasteful methods of villa farming led to decreased productiveness.

The Decline in Population. Increased luxury produced a lower birth rate, while the higher cost of living made for smaller families. The Asiatic Plague also caused the death of many.

Industrial and Commercial Stagnation. The lowered purchasing ability of country communities produced a consequent decline of city industries and increased unemployment. In order

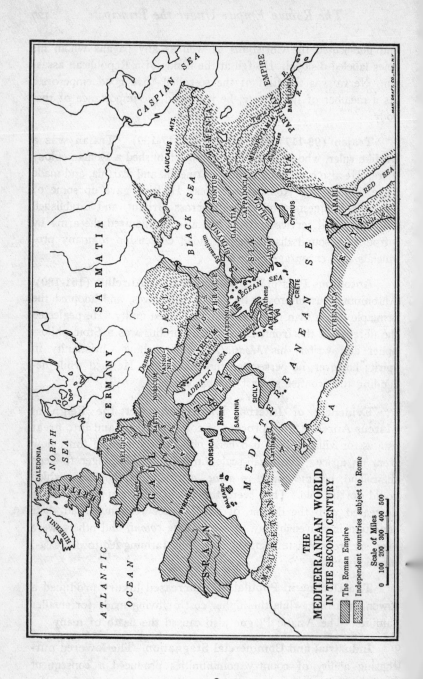

THE
MEDITERRANEAN WORLD
IN THE SECOND CENTURY

▨ The Roman Empire

▧ Independent countries subject to Rome

Scale of Miles

0 100 200 300 400 500

to remedy the scarcity of money, rulers resorted to debasing the coinage—a remedy that made matters only worse.

Demoralization of State and Army. Lacking money, the government paid soldiers in land and received taxes in grain. Because there was no law of succession, the army often put incompetent rulers into power. Because Romans would not serve, barbarian recruits were accepted.

The Political and Military Situation after Marcus Aurelius. So low did Rome sink that Julianus bought the throne at public auction (193). There were some signs of revival under Septimius Severus (193-211), but nothing permanent was accomplished. Eighty rulers occupied the throne within a period of ninety years, and most of them met death by violence. Goths from the East ravaged the coast; others overran northern Italy, Gaul, and Spain. The Gauls achieved independence, while a new Persia arose to threaten Rome from Asia.

ROMAN CIVILIZATION UNDER THE PRINCIPATE

Agriculture. In the period after 27 B. C. agriculture remained, as before, the chief source of wealth and activity. Slavery gradually began to decline, and was replaced by the institution of the so-called *coloni* on the one hand, and the increased labor of free tenants on the other hand. These *coloni* were neither freemen nor slaves. They closely resembled the serfs of medieval times, in that they were bound to the soil, formed the lowest level in the social order, and worked long hours for very little return. The Romans learned to fertilize the land with lime and manure. They were also accustomed to letting the fields lie fallow for one year out of every two or three. It was possible for a family to make a decent living on a farm of not more than twenty or twenty-five acres, but there were many estates that comprised from 50 to 200 acres, while stock ranches were much larger.

Trade. Commerce was manipulated on a larger scale than it had been in the time of the republic, owing to the maintenance of peace, the building of great networks of magnificent roads, the low customs dues that were exacted, and the uniform coinage. About the year 350 B. C. coinage was established by the Romans, the first of the coins being made of copper; after 250 B. C., some were of silver. In various parts of the empire, previously, many coins had been used, so that now the uniformity of the coinage was a great advance. Contact was made with both India and China, and from India the Romans obtained cotton, silk goods, linen goods, ivory, and spices; from China they brought home the valuable raw silk, which was not produced in Europe until after A. D. 550.

Industry. Commerce and industry expanded with the increasing size of the Roman Empire. Pottery, bronzeware, figures made out of silver and gold, glassware, furniture, and a great variety of woven and spun cloths were manufactured in the little shops throughout the empire. These were of about the same size as the establishments conducted by the Greeks. The articles of import and export already mentioned need not be enumerated again.

Trade Associations or Corporations (Colleges). In the cities of the Roman Empire, as well as in the old Greek city-states, it was customary for the men who were engaged in the same trade to have their shops in the same streets. This interesting custom was perpetuated throughout the Middle Ages. Skilled workers in a number of different trades organized into guilds called colleges, which maintained trade secrets, and secured for the respective members both political advantages and social entertainment. Like the masonic orders of today, they also provided financial support for needy members or their widows and orphans.

The Importance of Good Roads. In order to maintain peace and order, the government took care that all roads were kept in condition. An efficient postal service was established, in which use was made of relays of horses in the delivery of official dispatches.

The Freedmen. In the period from 100 to A. D. 235 large numbers of slaves were set free from time to time. These freedmen, although they were not admitted to citizenship, were allowed to fill subordinate positions in the civil service, and they were free to find whatever occupations that seemed suitable to them in other lines of work. Many grew wealthy, and from Tiberius on they were powerful at court.

Attempts to Restore Old Roman Life. During the same period laws were passed, especially by Augustus, to protect the sanctity of marriage and to banish the Oriental gods and restore the old religion. These had little effect. Moreover, old temples were rebuilt and new ones were erected.

Improvements in the Capital. New police, fire, and water departments were created, and beautiful theaters, public baths, and government edifices were built.

Architecture. In the fields of learning and art few changes were introduced in the period of the Principate. The buildings became larger, and the statues more abundant, but the character of Roman art remained substantially the same. Among the noteworthy examples of architecture may be mentioned the Pantheon, a beautiful temple constructed in Rome which differed from the typical Greek temple in that it was surmounted by a dome and was not rectangular but round. Beautiful triumphal arches were constructed in Rome, and in the famous marketplace, called the *Forum,* a great variety of structures were built. The Greek influence may be seen in the profusion of columns. The largest building in Rome was probably the great Circus Maximus, which seated approximately 250,000 persons. Another amphitheater was the Colosseum, which was much smaller, and built in a circular shape, while the former building was rectangular. In the second century A. D. Rome attained a population of about one million. Fabulous was the wealth of its prominent citizens, grandiose were its temples and palaces, magnificent its monumental arches. On what lines they were constructed may be gathered from the monumental work by Vitruvius, *On Architecture.*

Painting. Some of the Roman paintings on the walls of their buildings (frescoes) may be examined today among the ruins of ancient Pompeii, a city situated near the volcano called Mt. Vesuvius, in the vicinity of Naples. It was suddenly destroyed in the year A. D. 79. So swift was the work of destruction that many had no chance to leave their houses, and thus it is possible for scholars not only to study the architecture, sculpture, and paintings of the ancient city, but also the industrial and commercial life of its inhabitants.

Literature. Throughout the empire both Latin and Greek were the official literary languages. Greek scholarship and Greek literature retained their marked superiority, and it became fashionable for the wealthy citizens in Rome and elsewhere to employ Greek teachers for their children and to speak and write in the Greek language. Public schools were now maintained by the municipal governments. Large libraries were constructed in Rome, and a respectable literature was produced by Roman writers. Among the most famous writers was Vergil (Virgil), the author of the *Aeneid*. In this far-famed work he told of the adventurous and heroic exploits of Aeneas, who was depicted as the Trojan ancestor of Julius Caesar's family. It makes an excellent piece of thrilling epic poetry. Equally famous and influential was Horace, who composed lyrics in the Greek form called *Ode*, excelling in form and organization of the subject-matter. His *Satires* and *Epistles* also reveal the author's profound knowledge of human feelings and emotions. Livy was the writer of an excellent though somewhat uncritical history of Rome from its founding to the beginnings of the empire. Tacitus wrote three historical works of considerable importance, namely, the *Histories,* the *Annals,* and *Germania.* In the first two he depicted Roman history from the death of Augustus to his own time (A. D. 96). He spoke with bitter pessimism about the luxurious living of the wealthy and the lack of virtue among the rank and file of the people. The Romans he described as decadent, and contrasted them with the Germans (in the *Germania*), whose physical powers and high moral standards he extolled with exaggeration. Juvenal also criticized Roman society, but he was a satirical poet. Suetonius, his contemporary, introduced a fairly new form of literature in his biographical sketches entitled *Lives of the Caesars*. He did not scruple to condescend to gossip and to tell stories of decidedly popular interest bordering on the sensational. Ovid wrote poems of love. Plutarch, writing in Greek, composed the famous biographies of great men of the ancient world called *Parallel Lives,* since his plan called for a contrast, each Greek being compared with a Roman. Lucian also wrote in Greek. He specialized in biting and witty satire in the form of dialogues; he also wrote essays and narratives. Emperor Marcus Aurelius, as we already noted, composed a philosophical treatise entitled *Meditations*.

Science. Among the outstanding scientists in the Roman Empire were Pliny the Elder, the author of *Natural History;* and Ptolemy, who composed the *Geographical Outline.* Contact with India and China naturally enlarged the horizon of the peoples living in the Roman Empire, so that scholars like Ptolemy were able to draw better maps than the Greeks had done in earlier periods. In the field of medicine also we may note definite advancement. Galen, a Greek, visited Rome and wrote excellent treatises on medicine. Many public hospitals, possibly the first ever known, were built. Some successful attempts were made even to inaugurate public medical service, or socialized medical care. In each municipality a number of physicians were encouraged, through the exemption of taxes, to serve the poor free of charge.

Geography. Acting under the order of Augustus, the Roman general Agrippa made a survey of the Roman Empire. As a result he drew a map of the world which was exhibited on the square called Campus Martius in Rome. Distances from the city determined the location of various towns and regions on this map, instead of the principles of latitude and longitude. It was copied during the Middle Ages by numerous artists, one of whom prepared the so-called Peutingerian Table.

Progress in Roman Law. Roman law continued to be improved upon and provided with suitable commentaries. Early in the second century Emperor Hadrian set up a committee of jurists who were expected to advise the emperor whenever occasion arose. In the third century a number of exceptionally learned jurists brought the study of Roman law to its most fruitful period. Gaius composed the *Institutes,* covering the principles of Roman law. Perhaps the greatest of these men was Papinian, a Syrian Greek.

Bonds of Union. In spite of the vast extent and widely different peoples composing it, the Roman Empire existed for several centuries, and many considered it eternal. Evidently some strong ties bound it together. Perhaps one of the strongest of these bonds was the government itself. It was headed by an emperor who was deified after death, and regarded with reverence, and who was in theory all-powerful. It was active in maintaining order, establishing justice, and defending the boundaries. In some instances it provided even amusements and furnished food for its inhabitants. In the course of time it developed a superior system of law that was humane, uniform, just, and adapted to the needs of a complex society such as existed within the empire. The Roman law still exerts a profound influence on the world, for it is the basis of many modern law systems. Moreover, the government preserved a peace that was effective, most of the time, throughout its domain.

Education. Elementary, grammar, and higher schools were established in every town of importance, where teachers paid by the state taught popular subjects, such as law, medicine, Latin, Greek, rhetoric, and oratory. Though this education was chiefly for those of the upper and middle classes, nevertheless it acted as a unifying factor.

Religion. During the first and second centuries of our era, as the various conquered provinces became completely Romanized, the emperor decreed that the state cult of Jupiter Capitolinus should be introduced in all the urban communities in the Empire called municipalities. As a result, in numerous districts the original native cults could no longer be maintained, disappearing in some places, and merging in other places with the state cult. As mentioned above, the Emperor was worshipped in the city of Rome and the rest of Italy; after the citizenship was extended to the provincial inhabitants, they likewise were expected to worship the living emperor, in addition to his deceased predecessors. Since the state cult was enforced upon the populace, it lacked that vitality which accompanies real devotion. Consequently, millions of persons sought to satisfy their demand for a vital religion in the cults that were being imported from the Hellenized Near East. The Orphic mystery religion, the popular gods of the Greeks and the Oriental gods were all accorded reverence and support. Much attention was also paid to Mithra (Mithras, in Latin and Greek), who was widely worshipped in Asia Minor as the Unconquered Sun God. The Persians regarded him in somewhat the same light as the Christians later regarded Jesus of Nazareth, that is, as a personal savior. Some of the emperors and many of the soldiers participated in the worship of Mithras, for this practice did not in the least interfere with the deification of the emperors.

But this can not be said of the Jewish religion, since it insisted through the Ten Commandments of Moses (especially the first one) that one should worship only Jehovah, the God of the chosen people of Israel. The Jews were intensely attached to their own race and religious customs, and they would no doubt have been restricted in their forms of worship if it had not been for the active support they had rendered to Caesar and Augustus during the civil war that immediately preceded the establishment of the Roman Empire in 27 B. C. The Jews were not even required to participate in the worship of the Emperor. Although the brief rebellion which resulted in the destruction of Jerusalem in A. D. 70 as its aftermath naturally aroused the anger of the Emperor Vespasian, it was not long before the Jews once more had a licensed religion of their own. They were, however, required to pay a special head tax for this privilege.

Attitude of the Christians. The same might have happened also to the Christians if they had been willing to make some sort of a compromise with the imperial government. But they were adamant in their position, since their Founder had said that His kingdom was not of this world. They would rather lose their property and their lives than submit to anything that smacked of idolatry or worldliness. Thus they encountered opposition from the Roman officials and the orthodox Jewish clergy. They were often falsely accused of mysterious crimes and inhuman practices, and when in A. D. 64 Rome was almost totally destroyed by the great fire, the Christians were held responsible for its outbreak. It was then that the first persecutions were begun by Emperor Nero himself. Other emperors after him followed the same method, but generally the provincial governors were permitted to do as they saw fit in their treatment of the Christians. In a following chapter we shall see how Christianity was established and what its basic principles are.

CHAPTER XI.

FALL OF THE ROMAN EMPIRE IN THE WEST AND ITS SURVIVAL IN THE EAST

During the half century from 235 to A. D. 284 the Roman Empire was subjected to a number of terrible calamities from which it seemed at first unable to recover. A plague swept over the provinces and carried away several million inhabitants. Besides, a relaxation of discipline within the ranks of the armies and political chaos in Rome tended to disrupt the whole realm. A number of military dictators ruled as emperors, but most of them met with a violent death through assassination or battle. When the Germanic barbarians on the northern frontiers of the Empire learned of these developments, they proceeded to invade some of the provinces, and in several districts they made permanent conquests, notably in the region directly to the north of Gaul, subsequently known as the Netherlands. In the East the Persians once more grew restive and sought to revive their empire. To the north of the Balkan Peninsula the Goths stood ready to take advantage of any further weakness exhibited by the Romans. It was then that a great emperor arose to restore efficiency in the central government and discipline in the army. This was Diocletian, who ruled from 284 to A. D. 305.

POLITICAL DEVELOPMENTS

The Work of Diocletian. Diocletian made Rome into an undisguised Oriental monarchy. He deprived the Senate of all power and assumed the rôle of a god-king, dropping the title of *Princeps* and replacing it with that of *Dominus* (Lord). Thus he became like an Oriental despot. For administrative purposes, the government was divided into two grand divisions ruled over by Augusti, who further subdivided it and chose two Caesars as co-rulers; thus creating the Eastern and Western Empires. He also divided the provinces into four groups, reorganized their boundaries, and made them responsible directly to him. Finally, he engaged in the last and most bitter major persecution of the Christians in Roman history.

Results of His Work. Diocletian's reorganization infused new energy into the government, ended anarchy and lawlessness, and undoubtedly prolonged the life of the empire. Gaul now lost its independence, and in the East the puppet state at Palmyra, set up to keep the Persians in check but deemed no longer necessary, was destroyed. On the other hand, Diocletian brought about a more oppressive system of taxation to support the new Courts, ended all semblance of liberty and democracy, and paved the way for eventual separation of the East and the West.

The Successors of Diocletian in the West. Diocletian's plan of succession failed with the resignation of the Augusti in 305, and that period of civil war which followed was ended by the triumph of Constantine. This emperor (307-337) is chiefly important for two acts: the recognition of Christianity as the state religion, and the removal of the capital to Constantinople (formerly called Byzantium). Even in the west the city of Rome ceased to be the capital, for the emperors in this section ruled from Ravenna, in northeastern Italy, or Milan, in the Po Valley, or Trier, in western Germany. There were temporary reunions of the East and the West under Constantius (350) and Theodosius (379-395), but the period as a whole is a sad story of anarchy and confusion. In A. D. 476 the Roman Empire of the West

came to an end with the removal of the last Emperor (Romulus
Augustulus) and the bestowal of his powers on the Emperor of
the East.

Reorganization of the Army. The army was divided
into two major divisions, the field troops, which were quartered
at points of strategic importance, and the garrisons, which were
stationed at the frontiers, and in return for their services were
given land grants by the central government. More use than
formerly was now made of cavalry forces, which were protected
by chain mail, and of archers who fought on horseback. It also
became customary to have provincial garrisons commanded by
a so-called *dux,* or leader, the official who afterward was the *duke*
in some of the Germanic kingdoms. The title of count (*comes*)
was also used for the same officer at this time.

Development of a Bureaucracy. Owing to the vast size
of the Empire, the Emperor had to employ trusted ministers of
his own choosing who in turn were assisted by trained clerks and
messengers. The latter were all clothed in uniforms to indicate
their official position and civil service. Contrary to the men who
occupied the highest posts, and held their offices for but one year,
the subordinates had permanent positions, and for this reason
wielded greater influence in the long run. The advantage of this
system of bureaucracy was that it functioned continuously and
efficiently, regardless of what happened to the emperors and their
choice generals or ministers. On the other hand, its disadvantages
were clumsiness in management, expensiveness in operation, and
too little inclination toward necessary reforms. The men in office
tended to prefer individual to national interests.

The Senate and the Senatorial Order. All the officials
in government service who had reached a rank considered sufficiently high were admitted ex-officio (because of their office)
to the so-called Senatorial Order, but not in all cases to membership in the Senate itself. The latter body was made up, as before,
of the most prominent officials in the civil service, either past or
present, but its power had declined owing to the action of various
emperors who wished to be absolute monarchs. The higher officials received titles of nobility in keeping with their station in
the government and society.

Extent of the Roman Empire. The Roman Empire at one time included practically all the Mediterranean world. What are now Egypt, Syria, Palestine, Turkey, Spain, Portugal, France, the British Isles, Belgium, western and southern Germany, the Netherlands, and most of the Balkan states lay in its realm.

Diverse Nationalities. There were about eighty million people in this huge empire, and they consisted of almost every human race and tongue, from the rough barbarians to the highly cultured Greeks.

SOCIAL AND ECONOMIC CONDITIONS

Social Classes. After A. D. 250 the government saw fit to decree that nearly every person should remain in his respective occupation and retain his particular social status. Especially the agricultural workers called *coloni* found it increasingly difficult to leave the land to which they were tied, or their occupation. But even the members of the upper and middle classes were as a rule forced to remain in their respective positions. What was especially unpleasant was the custom inaugurated by the government of calling upon the wealthy members in each municipality to make up the deficits in the budgets. In this manner it frequently happened that large numbers of patricians lost all their property. Furthermore, whenever taxes could not be collected, the great landowners were held responsible. Some of the wealthy landowners, partly because they were enraged by the heavy burdens that had fallen upon their shoulders, made use of armed forces, and often became a serious threat to the whole community. As the estates of the wealthy increased in size, and the free men found it ever more difficult to make a respectable living, the latter were often impelled to sell their property to their more wealthy neighbors, or to exchange their property for personal services or protection.

Inflation of the Currency. The central government after A. D. 250 was seldom able to pay for all expenditures out of the customary revenues. Thus, inflation of the currency resulted, so that in the fourth century the old silver coinage had become thoroughly debased. Now it was a common practice for merchants to make payments not with single coins but with whole sacks filled with them, which would pass from hand to hand unopened.

It became necessary to introduce a new coin, made of gold and called *solidus,* and equivalent to one seventy-second part of a pound of gold.

Extent of Commerce. At the opening of the period now under consideration commerce was plied on an extensive scale. Both in Rome and in Alexandria products were exchanged from all parts of the civilized world. As long as the pirates were forcefully restricted in their operations, as long as the roads were safe for merchants and other travelers, and as long as the barbarians could not penetrate beyond the frontier defense of the Empire, the advantages of a new standard imperial coinage, and of low customs duties charged at harbors and at the frontiers continued to foster a healthful flow of commerce and industry. Most impressive indeed was the vast array of products that were brought by land and sea to Rome. Among these were grain from the provinces, raw materials for the local industries, and various other goods: Imports from Egypt were papyrus paper, silk goods, glass, linens, and grain; Asia Minor contributed steel, iron, and wool; Greece supplied figs, currants, olive oil, and marble; Spain sent from its mines copper, lead, tin, silver, and gold, besides such products as wool, finished cloth, oil, wine, and fish; Gaul also shipped wool and finished cloth, as well as grains and vegetables and meat; Britain provided iron, hides, gold, fleeces, oysters, and poultry; and Dacia added iron and iron products, hides, fleeces, and slaves. In exchange for these products from the provinces, Italy exported statues and implements of iron and bronze, finished cloth, glassware, and pottery. Not content with only provincial trade, the Romans also established contact with India, from which the merchants obtained copper goods, linen, silks, precious stones, spices, and ivory. As was the case with European countries that traded with India after the fall of the Roman Empire, the Romans had to pay the peoples of India with precious metals, especially gold and silver coins, as well as with such other metals as tin, lead, and copper, besides certain manufactured products and wine. India of the Middle Ages has aptly been called the "sink of precious metals." The spices and cotton of India were in such great demand that the European countries were constantly compelled to ship their newly mined gold and silver to India. Furthermore, the Romans also traded with China, from which they got some of their silks. As in medieval times, so in the days of the Roman Empire, the caravans crossed the deserts of Syria and Arabia, and the ships sailed along the coasts of the eastern Mediterranean, the Red Sea, and the Indian Ocean. No city of such size in early modern times could boast of so much commerce as did Rome and Alexandria in the closing centuries of the Empire.

Travel and Postal Service. The Romans imitated the Persians in establishing excellent roads and organizing a postal service, horses being supplied at relay stations. In this manner a speed of fifty miles a day and in certain special cases of eighty miles a day was maintained by messengers in the service of the imperial government. Other travelers, on the other hand, had to travel more slowly, at a pace from three to six miles an hour, but with an average speed of two or three miles an hour. Although traffic by way of the sea was more rapid than that on land, the merchants who shipped their goods on vessels had to encounter the danger of piracy, storms, and the loss of cargo and ships through ignorance of sand-banks and rocks. For that reason insurance rates were rather high. The flow of international commerce was indeed greatly restricted by such disadvantages. Conditions did not by any means resemble those that prevailed in the nineteenth century, nor of course those of our own. There was much less exchange of goods between provinces and countries than is the case today.

CULTURAL DEVELOPMENTS

The Languages Used in the Empire. Although the two official literary languages of the Roman Empire were Greek in the East and Latin in the West, many other languages continued to be used both in speaking and in writing. In Gaul, for example, the Celtic language did not disappear until the middle of the fourth century, while in certain parts of Brittany in the extreme west of what is now France, the language continued to be employed for many centuries later as a dialect. In northern Africa, especially in the vicinity of where Carthage once stood and where Carthage was rebuilt by the Romans, the Phoenician tongue remained popular until beyond the year A. D. 200. In Syria, including

Palestine, the Aramaic language, which is closely related to Hebrew and for that reason often referred to as that language, was also employed during the third and fourth centuries of our era. On the other hand, a popular form of Greek, known as *Koine,* readily supplanted the Aramaic tongue. Nearly all the books of the New Testament were originally written in *Koine.* In Egypt the old language also remained in use, but here, as in the other countries mentioned, the use of the native tongue was confined very largely to the peasant class and certain poor laborers in small towns. Latin underwent a change similar to that of classical Greek. Although the classical Latin continued to be used throughout the Middle Ages, this language was not spoken and consequently was no longer subject to change. But writers in the West, especially those beyond the Alps, were less scrupulous than certain dignified and well-trained authors. They did not care particularly how Cicero and Caesar used to write. They coined new words from time to time, they ignored rules of grammar, they changed the meter in poetry, and corrupted a large number of classical terms. Thus in the West, the written language altered; of course spoken language is always changing. In this manner both medieval Latin and the Romance languages were born. The Italians developed a dialect of the Latin tongue that was called Italian, the people of central Spain developed Castilian, which later was called Spanish, while in the country west of Castile a new kingdom arose by the name of Portugal, for which reason the language developed there came to be called Portuguese. Moreover, in Gaul the number of Romans remained always so great that even the Germanic settlers, such as the Franks, after whom France was named, were not able to affect to any great extent the native language of the Romans. Here, then, the French language was developed, meaning the language of the Franks, but in reality designating a Romance language. The true language of the Franks became modern Dutch and Flemish. Finally, in what is now Rumania, the troops stationed along the frontier intermarried with various peoples of Slavic or Teutonic descent, and were able to impose upon these people the Latin tongue; but during the course of centuries it has become the Rumanian language of today. At the close of the Middle Ages classical Latin was revived at the same time that classical Greek was revived. But, whereas medieval Latin fell into disfavor and eventually was no longer used in either writing or speaking, popular Greek used by the masses was never stamped out, so that today it is still current, though in a modified form. Classical Greek, with some alteration, is still the written and printed language of all Greeks; the pronunciation is greatly changed.

Literature. In the schools the great authors of the past continued to be read, but such was the stagnation in learning, literature, and art that few writers appeared to emulate Homer, Plato, Vergil, Cicero, or Caesar. Only one historian of importance need be mentioned here, namely, Ammianus Marcellinus, who flourished in the fourth century of our era. Although Greek was his native tongue, as he had become an officer in the Roman army, he preferred the use of Latin, and wrote historical treatises in imitation of Tacitus, covering the history of Rome from Tacitus' time to his own, that is, from 96 to A. D. 378. Only a few fragments of his works remain, but enough to indicate that he understood the nature of the decline of the Roman Empire. Since many important writers of the third, fourth, and fifth centuries belonged to the so-called Church Fathers, these will be mentioned in the following chapter.

Legal Studies. The Romans had made some of the greatest contributions in the field of political institutions and political theories, and they naturally continued to be active in this field, even in the period of their decline. It was during the third century that three jurists lived who belonged among the greatest law experts of all time. One of these has been mentioned—namely, Papinian. The other two were Paul and Ulpian. Papinian owed much of his learning to the famous law school in the city of Beirut in Syria. It is also important to note that under Emperor Theodosius in 438 the well-known *Theodosian Code* was promulgated. Appearing in a time of chaos and confusion, it was of immense practical value.

The Code of Justinian. Still more important was the code published in the reign of Emperor Justinian (527-565), called the *Corpus Juris Civilis,* or the Justinian Code. The *Code* itself was the body of imperial law still functioning; the *Digest* was another part of the whole code, being a collection of abstracts from the leading jurists; and the *Institutes* was a textbook intended for students of law. This code was studied and constantly interpreted in the three great law schools of the East Roman Empire, namely, those at Rome, Constantinople, and Beirut. In this manner Roman law was preserved for later generations, who, at the end of the Middle Ages, would participate in the *Renaissance*—a movement destined to help restore the knowledge of classical civilization.

Late Roman Art. Art, as well as literature, reflected the decadence of the time. Although certain buildings continued to be constructed, no important new styles of architecture appeared. Under Constantine a number of excellent arches were built, one of which is the famous Triumphal Arch in the city of Rome, though it must be noted that this is a composite of fragments of earlier structures. Interesting also are the baths of Diocletian and Constantine in Rome. Considerable engineering skill was exhibited in the construction of the subterranean reservoirs in Constantinople for storing its water supply. But the time was now past for the building of huge new temples, amphitheaters, palaces, and aqueducts. Not until after the fall of the Roman Empire in the West did a new period of culture set in, this time in the East rather than in the West. It was the good fortune of Constantinople to rise to new heights of wealth and learning and art, as Rome was sacked repeatedly, so that its population declined from more than a million to but a few thousands. When Rome lay almost entirely in ruins, the new Rome, that is, Constantinople, became the greatest city in the world. It is after the reign of Justinian that Byzantine history really begins, although it must be stated that much of the power and wealth of the Byzantine Empire was made possible largely through the excellent work of Emperor Justinian, whose career will be mentioned again in this chapter.

Christian Art. Since the Christians owed their artistic standards very largely to the classical models of ancient Greece and Rome, it seems fitting to discuss their art in this section. Although in many ways the Christians did break with the pagan past, they showed no great desire to do so in the field of art. During the first three centuries, when they were still more or less in disgrace, they were not able to make much progress or do important work in public, confining their work to the catacombs under the city and its vicinity, as well as to their own private homes. In some of the catacombs their painting and sculpture can still be examined. They made use of frescoes; notwithstanding the Ten Commandments of Moses, they frequently depicted human as well as animal figures. They were fond of symbolism, and since Jesus had said, "I am the vine and ye are the branches," they frequently depicted vine stalks. They also represented the dove, which stood for the Holy Spirit, although originally it symbolized the Christians' peace of soul, "the peace that passeth all human understanding." The fish stood for Jesus Christ the Savior, since the letters of the Greek word Ichtus (fish) are the initials of the Greek words "Jesus, Christ, Son of God, Savior"; the peacock stood for immortality, and the anchor for hope. Many are the paintings that picture the story of Moses, the wise men from the East, Abraham, Noah, David, Job, Daniel, Jonah, and above all the Madonna. The earliest Madonna known is in the catacomb of Priscilla, and shows Mary in the form of a healthy, youthful woman with large eyes and holding a child to her breast. The clothes and features and figure are all a reflection of the models left by classical art. The Christians did less with sculpture than painting, but interesting is the statue representing the good shepherd carrying the lamb, which reminds us of the "Calf Carrier" in the Acropolis Museum in Athens. The statue was produced during the first half of the third century. Some excellent sculpture was carved on the Christian sarcophagi, being relief work, a favorite type of pagan tombs.

The Christian Basilica. It was during the course of the fourth century that the Christians perfected a new style of architecture, the earliest Christian Church of the West. Whereas in the East the buildings were constructed after Syrian and Persian models, the Christians in Rome and its vicinity drew upon the architecture that was most familiar to them. They made use of the basilica, which was a structure used by the Romans as market halls or courts of justice. The basilica was constructed according to a very simple plan, consisting of a rectangular central hall called the nave, flanked by two rows of columns, and two or four aisles. Since the nave was much higher than the aisles at the sides, it was possible to have light filtered through the windows above the aisles. As a rule the roof was flat and made of timber, but the walls were constructed of brick or stone. In a few cases the roof was gabled. The entrance was at the front, and at the opposite end of the basilica was the apse, an enclosure in the form of a semi-circle. The Christians took over this plan, but in order to make the building in the form of a cross, they added between the nave and the apse a rectangular portion called the transept. They placed the altar in the extreme rear, so that the worshippers as they entered the church in the front could behold at the extreme opposite end of the building, far away from other portions of the church, the table with the candles where the priests placed the sacred elements representing the sacrifice of Jesus Christ upon the cross. An excellent example of the Christian basilica is that in the German city of Trier. Two other examples are those in Rome called respectively St. Peter's and Santa Maria Maggiore.

Early Byzantine, That Is, East Roman, Architecture. In the reign of Emperor Justinian one of the most famous of all Christian churches was constructed in the city of Constantinople. Its name was *Hagia Sophia,* or Holy Wisdom. It differed considerably from the Christian basilica constructed in the West. Hagia Sophia, unlike the basilica, had a round dome and two half-domes. The dome is supported on four huge piers, whose diameter is 108 feet, while the height of the piers is 175 feet. It was decorated with mosaics. But such was the fame of Constantinople and its buildings that throughout Russia and in the northern countries of Europe the Byzantine style was more popular than the Roman. It can be seen in some of the famous churches of Sweden, as well as in the chapel built for Charlemagne in the city of Aachen where he was buried. Even in Italy, since much of Italy was a part of the Byzantine Empire, the Byzantine church can still be seen, especially at Ravenna. For the same reason the famous church of St. Mark's in Venice is a Byzantine structure showing the dome, the profuse decorations, and the mosaics.

Education and Philosophy. In addition to the three great law schools noted above, there must be mentioned two universities founded in the city of Constantinople, one owned by the civil government and the other by the Church. Many of the emperors established centers of higher learning, and endowed chairs in the universities for the professors. In these universities philosophy was carefully studied. For a time Athens remained true to its pagan heritage and supported a number of excellent schools in which pagan philosophy continued to be taught. But during the second half of the sixth century the Emperor Justinian closed these schools, stating that, since Christianity had become the officially recognized religion of the Empire, it would not do any longer to teach pagan learning there. Early in the seventh century the pagan centers of learning in Alexandria and Constantinople were likewise closed. From 300 to A. D. 600 scientific study, like literature and art, deteriorated. It is sometimes alleged that the decline in scientific studies was the result of the coming of the Christian religion, since the Christians were satisfied with the account of creation presented in the book of Genesis in the Bible. But such a theory can scarcely be sustained, inasmuch as scientists as a rule do not limit themselves only to the question of the creation of the universe and of mankind. Furthermore, many of the Church Fathers had much to say about the creation of the world and in their opinion the opening chapters of the Bible are to be taken figuratively or symbolically. Such an explanation coming from the leaders in the Christian Church should have encouraged the scientists in their search for further truth. St. Augustine, in particular, was very liberal in his interpretation of important Biblical passages. Even the Apostle Peter stated that one day with God is like a thousand years. It has often been stated by certain historians that the study of philosophy was not considered safe during the declining years of the Roman Empire in the West, because the leaders among the Christians were always suspicious of heresy. But it should be borne in mind that while there have always been many classes of Christians, some tolerant and some less tolerant, yet there is nothing in the Christian religion to cause the decay of scientific study or of any other branch of learning.

Neo-Platonism. During the third century of our era a new school of philosophy was born, which is commonly called

Neo-Platonism, because it is said to be a revival of Platonism. But it should be noted, as one American historian has recently stated, that this system "supposedly a revival of Platonism, was in fact a pale reflection of what had been taught by the great Athenians." What was actually done is this. Plotinus, who died in A. D. 270, based a new system of thought upon Plato and other philosophers, including several who were not Greek at all. He also added certain elements of mysticism, which must be differentiated from Plato's mysticism. Emphasis was placed by Plotinus and his followers upon the Persian idea of the conflict between the forces of evil and the forces of good. In the opinion of the so-called Neo-Platonists the human body is evil and corrupt, so that it is desirable for the development of the soul to cultivate what is commonly called asceticism, that is, the mortification of the flesh for the intended benefit of the soul. It is often imagined by certain students of history that in this manner asceticism was introduced into the Christian Church. But those who have carefully read the epistles of Peter and Paul presented in the New Testament, together with the most important productions of the Church Fathers, will realize perfectly that, long before Plotinus lived, certain mild features of asceticism were present in the Christian Church. On the other hand, the Christian religion does not necessarily lead to asceticism at all.

The Mystery Religions. During the third and fourth centuries the mystery religions continued to gain favor with many millions of persons within the Roman Empire. The followers of these mystery religions taught that men must undergo a process of purification, in order to be fit for the realm beyond the gates of death. Sometimes the process of purification was called regeneration, or rebirth. In most of the religions there was the element of a sacrificial meal, commemorating a supposed sacrifice made by a certain religious leader or certain mysterious persons. Those who participated in the ceremony were said to partake of a divine substance. As a rule the religion included also certain elements of Babylonian astrology, exactly as is the case today in a large number of spiritualistic churches both in Europe and in this country. The Platonic idea of reincarnation or the transmigration of souls, which also is a feature of the Hindu religion, likewise entered the mystery cults. For that reason it is not at all surprising that we read in the New Testament of certain Jews who, when they heard of Jesus of Nazareth and His miracles, together with His familiar teachings, thought that He was Elijah, who had returned to this earth and had gone through the process of reincarnation. Others thought that John the Baptist was Elijah reincarnated.

THE CAUSES OF THE DECLINE OF THE ROMAN EMPIRE

Some Causes. Among the causes of the fall of Rome must be mentioned the prevalence of slavery, the loss of the fertility of the soil, the deterioration of the army, the intermingling of races, the invasions of the barbarians, and the Christian religion. Though these were not the only causes, it is well to analyze them. To begin with the question of slavery, Rome brought home conquered slaves from the borders of the empire. This element, often in revolt, was a permanent source of disaffection, so that there is close connection between the institution of slavery and the decline of Rome. The progressive denuding of Italy's timber (for shipbuilding) and the gradual exhaustion of the soil of Italy, Sicily, Sardinia, and Africa were one of the chief internal sources of imperial decline. Again, to say that the army of Rome deteriorated is to admit that leadership was lacking and discipline relaxed, though the decline of discipline in the army was a symptom of general decline in the government and in society as a whole. Furthermore, the invasion of the barbarians was simply the result of the weakness of Rome. The barbarians had always been anxious to pierce the frontiers of the Roman Empire. Even before the Empire had been founded, some Germanic tribes had invaded Gaul and reached the southern portion of that province. In the reign of Augustus, as we saw, Roman legions under Varus had been defeated by Arminius and a German army; Augustus is supposed to have cried out, "Give me back Varus and my legions!" It is also known that in 387 B. C. Rome was sacked by barbarians. That it was never sacked between 387 B. C. and A. D. 370 is much to the credit of the Romans, not a sign of weakness on the part of the barbarians. The intermingling of Germanic and Roman races should have instilled new blood into the arteries of a decaying race. As a matter of fact it did, but the aliens never really assimilated Roman culture nor acquired devotion to the Roman government. Finally, the Christian religion is not of such a nature as to produce the characteristics exhibited by the Romans during the third, fourth, and fifth centuries, but its insistence on the worship of one God together with its teaching that war was a sin tended to sap the morale of the Roman military establishment.

The Nature of the Political Decline. Many historians have correctly pointed out that Rome was originally a small city-state, and its whole government was framed to have one city control the whole of the civilized world. It is almost a miracle that Rome was able to control so huge an empire for so long a time. No other nation had been able to do that, nor has any other power since that time duplicated this feat. For 600 years Rome controlled nearly the whole of the civilized world. It had learned much from the Persians and the Greeks. It had created a magnificent system of law. It had built excellent roads. It was served by the finest military organization that the world had ever seen. Nor was its provincial government to be despised. Perhaps the Roman Empire would have lasted for 600 years more had it not been for the factors just discussed and certain others which may now be analyzed.

The Nature of the Economic Decline. It would seem that the most important factor in the fall of the Roman Empire is the economic decline. This decline was reflected in political and social deterioration. Perhaps it also affected literature, learning, and art. At any rate, no historian can properly analyze the causes of the decline of Rome without considering carefully what were the economic problems facing the Roman government and the people as a whole. As was just stated, it seemed that the soil could no longer produce abundant crops. Everywhere pirates turned up to endanger merchants, both on sea and on land. To make matters worse, the imperial government became so expensive that it could no longer raise taxes sufficient to meet the required expenditures. Unlike the nations of our day, the Roman government did not resort to the issuing of bonds or the borrowing of money on an extensive scale. It kept on spending more than it received, and consequently it ran hopelessly into debt. As a result the currency was inflated until it became practically worthless. Although Diocletian restored the coinage, he did not thereby return to the masses the wealth they had formerly possessed. The government had to have cash, and cash was no longer available. But the government had to be run somehow, and when cash was no longer available it compelled its subjects to surrender to it man power for the army, horses for the cavalry, wagons for general transportation, and raw materials of all sorts. As long as these methods were followed by men of integrity and honesty, the populace realized that such things had to be done. But in many cases unscrupulous officials enraged both wealthy and poor alike. As economic conditions grew worse and worse, the members of the trade *colleges* became panicky and refused any longer to sign any business contracts either for the government or for private capital. When this method was resorted to, the government officials took active measures to compel these businessmen to carry on as before. No member of such a trade college was permitted to leave the college, while even his heirs were obliged to assume his responsibilities in this direction. Peasants and merchants, soldiers and artisans were all servants of the state. One would almost imagine that Germany, Russia, and Italy between 1933 and 1940 had deliberately determined to imitate the officials who ruled the Roman Empire during the third and fourth centuries of our era. A study of the decline of Rome is certainly very instructive for all students of history who are seriously interested in the future of the European countries of today.

Sad Fate of the Urban Aristocracy. It was bad enough to see the peasant tied to the soil, so that he lost his liberty of action and became a slave to the state, but it was worse to see the greatest thinkers and the greatest businessmen of the Empire reduced to servitude that must have weighed more heavily upon their shoulders than it did upon the shoulders of the peasants in the country and the laboring classes in the cities. After all, the more intelligence a person possesses, the more he is aware of injustice, the loss of property, and forced servitude. There had been a time when the municipalities within the Empire had been prosperous and well governed. In each municipality certain men of integrity and social prominence had gladly assumed the duties of municipal government. It was an honor to belong to the so-called urban *curia*. One might enter such a *curia* through one's own social prestige, but as a rule extensive real-estate holdings were required. In the days of prosperity and good feeling these officials of the municipal governments had been very proud of their official duties, and they had assumed the obligation of enriching the town with public buildings, libraries, and schools. In this manner they resembled the Rockefellers, Carnegies, and Fords of recent times who, after having grown wealthy through free enterprise and competition, as well as through their own industry and integrity, have rewarded the general public with various institutions. On a humbler scale the Romans of the first and second centuries of our era had thousands of such public benefactors. Then came the terrible economic depression, which appeared in the first half of the third century and lasted for about two hundred years. The men of wealth suffered together with the members of the poorer classes. Even in the third century it was fashionable to "soak the rich." The taxes that could not be collected by a municipality had to be advanced by the members of the municipal council. When they tried to evade their duties, they were told that they could not leave the city nor resign their office. It seems that there was only one class of persons who escaped the general misery—the members of the senatorial order were not liable for municipal offices. Many members of this order owned large estates in the country and left their homes in the cities, in order to escape inevitable conscription of services and property. Out in the rural districts these landholders exploited the peasants in the country and even employed armed forces in order to protect themselves against the desperate officials in the municipalities who were bound to find some means of collecting money for the imperial government of Rome. For all these reasons a number of historians in recent years have come to the conclusion that the economic factor in the decline of Rome is the heart of the whole problem.

Moral Disintegration. But now the question still remains. Why did all these dreadful things have to happen all at once? Why would the peasants become so discouraged as to let weeds grow among their grain? Why were the fields no longer efficiently cultivated? Why did pirates suddenly abound on sea and land? Why did there have to be so many unscrupulous officials in the civil government? Why did there have to be so many military dictators during the third century? Why was the currency permitted to be inflated, as it was permitted to be inflated in Germany and Russia after the First World War? Why did the government officials suddenly find a right to force the subjects to turn over their personal services as well as their private property? Moreover, why have these things happened of late in certain European states of great importance? Could perhaps a parallel be drawn between these recent conditions and those that prevailed in Rome as the great empire went to pieces? The answers to all these questions appear to have been given by one of the greatest authorities on Roman history in the world, namely, Professor Rostovtzev of Yale University. In his famous work entitled *The Social and Economic History of the Roman Empire,* he points out that "the men who inhabited the Roman Empire had utterly lost their balance." He adds that hatred and envy ruled everywhere: The peasants hated the landowners and the officials, the city proletariat hated the city bourgeoisie, the army was hated by everybody, even by the peasants. The Christians were abhorred and persecuted by the heathens, who regarded them as a gang of criminals bent on undermining the state. Productivity was declining in agriculture, in industry, and in commerce. The seas and the roads were no longer secure, industry refused to prosper any longer, the purchasing power of the masses of the people was diminishing. The system of taxation, which had once been admirable, was now in a state of chaos which seems almost unbelievable to modern historians. Professor Rostovtzev continues by saying that "the relation between the state and the taxpayers was based on more or less organized robbery." (This, however, had been true even in Cicero's day.) He severely criticizes the government officials that replaced the older type. The latter knew that their ultimate doom was not far away, as did Louis XVI of France when he said, "After us the flood." They enjoyed themselves as much as possible in the exercise of their powers to exploit the people below them. Especially wretched were the city bourgeoisie, who were maltreated, persecuted, and cheated. At the same time the municipal aristocracy was ruined by confiscations and the responsibilities that we have just described. Professor Rostovtzev concludes his survey with these pregnant words, "The most terrible chaos thus reigned throughout the Roman Empire."

THE CONTRIBUTIONS OF THE ROMANS TO THE MAKING OF WESTERN CIVILIZATION

Why It Is Relatively Simple to Enumerate and Analyze These Contributions. The Romans made very real and concrete contributions to the growth of western civilization. It is easy to determine where they borrowed from and imitated the Greeks, that is, in the fields of literature, art, science, mathematics, philosophy, and religion.

Roman Law and Political Institutions. Perhaps the greatest contribution made by the Romans is in the form of the magnificent Code of Justinian, together with the old codes of law. Moreover, the Romans showed the world how they ruled many subject peoples through the iron hand of army discipline, excellent provincial government, efficient administration in the capital, high standards of living and social duties, and devotion to the state. In the early days of the Republic, Rome also exhibited an excellent understanding of the principles of democracy, when in the popular assemblies all men of good standing in the city were permitted to vote. At one time there was practically universal manhood suffrage and direct representation in this great city Rome also demonstrated to the world that it is possible under an absolute monarchy to have a great civilization, to maintain order to promote commerce and industry, and foster the arts and the sciences.

Imitation of the Greeks and Other Peoples. The Roman also rendered a great service to later countries by knowing how to take over from the Greeks and other civilized peoples their system of government, their greatest literary contributions, th flower of their philosophy and science, and their way of solvin economic and social problems. Through the peace introduced b

Rome the fruits of Greek civilization and of the Christian religion were permitted to spread over the Western World. Greek philosophy was thus preserved, and Greek science was given an honorable place among medieval and modern peoples. All of this was very creditable.

Road Building and Architecture. The Romans surpassed the Greeks and other peoples of antiquity in their magnificent system of roads, in their enormous aqueducts, their use of cement in the building of huge bridges and aqueducts, the perfection of triumphal arches, and the building of great amphitheaters.

Family Life. When Rome was great, it owed much to its admirable home life. The Romans correctly reasoned that virtue and religion can best be practiced in the family. The relation between father and children and between husband and wife, when properly functioning, formed the greatest pillar of prosperity and good government. When home life is sound, the nation will remain prosperous and secure. When home life is undermined by immoral teachings, by constant quarreling and by selfishness, the disorders in the home are magnified in the larger groups that make up society as a whole. Thus Rome taught the peoples of antiquity a good lesson. Where the Greeks had failed notably was in their lack of interest in the home. Women were relegated into such a subordinate position in society that they were deprived of the opportunity to become educated and to mingle freely in society. Thus they became dwarfed and miserable, and could not make the proper contributions to a wholesome culture. The Romans, on the other hand practiced stern discipline, accorded women a respectable place in home and in society, were intensely patriotic, believed that "piety" consisted partly in proper observance of family duties, and knew how to govern both themselves and their subjects.

The Latin Language. The use of the Latin language during medieval and early modern times was such that it may be said to have been the most important language of all Europe during some fifteen centuries. Moreover, the English language owes more than one-third of its vocabulary to the Latin, being a trifle more strongly Anglo-Saxon than Roman. Latin used to be the language of instruction in all the great European universities, and governments used to promulgate their decrees in Latin long after the fall of the Roman Empire in the West. Today innumerable scientific terms are still entirely or largely of Latin origin. Latin is also the parent of all the Romance languages.

Latin Literature. Although the Romans imitated the Greeks in the field of literature, they produced many masterpieces of their own which are still widely read. Medieval literature was greatly enriched by Latin literature, and it was for centuries studied in the secondary schools of Europe and America to the exclusion of nearly all other types of literature, including that in the vernacular.

THE INVASION OF THE BARBARIANS

Early Invasions of Rome. The Gauls made several incursions into Rome and once sacked the city. Hannibal enlisted many barbarians in his army while he was in Italy. Marius earned the proud title of Savior of the Country because he defeated the Cimbri and Teutons. Other barbarians entered Rome peacefully and became soldiers or coloni. These early barbarians came for various motives—booty, plunder, adventure, or homes.

Origin and Native Homes of the Early Germans. The German barbarians lived in the vicinity of the Baltic Sea before they invaded Rome. Some historians trace them to an Indo-European origin similar to that of the Persians, Greeks, and Romans. More about their early history will be covered in a following chapter.

The Goths. Driven by the Huns, these people sought to cross the Danube River into Rome, and succeeded in doing so. They defeated the Romans at Adrianople (378) and later, under Alaric, sacked the city of Rome (410). The West Goths (Visigoths) settled in Spain and southern Gaul, where they founded a kingdom and helped the Romans defeat Attila at Chalons (451). They also ended the Empire of the West in 476. The East Goths (Ostrogoths) under Theodoric set up a kingdom in Italy (493), which lasted until 553.

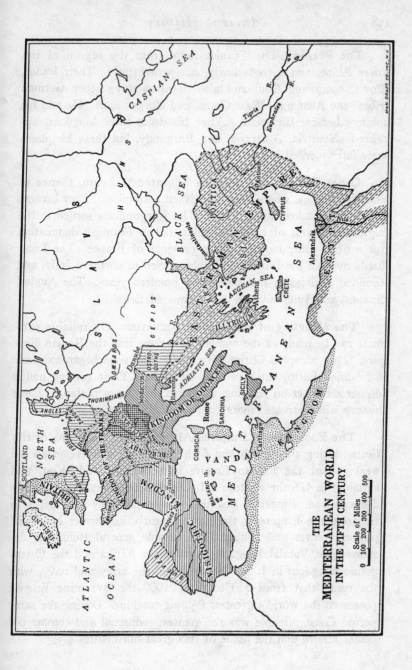

THE MEDITERRANEAN WORLD IN THE FIFTH CENTURY

Scale of Miles
0 100 200 300 400 500

MAP DRAFT CO. INC., N.Y.

CASPIAN SEA

BLACK SEA

Tigris R.

Euphrates R.

Nile R.

EASTERN ROMAN EMPIRE

PONTICA

CYPRUS

EGYPT

Alexandria

Antioch

PERSIA

Constantinople

THRACE

AEGEAN SEA

Athens

CRETE

ILLYRICUM

ADRIATIC SEA

MEDITERRANEAN SEA

Ravenna

Rome

SICILY

SARDINIA

CORSICA

VANDAL KINGDOM

Carthage

BALEARIC IS.

KINGDOM OF ODOACER

NORICUM

OSTRO-GOTHS

GEPIDS

Danube R.

LOMBARDS

THURINGIANS

BURGUNDY

KINGDOM OF THE FRANKS

VISIGOTHIC KINGDOM

Toulouse

Bordeaux

SAXONS

FRISIANS

ANGLES

BRITONS

BRITAIN

SCOTLAND

IRELAND

NORTH SEA

ATLANTIC OCEAN

SLAVS

HUNS

The Franks. The Franks came from the region of the lower Rhine, and spread slowly, but permanently. Their leader, Clovis, conquered Gaul and also defeated three other German tribes: the Alemanni, West Goths, and Burgundians. He and his soldiers became Christians. After his death three kingdoms appeared: Neustria, Austrasia, and Burgundy, but these kingdoms were later merged under Pippin.

Other Tribes. The Vandals migrated to Spain, thence to northern Africa, where they established a kingdom. They became pirates and sacked Rome (455). The Burgundians settled in the region northwest of Italy, but submitted to Frankish domination for a time. Burgundy became a province of France. The Lombards overran the Italian Peninsula, settled in northern Italy, and founded a kingdom that lasted two hundred years. The Angles, Saxons, and Jutes invaded and conquered Britain.

The Mingling of Roman and Barbarian. No reliable estimate can be made of the number who came into the Roman Empire. They accepted Christianity readily and soon began to speak a modified Latin, but kept their own laws. Their coming had a disastrous effect on learning, of which they knew nothing. Their history will be treated more fully in a subsequent chapter.

The East Roman Empire. Although the invasions of the Goths during the fourth and fifth centuries clearly revealed the weakness of the Roman Empire in both East and West, and although in 476 the western half of the Empire was permanently dismembered, Emperor Justinian was remarkably successful in restoring the Empire in the East to nearly its former height of physical power and culture. His capable general Belisarius destroyed the Vandal Kingdom in northern Africa and the Ostrogothic Kingdom in Italy. He perfected the army and navy, with the result that from 530 to A. D. 1000 the Byzantine Empire possessed the world's greatest fighting machine. During the same period Constantinople was the greatest industrial and commercial center known and the home of two great universities.

CHAPTER XII.

THE RISE OF
THE CHRISTIAN CHURCH

Since for more than a thousand years practically all Europeans were born automatically into the Christian Church, and since even today half of the inhabitants of the United States still claim affiliation with various denominations of Christendom, it can easily be seen that the rise of the Christian Church forms the most important chapter in the history of the ancient world. The Christian religion was not merely one of the religions that have come out of the Orient, but one that profoundly altered the social and economic order bequeathed by classical Greece and Rome.

THE SOURCES OF THE CHRISTIAN RELIGION

The Importance of the Old Testament. In the chapter devoted largely to the Hebrews we saw that their Old Testament was adopted by the Christians as a part of their sacred book, the Bible. The Christians believed that, since the Jews had refused to accept Jesus of Nazareth as the Messiah (Christ is a Greek translation of the Hebrew *Messiah*), they had forfeited the right of being the chosen people of God. The Christians were thought to have taken their place in this respect, and they accepted the

159

Ten Commandments of Moses as binding upon themselves. They were of the opinion that a number of prophecies in the Old Testament referred very clearly to Jesus, while in the four Gospels it is stated that in the opinion of Jesus, Moses spoke of Him. Significant especially is the story of the two disciples who on their way to Emmaus were told by Jesus how the Scriptures had predicted His suffering and death for the redemption of the world. The Hebrew sources were called the "Scriptures." It was frequently stated that "the Scriptures must be fulfilled."

The Religions of the Persians and Other Peoples of the Ancient Near East. In a preceding chapter reference has been made to the resemblance between the Persian religion and that of the Christians. The Persians, like the Christians, developed the idea that there was a conflict between forces of good and those of evil, that eventually the good forces will overcome the evil ones, that a savior will redeem sinful mankind, and that eternal life and eternal punishment will be meted out respectively to virtuous and wicked persons. Moreover, a certain sect called the Manichaeans added other elements to the Persian religion to make it seem even more like the Christian faith. St. Augustine, before he was converted to Christianity, was a Manichaean, for example. Later cults made use of a baptism and a ceremony of eating food that enabled devotees to partake of eternal life. For this reason it has seemed to a number of well-known writers that the Christian religion developed naturally out of these religious practices and beliefs.

The Influence of the Greek Religion. The Greeks spoke of the *logos,* as the principle and power that resided in the universe as a part of God. In the Gospel of St. John this *logos* is mentioned and called the Christ, while the author makes the assumption that Jesus of Nazareth was the Christ. Since the Apostle Paul was educated in Tarsus, a Greek town in Asia Minor where Greek education held sway, he is thought to have introduced into the New Testament and thence into the Christian religion certain features of the Greek religion. The Neo-Platonists, as mentioned previously, are also said to have made important contributions to the development of the Christian faith. The leaders among the early Christians were well aware of these facts and sought to account for them by saying that the pagans had prepared the way for Christ, but that they had not made important contributions to His religious teachings. These were of divine origin.

The Explanation of the Greatest Church Fathers. In addition to Clement of Alexandria, Justin Martyr, and Irenaeus, who were well known for their attacks upon Greek philosophy and the Greek religion, many prominent Fathers followed who went even further in their condemnation. One of these was the Athenian philosopher Athenagoras, who in the year 177 presented to Emperor Aurelius a work entitled *Apology,* or *Plea for the Christians.* He pointed out the ridiculous conception the Greeks had of their gods, and how they tolerated immoral practices and adultery. He considered Aristotle as a Deist, who thought that God is not interested in individual human beings. Significant also is the work of Hippolytus called *The Refutation of All Heresies,* which was written in the first quarter of the third century. Since Hippolytus was a pupil of the famous Irenaeus, he repeated the views of this great leader. He condemned and criticized the following authors: Thales, Pythagoras, Empedocles, Heraclitus, Anaximander, Anaximenes, Archelaus, Parmenides, Leucippus, Democritus, Xenophanes, Ecphantus, Hippo, Socrates, Plato, Aristotle, the Stoics, Epicurus, the Academics, the Brahmans, the Druids, and Hesiod. He showed that a large number of heretics among the Christians had derived their opinions from Plato and Pythagoras. He also condemned a number of Neo-Platonists who claimed to be Christians. Noteworthy also are the remarks by Theophilus in his book called *Address to the Greeks.* In his opinion the Greeks were much too conceited and refused to admit that they had been taught by the Barbarians. He pointed out all the contributions made to Greek civilization by the peoples of the ancient Near East. He mentioned in particular the Babylonians, the Egyptians, the Persians, and the Phoenicians. Of Heraclitus he said that this philosopher led such a foolish life as to become afflicted with dropsy; he then plastered himself with manure, which as it hardened, contracted his flesh in such a manner that he was pulled to pieces, and thus he died. He also condemned the teaching of the transmigration of souls taught by Zeno. Theophilus argued that the teachings of the Hebrew prophets were confirmed by the Greek poets and philosophers. The Christians owed their points of view to the Hebrew prophets rather than to the Greek philosophers and poets. Yes, what did it profit Homer to have composed the story of the Trojan War, and to have deceived so many? Of what use were the searchings of Empedocles and Epicurus, who denied a divine providence and taught atheism? Why should Socrates have sworn by the dog, the goose, and the planetree? Especially severe was the famous Church Father called Tertullian, who lived in the third century, and who is often considered as unreasonable in his attack upon the Greek philosophers and the Greek religion. But even the sweet-tempered Lactantius, who was born about the middle of the third century and died about the year 325, was very frank in his condemnation of Greek philosophy and Greek religion. In his famous work, *The Divine Institutes,* he made numerous references to the errors committed by pagan authors. He devoted a whole book to the subject "The False Wisdom of Philosophers." The doctrine of Platonism is carefully analyzed in two separate chapters, and is absolutely condemned. The author is scandalized especially by Plato's recommendation that decent family life must be abolished. Lactantius sums up the position of the Church Fathers in these words: "Wherefore all the sects of philosophers must be far removed from the truth, because they who established them were men; nor can those things have any foundation or firmness which are unsupported by any utterances of divine voices."

JESUS OF NAZARETH

His Place in the History of Western Civilization. Whatever one may think of the nature of the Christian religion and of the personality of Jesus Christ, few students of history can deny that He was by far the most important person in the history of the human race. Even if the story of His life recounted in the four Gospels is entirely false, and even if the Epistles of St. Paul and St. Peter are filled with lies and errors, the historian would still have to grant that the mere story of His life was of immense importance and influence in developing not only religious ideas among all the peoples of Europe and America, but also a social gospel which has had profound effect upon the lives of untold millions of men and women.

His Career. Believers and unbelievers, Christians and pagans, all writers pay testimony to the greatness of Jesus Christ whenever they date a letter. The date upon this letter is supposed to indicate how long it is since the birth of Jesus of Nazareth. Since He chose to lead a quiet life, there are certain textbooks on the history of Rome that do not refer to Him even a single time. But that does not alter the fact that He lived His life and found His followers in ancient Palestine. He was no doubt a Jew, and all of His disciples were likewise Jews. The same may be said of all the apostles, who became the first of the Christian missionaries. Few persons doubt that He was crucified under Pontius Pilate and died about the year A.D. 31. His teachings, as recorded in the four Gospels of the New Testament, have been proclaimed by practically all learned scholars as unique. The only thing that history cannot decide upon, being only a science, is the question of His virgin birth and His resurrection. Naturally there are also other major questions, such as those concerning His miraculous cures.

The Epistles of the Apostle Paul. As has been stated, St. Paul became the first of the great Christian missionaries. There could also be no doubt that St. Paul was a historical figure, even more so in the eyes of historians than was Jesus of Nazareth Himself. Few scholars question the genuine character of the records presented in the New Testament under the title of the Epistles of Paul. Unlike the twelve disciples, he was an eloquent teacher. Having been taught by the Jewish sect called the Pharisees, he had imbibed their teachings concerning the law and the Jewish practices. What is less certain in his career is the alleged influence exerted upon him through the environment in the city of Tarsus, his native town. There is very little in his own epistles to prove that he had become Hellenized himself. On the contrary, he was a Jew of the strictest sect and referred constantly to the teachings of the Pharisees, and does not seem aware of any important influence exerted upon him by Greek philosophy or Greek religion. His line of reasoning is always thoroughly Jewish or Christian. Some of his important experiences are recorded in the Acts of the Apostles, while he himself adds other particulars in these epistles. He tells how he was converted one day when he was on his way to Damascus to persecute the Christians. He was struck blind when he saw Jesus Christ in a vision, and he was conducted to a humble home of a Christian in the city of Damascus. After a short residence in this city, he was absent for fourteen years, during which time he must have studied most in Arabia. While he says himself that he went to Arabia, he does not mention an interest at this time in the religion of the Greeks. It is controversial whether Paul's theology differs considerably from that expressed in the four Gospels and the epistles of the apostles, Paul, Peter, James, Jude, and John.

The Epistles of the Other Four Apostles. The most important information is given in the two epistles by Peter, because he is said to have been Christ's representative upon this earth. In the Gospel of John we are told that at the resurrection of Jesus, He asked Peter three times in succession whether he loved Jesus, and after having received the answers from Peter, He said that he should feed both the sheep (the clergy) and the lambs (the lay members of the Church). In nearly all the epistles in the New Testament the same theory is presented concerning the mission of Christ upon this earth. We are told repeatedly that Jesus came to lay down His life for His followers, in order that they might be redeemed from the power of Satan, sin, and death. They were to be rewarded with eternal life in heaven, while the unbelievers were to be punished in a supposedly eternal state of hell.

The Social Gospel of Jesus. Jesus of Nazareth recapitulated the Ten Commandments of Moses in the Two Commandments of His own. He stated in these Two Commandments that a person should love God above all things, and his neighbor as himself. He placed the love of God above the love of men, but He added that the second commandment was like unto the first. He made it very clear that the rich had great duties to perform and were weighed down by heavy responsibilities. In His opinion it was difficult for a rich person who was attached to his riches to inherit the kingdom of heaven. When a rich young man came to ask Him for advice, He told the young man to sell all his goods and give the proceeds to the poor. He advised His disciples to serve fellow-men to the limit of their ability and their energy. He pointed out that the law of Moses was in part antiquated and that the idea of "an eye for an eye and a tooth for a tooth" no longer held true for the disciples. No one ever had the right to seek revenge or rectify wrongs inflicted upon him. This was to be left to God alone, the only one permitted to judge anyone. Jesus complained frequently about the popular habit of criticizing other persons, and also about the almost universal practice on the part of people of seeking to take the law into their own hands. He claimed that two wrongs could never make a right. A person should love even his enemies, and do good to those that hated him. All these teachings were faithfully repeated by the apostles in their sermons and in their letters. Jesus also stated that a person should render services to the civil government and other services to God. The Christians were to pay taxes to the civil government, as all other people did. Parents and children, husbands and wives, employers and employees, masters and servants, superiors and inferiors, government and subjects, and partners in any and every establishment should learn to cooperate with each other to the limit of their ability. Taking advantage of one's partner or even of one's enemy was both improper and foolish. He condemned divorce in the plainest of possible terms. He disapproved of all manner of quarreling and strife. He said to Peter that he that taketh up the sword shall perish by the sword. Only in one instance is there a reference that might be construed to show that He was not opposed to warfare, namely, when just before His betrayal and crucifixion He suggested that the disciples might procure some swords. When He was informed that they already had two, He said that this was sufficient. Most Bible commentators point out that this merely refers to the opportunity thus presented to Peter to hew off an ear of a certain soldier in order that the "Scriptures be fulfilled." This enabled Jesus to make His famous statement that he who takes up the sword shall perish by the sword.

THE CHURCH DURING THE FIRST CENTURY

Reasons for the Success of the Early Christian Church. First of all, it possessed a book, the Bible, that was considered the divinely inspired Word of God. In the second place, the members of the Church believed that Jesus Christ was the only-begotten Son of God, and since He was the Founder of the Church, the Christian religion surpassed all others. Thirdly, the

Christian religion proclaimed the highest code of ethics that the world had ever known, including the Ten Commandments of Moses and the Two Commandments of Jesus. Fourthly, to all human beings who wished to accept Jesus Christ as their Savior, it held out the hope of redemption from sin and the devil and of eternal life hereafter. Fifthly, it promised the resurrection of the body, not merely eternal life. Sixthly, it taught that God was the Father of all human beings, and that He was sincerely interested in the welfare of every one of them. Seventhly, it raised the status of women and it proclaimed that all human beings, in a certain sense at least, were equal before God. Finally, it gave to its members an enlightened point of view concerning their duties toward rulers, superiors, inferiors, and in short toward all other human beings. As a result Christians became respectable and orderly citizens of all nations in which they lived though refusing to worship the Emperor.

The Story of the Crucifixion and the Resurrection of Christ. It is remarkable how much the disciples and apostles made of the significance of the crucifixion and the resurrection. The week before the crucifixion and the two days after the crucifixion, making a total of only eight days out of thirty-three years (which comprise the life of Christ upon this earth), were considered so important by the authors of the four Gospels that Matthew devoted eight chapters to them of twenty-eight; Mark, six out of sixteen; Luke, five and a half out of twenty-four; and John nine out of twenty-one chapters. The reason for this phenomenon is very simple. The primary aim of the coming of Christ, according to His own words and to those of His disciples, was to fit His followers for the life everlasting. That was also the testimony of the leading apostles, especially St. Paul and St. Peter.

Pentecost. The first recorded spoken testimony relating to the completed task of the risen Christ is that by Peter, when he stood in the midst of about one hundred and twenty disciples, and told them that one man must be ordained to take the place of Judas Iscariot, in order to "be a witness with us of His resurrection." The next event mentioned in the Acts of the Apostles is the outpouring of the Holy Spirit, in accordance with the prediction of Jesus. After the apostles had spoken in such manner that every auditor had heard the words as if they had been spoken in his own native tongue, Peter explained that, contrary to the opinion of skeptical auditors, he and his companions were not drunk but had actually talked in foreign languages, since they had received that great power from the Holy Spirit. He added that Jesus, whom the Jewish leaders had crucified, had risen from the dead, and had been made by God "both Lord and Christ."

The Work of Peter. The third recorded speech is also by Peter, in which he said that he and John had made a lame man walk through the power of the Holy Spirit. He added that God had "raised His Son Jesus from the dead; whereof we are witnesses." God would send Jesus once more from heaven; it was He who before had been preached to the Jews; "Whom the heaven must receive until the times of restitution of all things. . . . Yea, and all the prophets from Samuel and those that follow after, as many as have spoken, have likewise foretold of these days." The fourth recorded speech was delivered by Peter to the High priest and his kindred, who had asked the apostles by what power they had done the miracles of which they had heard. It was "by the name of Jesus Christ of Nazareth, whom ye crucified, whom God raised from the dead. . . . This is the stone which was set at nought of you builders, which is become the head of the corner. Neither is there salvation in any other: for there is none other name under heaven given among men, whereby we must be saved." We are informed here that Peter was filled with the Holy Ghost when he made the statement just reproduced. There is no other name under heaven, said Peter, but that of the only Savior, Jesus Christ. How ready was Peter now to suffer for Jesus!

Stephen, the First Martyr. In the seventh chapter of the Acts of the Apostles we find the eloquent account by Stephen of the promises made by God to the people of Israel, the persecution of the prophets by the Jews, and the final act, the death and resurrection of Christ. He remarked that he saw the heavens opened and the Son of man standing on the right hand of God. This confession so enraged his auditors that they stoned him to death, as they laid their clothes at the feet of Saul of Tarsus. What must have gone through Saul's mind when he beheld that dreadful scene?

The Founding of New Churches. After the Church had been established at Jerusalem, the apostles set forth to convert both Jews and Gentiles at other places. It was at Antioch where they were first called Christians. In Asia Minor a large number of churches were likewise founded, notably in the great city of Ephesus. From Asia Minor Paul went to the Balkan Peninsula, where he also established important congregations of Christians. The most important church in this region seems to have been that at Corinth, and the two epistles of St. Paul to the Corinthians are a result of his missionary activities in this city. In the first chapter of the first epistle, Paul states that "the Jews require a sign and the Greeks seek after wisdom." But he continued to preach Christ crucified, which was to the Jews a stumbling block and to the Greeks foolishness. He continued that God had chosen the foolish things of the world to confound the wise. In the second chapter he made this significant observation: "For I determine not to know anything among you, save Jesus Christ and Him crucified." Paul also preached in the city of Athens. A crowd assembled there upon the Acropolis, and the auditors asked him what that new doctrine of his was. At first they listened eagerly, but when he referred to the resurrection of the dead, some mocked, while others said, "We will hear thee again of this matter." So Paul left them, realizing how profound was the difference between the Christian religion and that of the learned Greeks in the city of Athens.

The Christians in Rome. No doubt the largest congregation of Christians during the first century of our era was that established in the city of Rome, where enormous numbers of Jews were living at the time. After the apostles had labored faithfully among the Jews, they turned to others. According to a tradition, both Peter and Paul spent several years among the Christians in Rome, and both were martyred there in the reign of Emperor Nero. The lives of these Christians are well depicted by Henry Sienkiewicz in his world-famous novel entitled *Quo Vadis*. We read how Peter became discouraged and finally decided to leave the city of Rome, but on the road not far from the gates of the city he saw Jesus in a vision. The latter asked, "Quo Vadis?" ("Where are you going?"). When Peter told Jesus that he was going to leave Rome and desert the Christians there, Jesus said that unless he returned at once Jesus would go to Rome Himself and be crucified a second time. No one can fail to be moved to sympathy for the early Christians, who, stirred by the fire of a new religious faith, surmounted the dangers of persecution. Many were thrown before the wild beasts in the arena, while others were covered with pitch and burned upon crosses. But it was said among them that "the blood of the martyrs is the seed of the Church." It is true that whenever the persecution raged most fiercely, the numbers of the faithful increased rapidly.

The Churches in Alexandria and Constantinople. Owing to the fact that it was one of the greatest centers of commerce during the first and second centuries of our era, Alexandria had a large colony of Jews. Some of the apostles labored among them while others worked among the Gentiles present. As a result, a large congregation of Christians was established in the city, and several important Church Fathers lived here during the second and third centuries. Likewise, since this city also was an important center of industrial establishments, Constantinople became the home of an enterprising congregation of Christians. During the sixth century, when Rome declined, it looked as if Constantinople would take precedence over Rome as the chief center of the Christian Church. At no time was the head of the Christians in Constantinople, who was styled officially the patriarch, willing to accept the headship of the bishop of Rome in the Christian Church. This is the chief reason that during the eleventh century the Eastern Church separated from the Church in the West. Ever since 1054 the two branches of the old church have remained separated.

THE NEXT THREE CENTURIES OF CHURCH HISTORY

Continued Persecution of the Christians and the Edict of Milan. How the Christians were persecuted during the second and third centuries has been narrated in a preceding chapter. But these persecutions were officially terminated in the year 311 when Emperor Galerius issued an edict of toleration of the Christians. The edict of Galerius was preserved by the Church Father Lactantius, who has already been mentioned. Lactantius reports that Galerius in the eighteenth year of his reign was struck

with an incurable plague. "A malignant ulcer formed itself . . .
and spread by degrees. The physicians tried to eradicate it. . . .
These things happened in the course of one year; and at length
overcome by calamities, he was obliged to acknowledge God, and
he cried out aloud, in the intervals of raging pain, that he would
re-edify the church, which he had demolished, and make atonement
for his misdeeds." Consequently, just before his death, he promulgated his edict. Thus ended the last important persecution
of the Christians although there were to be a few others during
the fourth century. Lactantius also reports that Emperor Constantine saw a vision of the Cross in a dream at night, and was
thus moved to assist the other emperor in protecting the Christians. It is possible that the two emperors happened to be in
Milan when this edict was issued, probably in 313. But the official
document is no longer extant. Galerius was already dead, and
his place had been taken by Licinius. In the writings of Lactant-
tius there appears the following statement: "When we, Constantine and Licinius, emperors, had an interview at Milan, and
conferred together on the good and security of the common-
weal, it seemed to us that amongst those things that are profitable
to mankind in general, the reverence paid to the Divinity merited
our first and chief attention, and that it was proper that the Christians and all others should have liberty to follow that mode of
religion which to each of them appeared best." The famous
Church historian, Eusebius, on the other hand, in his biography
of Constantine gives the impression that Constantine, rather than
Galerius or Licinius, was responsible for the Edict of Milan.

The First Council of Nicaea (325). This was an assembly
attended by the leading clergy throughout the Roman Empire,
and was called together by Emperor Constantine. Among the
many decisions made was the condemnation of the heresy of
Arius, who taught that God the Father is from eternity, but that
God the Son and God the Holy Spirit are His creations. The
Council adopted a formula with anathemas as a test of faith;
the touchstone of this test was the consubstantiality of the Son
and the Father.

Final Conquest of the Christian Religion. During the
course of the fifth century, after Emperor Julian had completely

failed in his undertaking to restore paganism to its ancient position of power within the Roman Empire, the Christian religion became the only legitimate religion in the empire. The emperors themselves accepted its teachings, and a large number of the officials in the Empire also called themselves Christians. Unfortunately for the Church, the adherence of so many wealthy and influential persons tended to make the Church more worldly and hence less interested in purely spiritual things. Furthermore, the Church also received an immense number of real-estate holdings, which were bequeathed by persons anxious to have prayers said for them after they had passed away.

Church Government. Each congregation had a minister or pastor, who was originally called a bishop (*episcopus*) or elder (presbyter). The word "priest" was derived from the term *presbyter*. The pastor as a rule was assisted by elders and deacons. The latter were in charge of the finances of the congregation, and also visited the poor and needy. The elders often substituted for the pastors in the administration of the sacraments and in preaching. They also helped in visiting the sick. A number of congregations were united into a district called an episcopate, governed by an official called "bishop." Furthermore, a number of bishoprics, or dioceses, were grouped into a larger unit which was called an archbishopric, and was governed by an archbishop. This unit was also called a "province." Gradually the democratic features of early Church government made room for a monarchial system of government, which afterwards was called the "hierarchy."

THE BEGINNINGS OF MONASTICISM

Origin and Spread. The idea of separating from the world to avoid its snares and pitfalls is of pagan origin, but early found vogue among the Christians. Some devotees of the practice lived as hermits, but the more common method was to live in groups, or monasteries. St. Basil early founded such communities, and others took up the idea and spread it throughout Europe. Monastic life attracted many. Those who wished to mortify the body, to escape from the Barbarians, to spend a life in study and contemplation, or to flee from crime and disgrace—all such found a refuge in monasteries.

Monastery Life. St. Benedict formulated a set of rules for monastic life that others widely copied. According to this system, a person who entered a monastery took the vows of poverty, obedience, and chastity. He spent his time in a regular routine of meditation and prayer, farming, draining marshes, copying manuscripts, writing, and similar activities. The monastery strove to be a complete economic and social unit.

Influence of the Monasteries. These organizations produced many church leaders and upheld the Popes in all matters. They also kept alive learning, dispensed charity, taught new methods of farming, gave new dignity to manual labor, and sent out missionaries. It was Augustine (Saint Augustine of Canterbury) and forty followers who went as missionaries to the British Isles and converted King Aethelbert (597). St. Columban acted as a missionary to the Gauls and Lombards; St. Boniface established churches and monasteries among the Germans. These were but a few of the missionary activities of the monks.

THE RISE OF THE PAPACY

Relation of Church and State. Mention has been made of the growth of the primitive religion until it became the state religion under Constantine. After that time it not only grew in size and complexity of organization, but also began a persecution of pagans and Arian Christians. At first, church and state cooperated, for the church was dependent on the Emperor, who rewarded it and punished its enemies. But as the Empire grew weaker from Barbarian inroads the Church tended to become more independent of the government, and even to assume certain governmental functions, such as the dispensing of charity, the defense of widows and orphans, and the control of education, marriage, and divorce.

Origin of the Powers of the Pope. The term *Pope* is not mentioned either in the Bible or in the early church codes. Catholics, however, maintain that Peter was leader among the apostles and was first bishop of Rome, and that his powers were handed down to subsequent bishops of that city, or to the Popes. Historically speaking, it is easy to understand how the bishop of Rome came to be leader of the church. Rome had been the capital of the old world, and people had become used to looking to it for leadership. The fall of the Empire of the West increased the prestige of the Pope in that direction. One bishop in particular—Leo (440-461)—greatly increased the powers of his office. He persuaded Valentinian III to issue a decree recognizing the supremacy of the bishop of Rome over other bishops. This active bishop also turned back Attila and helped to save Rome from destruction. The name *Pope* finally came to be applied only to the bishop of Rome. The leading prelate in the East was called the Patriarch.

Gregory, the First Great Pope (590-604). Raised in a pious home, Gregory was well-educated and early entered monastic life. When he became Pope he revolutionized the administration of affairs in the city of Rome, and increased the private patrimony of the Pope. He also made peace with the Lombards and even converted the king, thereby ridding Rome of a troublesome enemy. He established numerous ecclesiastical courts and gained control over many bishops. He also was a leading writer of the day.

THE CHURCH FATHERS

Apostolic Fathers. The Church Fathers who lived in the first century of our era were commonly referred to as Apostolic Fathers. Among them may be mentioned Clement of Rome, who is considered, at least by the Roman Catholics, as one of the early popes. He wrote influential letters to the churches in the Near East, and in this manner he kept in close touch with them.

The Defense of the Christian Religion. A large number of Christian writers of prominence wrote treatises called *Apologies,* in defense of their religion. They tried to show that the Greeks had been poorly led even by so great a thinker as Plato. They condemned the immoral teachings of the mystery religions of the ancient Greeks, and they pointed out that the polytheism of both the Greeks and the Romans was an abomination in the sight of God. They compared the virtues of the Christians with the immoral lives of the greatest thinkers among the Greeks, including Plato, whose ideal state included the abolition of the family. Many of them made elaborate lists of all the heresies, both among the Christians and among the pagans. Among these apologists may be mentioned Irenaeus.

St. Ambrose. Perhaps the most influential Church Father in the fourth century was St. Ambrose, who not only wrote important books, but also exercised much influence in his capacity as the Bishop of Milan. At that time the Emperor lived in Milan instead of Rome, and for that reason the position of Ambrose was of great importance. The emperor at this time was Theodosius, who at least on one occasion was severely reprimanded by Ambrose for massacres that had been perpetrated at his command.

St. Jerome. This great writer lived at the end of the fourth century and at the beginning of the fifth century. He was a great linguist and he made a new version of the Bible which is commonly called the Vulgate, written in the Latin language, and translated out of the original Hebrew and Greek tongues.

St. Augustine. He was the most important among all the Church Fathers, for his books, including his famous *Confessions* and *The City of God,* were read by more persons in the Middle Ages than the books of any other person. In *The City of God* he told about the Christian Church, which he contrasted with the Roman Empire. He pointed out that all nations were full of corruption, and all would in time pass away, but that the Christian Church had an eternal inheritance reserved for it in the heavens. St. Augustine also became famous for his excellent exposition of the most important doctrines that comprised the Christian faith, or the Christian creed. Like Plato, he believed in "realism." He also taught the doctrine of predestination, according to which God determines in advance what shall be the fate of human beings as far as their salvation is concerned. However, St. Augustine has often been misunderstood, and it should be remembered that he did not teach that God forced people into heaven or hell, but that there was a real cooperation between God and man, although man was not able to do very much.

CHRISTIANITY IN THE REALM OF POLITICS

Importance of the Church in the Middle Ages. In the Middle Ages the Church was the greatest and the most stable institution in Europe. Except for a comparatively small number of Jews and Mohammedans, every European was technically born into the Church, and, of even more significance, throughout his life he was affected by it in varying degrees. He had to be baptized soon after birth by a member of the clergy, and when he reached the age of discretion he was confirmed as a full-fledged member of the Christian Church. Marriage was a sacrament, and burial was usually restricted to consecrated ground (the churchyard). At the end of his life the Church offered the sacrament of extreme unction. At stated intervals every member of the Church was expected to confess his sins to his priest, and there was an obligation upon every member regularly to attend mass, or the communion service, of his local church.

The Temporal Power of the Church. Since for about a thousand years the Pope was the civil ruler in a large area in central Italy called the Papal States, or the States of the Church, in this capacity he wielded temporal power. Furthermore, in the Age of Feudalism, that is, from about 900 to 1400, the bishops and abbots who were ruled by him, functioned as feudal lords. It was very difficult to distinguish between their spiritual and temporal power. The greatest of all the popes, Innocent III, made even King John of England his vassal; John had to surrender England to the Pope, and had to accept England as a fief of the Church. All through the Middle Ages various writers contended that the Pope was above the Emperor, and that no Emperor in the West had attained his office legally until he had been crowned and anointed by the Pope. Such was the custom in the Holy Roman Empire until the year 1530. Finally, since the kings as well as the emperors were officially members of the Church, they fell under papal jurisdiction. In several cases a Pope compelled a wicked king to take back his divorced wife, and in other cases he instructed the nobles under the king to disobey him until he had made a reconciliation with the Pope. This was done, for example, by Pope Gregory VII, who is famous for his struggle with Emperor Henry IV.

The Political Theories of the Apostles Paul and Peter. There can be no doubt that the Christians of the second and third centuries took to heart the admonitions of their great missionary and teacher, St. Paul, who advised them to love their neighbors, for "the greatest thing is love" (see I Cor. XIII). In the Epistle to the Romans, Ch. XIII, the apostle said in plain words that everybody should be subject to the powers which happen to be established. His brief treatise is the most influential pronouncement about political science written in the first seventeen centuries of the Christian era, for it was implicitly adhered to by nearly all the great writers and teachers of the Christian world before the eighteenth century. He had written thus: "Let every soul be subject unto the higher powers. For there is no power but of God: the powers that be are ordained of God. Whosoever therefore resists the power, resists the ordinance of God; and they who resist shall receive damnation." St. Peter also enjoyed great authority among the early Christians, and his words were likewise of considerable social and economic importance. He said, "Servants, be subject to your masters with great fear; not only to the good and gentle but also the perverse" (see I Peter II, 18). "Submit yourselves," wrote he in the second chapter of his first epistle, "to every ordinance of man for the Lord's sake: whether it be to the king, as supreme; or unto governors, as unto them that are sent by him for the punishment of evildoers, and for the praise of them that do well. . . . Fear God. Honor the king."

The Social Gospel of the Apostles Paul and Peter. The thirteenth chapter of the First Epistle to the Corinthians and the thirteenth chapter of Romans are of primary importance in the political and social history of Europe. Although all Christians were deemed equal before God, they were exhorted to remain peaceful and patient amidst tribulation and oppression. The slaves were therefore persuaded to desist from rebellion or revolution, the poor laborers were enjoined not to fret about low wages, and the rich were admonished to give freely of their substance, though they were not asked to give up all they owned. In short, political or social equality was not preached by the chief missionary of the Church in the Roman Empire.

The Sanctity of Work. The following words of St. Paul have long been the subject of controversy among modern Catholics and Protestants: "Let every man abide in the calling wherein he was called. Are you called being a servant? Care not for it, but if you may be made free, use it rather. For he who is called in the Lord, being a servant, is the Lord's freeman; likewise also he who is called being free, is Christ's servant. You are bought with a price" (I Cor. VII, 20-23). Whatever the theologians may think of these words, it is certain that before the end of the Middle Ages the people of Christian Europe saw in them little justification for revolt against established authority in the political, social, or economic order. Chrysostom remarked in his commentary on these texts that one gains little by being set free by masters of this world: "You are the slave of Christ, just as is your master. Joseph was also a slave, but he was nevertheless the most free of all men." Moreover, manual labor, which had not been honored adequately by the ancient world, was treated with much respect by the early Christians. Since Christ Himself had been a carpenter, and since St. Paul gloried in his ability to make tents for a living, the Christians in Rome and elsewhere thought so much of their daily labor that in the catacombs their tools were frequently buried with their bodies. The members of the grain corporation which distributed the grain among the populace, those who weighed and measured the grain, honored their vocation by having the grain measure placed upon their graves as a fitting emblem. Furthermore, in the catacombs under Rome and its vicinity may be seen the emblems of the associations of wine growers, skippers, bakers, and carpenters.

The Social Teachings of the Early Christians. The Christians lived among the heathen, and tried to dissolve Roman customs by infusing the Christian spirit, so that the gifts of God's grace could be poured out into the activities of mankind. A sanctification of the calling, or vocation, may thus be recognized. There is a diversity of gifts, says St. Paul, but they all proceed from one and the same spirit. True, there were degrees of value, and the spiritual powers were higher than the temporal powers. That which is higher objectively is not necessarily higher subjectively. Each person can attain the greatest degree of sanctity in his respective vocation. This is what the Middle Ages taught, as may be gathered on every hand in the theological treatises and the books of sermons. To flee the world was a novelty in the time of St. Anthony (*ca.* A. D. 285). Asceticism was neither new then nor widespread.

Worldliness and Asceticism. There was, however, such a wide variety of belief and practice within the confines of the Christian Church of the third and fourth centuries that generalizations are apt to be misleading. On the one hand we meet with extreme forms of asceticism which impelled the devout to spend their lives upon pillars in the desert or in lonely huts, while on the other hand we can note a widespread relaxation of discipline and religious fervor in all the important sources. One of the best church histories states, "There were fewer marks of mystery in the lives of the Christians in the third than in the second century, and, consequently, the Christians were better known in the third century." It is pointed out that in spite of the moral restrictions, which continued to limit the participation in public functions, this participation proceeded apace. Many official duties were performed by the Christians, both in the lower ranks and in the imperial court. As the numbers of the Christians increased, the contagion with the world also increased. Many of the leading writers and preachers among the Christians, whom both the Catholics and the Protestants call the Church Fathers, continued, however, to warn against the spirit of worldliness that was stealthily creeping into the Church at large. For example, the eloquent Chrysostom, in his second Homily on Paul's Epistle to the Hebrews, wrote these interesting words about wealth and poverty: "Neither wealth nor poverty is excellent in itself, but through those who use it. The Christian shines out in poverty rather than in riches." Tatian said, "Not only do the rich among us pursue our philosophy but the poor enjoy instruction gratuitously: for the things which come from God surpass the requital of worldly gifts."

The View of St. Augustine. St. Augustine, the most influential writer among the Fathers, expressed certain views which may be considered as typical of the patristic school of Christian authors and doctors for the period between 200 and 450. In his sermon on Matthew XIX, 17, he made this significant remark: "If then they ought not to 'trust in riches,' not to confide in them, 'but in the living God,' what are they to do with their riches? Hear this: 'Let them be rich in good works.' . . . Must they then lose all they have? He said, 'Let them communicate,' not 'Let them give the whole.' Let them keep for themselves as much as is sufficient for them, let them keep more than is sufficient. Let us give a certain portion of it. What portion? A tenth? The Scribes and Pharisees gave tithes, for whom Christ had not yet shed His blood. . . . 'Except your righteousness exceed the righteousness of the Scribes and Pharisees, ye shall in no wise enter into the kingdom of heaven.' He does not deal softly with us; for He is a physician, He cuts to the quick . . . I have admonished the rich; now hear, ye poor. Ye rich, lay out your money; ye poor, refrain from plundering. Ye rich, distribute your means; ye poor, bridle your desires."

How Far the Christian Was to Obey the Government. We read in the fifth chapter of the Acts of the Apostles that some apostles, imprisoned by the high priest at Jerusalem, were set free by an angel, and were called before the high priest and his council. The high priest was very angry at the apostles, and said: "We strictly charged to you not to teach in this name: and behold, you have filled Jerusalem with your teaching, and intend to bring this man's blood upon us." Now what were the apostles to do in this case? Peter stated that they had to "obey God rather than men." The Christians also took to heart the examples set by pious Hebrews as recorded in the Old Testament. There we read, for example, in the sixth chapter of Daniel that this great Hebrew prophet had refused to obey King Darius, because this king had commanded the faithful believers to do something that was contrary to the will of God as expressed in His Word. Daniel refused to ask petitions only of him, insisting that he should always ask them of his God. Consequently, he was thrown into the den of the lions and continued his prayers to his God. After he had been set free, he could report that, "My God hath sent his angel, and hath shut the lions' mouths, and they have not hurt me: for as much as before him innocence was found in me." We also read in the Old Testament that when King Jeroboam made a golden calf and commanded that the people should worship it, a prophet appeared and condemned the actions of the King, making it clear that in this case the subjects should not obey their ruler. The prophet Hosea also complained about obedience that was wrongfully rendered by the Israelites to their king. For this reason the Christians in Rome, although they were not distinguished in their walks of life from the pagans around them, steadfastly refused to offer sacrifices to the gods worshipped by the Romans, and to accord to the Emperor reverence befitting a god.

The Political Theories of St. Augustine. St. Augustine stated in his work *The City of God* that the civil government is independent of the Church, and the latter is independent of the State. All Christians must obey all the laws of the civil government, except where commanded to do something that would be contrary to the Bible and to the teachings of the Christian Church. He said that the highest and greatest law in the State was the commandment of God that one should love God above all things and one's neighbor as one's self. The ideal state was that in which the civil government and the Church cooperated with each other to the fullest possible extent. Each person was a member of both the State and the Church. Each would promulgate its respective laws independently, but was expected to assist the other in the enforcement. According to St. Augustine, who quoted several examples from history, warfare was permissible. In his day, and in fact from about 324, when Constantine made Christianity the state religion, many of the Christians served in the ranks of the armies and in the imperial government. Several of the Church Fathers looked with favor upon this action. The civil rulers had received their powers directly from God and were retained in their position as long as it pleased Him. Sometimes even bad emperors retained power for a long time, but nevertheless the Christians should obey them in all purely civil matters.

The Question of Slavery. Most of the early leaders in the Christian Church condemned the institution of slavery as contrary to the will of God, but at the same time they exhorted the slaves to remain patient in their suffering and affliction. They were never to rise against their masters as individuals. Chrysostom wrote: "The laws of the world recognize the difference between the two races, but the law of God ignores it; for God has made all things for everybody; He opens the heavens to all without discrimination." And St. Augustine wrote: "The Christian slaves do not demand of their masters liberation of their servitude, for the apostolic authority commands the slaves to remain obedient to their masters, for fear that the name of the Lord may be blasphemed." Very interesting are the words of Lactantius, who was a learned church Father. He exercised tremendous influence during the fourth and fifth centuries of our era. He wrote thus: "God, who created men, wished to have them all equal. Just as He has distributed to all an equal measure of His light, so He has given to all equity and virtue. Before God there is neither slave nor master; since He is our common Father, we are all free. Before God there is no poor person, except him who is wanting in justice; and there is no rich person, except him who is full of virtue." In the opinion of Lactantius the chief cause of the downfall of the Roman Empire was the extensive wealth owned by the rich as contrasted with the excessive poverty endured by the poor. That explanation of his certainly came near to the truth.

The Question of Religious Toleration. During the second and third centuries the majority of the Church Fathers believed that Christians ought to be permitted to worship God as they saw fit. This was a natural attitude to follow, as long as the Christians were being persecuted. But in the time of St. Augustine, about the year 400, a number of heretics preached their doctrines among the ranks of the Christians. For that reason St. Augustine appealed to the emperor and others, suggesting that hereafter heretics ought to be punished by the civil government. As early as the first half of the fourth century, at the Council of Nicaea, Emperor Constantine had looked with favor upon the restrictions put upon such heretics as the Arians. St. Augustine argued that it is a good thing to stop the heretics. He said that if we were to see one of our enemies running toward a precipice in order to hurl himself down into the abyss below, would it not be our duty to stop him from doing this? Likewise, a heretic must be restricted in his speech and writing. He referred to a text in the fourteenth chapter of the Gospel of Luke, where, according to Christ, the disciples should compel the unbelievers to "come in." St. Augustine was followed by St. Thomas Aquinas, who expressed similar views. It is well known that John Calvin, Protestant reformer, during the sixteenth century had a number of persons burnt at the stake because they differed from him in certain theological views. In the same century Queen Mary of England had persons persecuted because they were Protestants, and her successor, Queen Elizabeth, had persons beheaded because they were not Protestants. But during the seventeenth century, owing very largely to the attitude of the Baptists and some Congregationalists, as well as some Presbyterians, religious toleration was restored in the western world. During the eighteenth century the United States led in the march toward perfect religious toleration.

Church and State during the Early Middle Ages. Emperor Justinian made himself head of the Christian Church in the East Roman Empire. At the same time the kings in the Germanic kingdoms made themselves heads of the church in their states. But the leaders within the ranks of the Roman Catholic clergy for centuries fought against this attitude adopted by the civil rulers. Nevertheless, in the first half of the sixteenth century King Henry VIII of England proclaimed himself head of the church in his country. A little later the German princes assumed the same right in their respective states. On the other hand, leading Calvinists strenuously objected to the principle of placing the civil government above the Church. In general it may be said that the principles of the Christian religion favored those expressed by the early Church Fathers, who claimed, as John Calvin also did, that both the Church and the State should make laws independently of each other, but should assist each other in the enforcement of those laws. It is erroneous to state that Calvin or the Puritans in New England established a theocracy, because a theocracy is a form of government in which the Church controls the State. The Israelites had a theocracy before they had their first king, as did also some of the other peoples of the ancient world. But there were no theocracies in the West in early modern times, although this is often erroneously assumed. Since Jesus Christ paid no attention to the forms of government prevalent in his day, saying that the Gentiles had kings to rule over them, but that the Christians should not have, His early followers paid comparatively little attention to the question of what form of government is the most suitable. But St. Thomas Aquinas, who is generally considered the greatest thinker of the medieval world, was of the opinion that a limited monarchy was superior to all other types of government. Luther, the first great leader among the Protestants, was upon the whole satisfied with the imperial rule in the Holy Roman Empire, such at it was in his day. He showed comparatively little interest in this problem, and only when he had been forced by some of his followers to take a definite attitude for or against the right of the princes to rise against the

Emperor, was he willing to state that they had that right, since it was so stated in the constitution. He consistently disapproved, however, of the actions of private individuals who attacked the government or their masters. John Calvin preferred an aristocratic republic, but believed that members of municipal councils or national legislatures had the right to rise against their kings. Largely as a result of his attitude, the Dutch Calvinists in the sixteenth century revolted against the king of Spain, the English Puritans in the seventeenth century overthrew the government of Charles I, and the Americans in the eighteenth century formed an independent republic. Some Calvinists favored aristocratic church government, others more democratic control, while the Baptists contributed much to the rise of both democracy and religious toleration. Roman Catholics are of the opinion that the form of government does not matter so much as long as government officials and subjects are moved by the spirit of brotherly love, as taught by Jesus Christ. For this reason we may conclude that neither the Catholics in particular nor the Christians in general are partial to any special form of government.

CHRISTIANITY AND CAPITALISM

The Attitude of Jesus and His Disciples. Jesus of Nazareth chose his earliest followers from among the lower classes in the social order. His disciples were all very ordinary persons before the fire of missionary zeal began to course through their veins. Gradually, however, some of the leaders in the Jewish churches, lawyers, centurions, and patricians adopted the essential principles of the primitive Christian faith. Rich and poor, strong and weak, Jew and Gentile, learned and ignorant—everybody was welcome in the church of the Nazarene.

So-Called Communism in the Church of Jerusalem. According to the Acts of the Apostles about three thousand persons were converted on the day of Pentecost, and a few days later two thousand joined the ranks of the Christians. For a short time the Apostolic Church was marked by a practice that closely approached communism, but it should be observed that the giving of alms and the sale of property by the Christians were voluntary. St. Peter said to Ananias, "While your property remained, was it not your own? and after you had sold it, was not the money yours?" Even the Anabaptists of the sixteenth century admitted the truth of this observation, although Calvin, Melanchthon, and Luther felt obliged to enlarge upon it.

Subsequent Events. In a relatively short time the attempt to hold all or nearly all property in common proved very difficult of accomplishment. Society in the Roman Empire was too complicated for that, and gradually the Christians accommodated themselves to the social, political, and economic conditions prevailing all about them. In such great centers of commerce and industry as Rome, Alexandria, Ephesus, and Antioch the simple tenets of the faith of the first disciples were modified. Many of the Christians served in the imperial armies, while eventually many others joined the associations or corporations of bakers, skippers, wine growers, carpenters, and the like.

Teachings of the Church Fathers. Commerce was regarded with respect by the early Christians. Although Clement of Alexandria, Ambrose, Cyprian, and Augustine saw great danger in the type of society built up by commerce and industry when plied on an enormous scale, as was the case in Rome and Alexandria, they did not thereby condemn trade in itself. Such is still the official teaching of the Roman Catholic Church. There is also little sense in denying the obvious fact that the church after its very early days did not object to the unequal distribution of the world's goods. No protest of any importance has yet come to light. Clement of Alexandria derived the existence of private property from the friendship between God and man: "God grants temporal goods to mankind in order to bestow benefit upon it." The consensus among the Church Fathers was that earthly possessions were of little importance and might easily distract the mind of the devout Christian. But they were not evil in themselves. It was excessive attachment to them that resulted in sin.

The Question of Usury. A few passages from the works of several Church Fathers will indicate what was meant by *usury,* and what was the attitude of the leading Fathers toward worshippers of Mammon. Cyprian, in his treatise *On the Lapsed,* wrote thus: "Each one was desirous of increasing his estate; and forgetful of what believers had either done in the times of the apostles, or always ought to do, they, with the insatiable ardor of covetousness, devoted themselves to the increase of their property. Among the priests there was no devotedness of religion; among the ministers there was no sound faith; in their works there was no mercy; in their manners there was no discipline. In men, their beards were defaced; in women, their complexion was dyed: the eyes were falsified from what God's hand had made them; their hair was stained with a falsehood. Crafty frauds were used to deceive the hearts of the simple, subtle meanings for circumventing the brethren. . . . Very many bishops who ought to furnish both exhortation and example to others, despising their divine charge, became agents in secular business, forsook their throne, deserted their people, wandered about over foreign provinces, hunted the markets for gainful merchandise, while their brethren were starving in the church. They sought to possess money in hoards, they seized estates by crafty deceits, they increased their gains by multiplying usuries."

The Opinion of Lactantius. Lactantius, who lived in the first half of the fourth century, left two interesting statements about loaning money at interest. In the *Divine Institutes* he outlined the duties of a Christian, and argued as follows: "If he shall have lent any money, he will not receive interest, that the benefit may be unimpaired which succors necessity, and that he may entirely abstain from the property of another. For in this kind of duty he ought to be content with that which is his own; since it is his duty in other respects not to be sparing of his property, in order that he may do good. But to receive more than he has given is unjust, and he who does this lies in waiting in some manner, that he may gain booty from the necessity of another." Again, in the *Epitome of the Divine Institutes,* Lactantius wrote, "He will not give his money to usury, for that is to seek after gain from the evils of others; nor, however, will he refuse to lend, if necessity shall compel anyone to borrow."

Usury and Capitalism. It will be seen, then, that the name *usury* was applied to every form of interest exacted on money lent to anyone. The ancient world was not familiar with conditions such as have prevailed since the close of the Middle Ages. It is for this reason that most authorities in the field of economics do not speak of capitalism until we have reached the fifteenth century. Again, since capitalism developed side by side with Protestantism, it has frequently been argued that Protestantism was partly or largely responsible for the rise of capitalism. But such reasoning is false.

How the System of Capitalism Originated. In the period of the Crusades, however, practical considerations often led to actions which were not in keeping with the words of the Canon Law and the Church Fathers. Closer contact with Constantinople also drove an ever-deepening wedge between theory and practice. Led by the Italian merchants, the businessmen of all western countries began to talk more and more about the theory of a just price, which was the price they could reasonably ask for their goods when consideration was given to the amount of time they spent and the risks they had to take. Gradually the principles of law and equity assumed their proper place beside moral and religious requirements. When capital was needed to increase the stock of a merchant, and when he made a decent profit with the money borrowed, it seemed only logical and fair that both parties concerned in the loan should share in the profit thus acquired. On the other hand monopolies, or trusts, which engineered the artificial rise in prices, and all manner of unjust profit were still generally condemned by clergy and laymen as deceit and robbery. The real meaning of the old word *usury* was applied in practice to the latter evils, and the word *interest* was introduced to indicate the essential difference between the former significance of usury and the later connotation.

Attitude of the Modern Churches. The Roman Catholic Church teaches now, as it always has done, that rich people may live side by side with the poor, as long as the rich are not unduly attached to their wealth. The workmen are permitted to organize into unions and seek collective bargaining from their employers, but both employers and employees must come to the conclusion that financial profit must be subordinated to brotherly love and cooperation. The attitude of practically all the other large denominations of Christendom is the same as that of the Roman Catholic Church. When Jesus said that His kingdom was not o this world, He implied that His kingdom was a higher kingdom

He realized perfectly that all human beings are in this world for a certain purpose, and that a Christian must not despise either his body or his physical environment. The books of the New Testament do not insist upon asceticism, nor upon persecution in any way. Many believe that the social gospel of the Christian churches, when practiced by both husbands and wives, by both parents and children, by both employers and employees, by both the government and its subjects, will limit divorce, murder, strikes, war, and social injustice—briefly it will revolutionize the social order of the modern world. Such an opinion is certainly of great historical importance.

Conclusion. We may quote the admirable words in a textbook of medieval history, one recently used with marked success in the elementary course of history at Harvard University. The co-authors of this book write thus: "In considering Christianity, therefore, we are considering one of the most important of all historical phenomena, no less important today than it was fifteen hundred years ago. For Christianity is not a chapter in the decline of the Roman Empire; it forms the very warp and woof of all the history of that western Europe which immediately followed upon Rome. The whole intricate complex of our present political, social, and even economic life is shot through and through with Christian rites and Christian teachings."

CHAPTER XIII.

THE GERMANIC MIGRATIONS AND KINGDOMS

The Germanic tribes that invaded the Roman Empire from the north have often seemed important merely because of their dramatic exploits and adventures. But there is a much more potent reason for studying the history of their migrations and settlements. They were greater and more important in their peaceful pursuits when living side by side with the cultivated Romans than in their work of destruction and devastation. It frequently happens that both newspapers and textbooks of history pay far too much attention to persons or people who disturb the peace than to those who promote the cause of peace; it is the peacemakers who are instrumental in the expansion of commerce and industry and in the fostering of learning and art. We shall observe that the greatest among the Germanic peoples were exactly those that caused the least destruction. Whereas on the one hand the restless wanderers like the Visigoths and the Ostrogoths and the Vandals soon disappear in history, leaving hardly a trace of their own type of civilization, others, like the Angles, the Saxons, and the Franks founded great nations and made fruitful contributions to the development of western civilization.

188

THE GERMANIC TRIBES BEFORE THEIR MIGRATIONS

The Region Where They Lived Originally. It is practically a consensus that the Germans lived originally in the countries that border the western shores of the Baltic Sea. But historians are not agreed upon the question whence the Germans came before they inhabited this area. In some of the original sources there are, however, references to migrations that occurred between 1000 and 500 B.C., when presumably a number of adventurous wanderers moved from northwestern India or southern Mesopotamia to northwestern Germany and southern Scandinavia.

Sources of Their History. Since these Germanic tribes did not know how to write, they left no written records of their early history. On the other hand, from the household utensils, weapons, and pottery we learn much about their type of civilization. Some of the tribes were accustomed to bury their dead in hollow trunks of trees, which permitted them to keep the dead bodies in an excellent state of preservation. A large number of such bodies have been unearthed in recent times and are in the Ethnological Museum in Berlin. From these remains we gather that the Germans were sometimes in the habit of burying their dead fully dressed in textiles of excellent manufacture. On the other hand, it is also known that some of the Germans were dressed in skins of wild animals. The Romans have left two most important sources: the first is *The Gallic Wars* by Julius Caesar; and the other, much more important than that by Caesar, is the *Germania* by Tacitus.

The Germans and the Celts. It seems that the Germanic tribes in northwestern Germany and southern Scandinavia were closely related in prehistoric times to the Celts, who inhabited what is now France, the Netherlands, and the British Isles. But after 500 B.C. the Celts are distinguished from the Germans in being darker of complexion and smaller in stature. The Celts were called Britons in the British Isles, and both the words "Great Britain" and the "British Isles" are derived from the name for the Britons. Likewise, the peninsula in western France called Brittany was named after them. Those who inhabited Ireland, Wales, and western Scotland were called Gaels. To a certain extent the native tongue of the Irish, which since about 1893 has been revived as a literary language, goes back to the language of the Gaels. In what is now France the Celts were called Gauls, and their country was named Gaul. Caesar called this country Gallia. It appears that shortly after 500 B.C. the Celts were driven back from western Germany and the Netherlands into France and the British Isles. Since the climate of southern Scandinavia is not favorable to agriculture on a large scale, and since the Germanic tribes seem to have exhausted the supply of game and fish in this region, while their cattle seem to have denuded the pasture lands available, they pressed upon the Celts and gradually followed them into western Germany, the Netherlands, and northern France.

The Germans Described by Caesar. Caesar made his book *The Gallic Wars* known to the world in 51 B.C. He described the Germans he had encountered in what was then called Gaul. According to him, they were more interested in hunting and warfare than in peaceful occupations, such as keeping domestic animals and tilling the fields. But they did practice a certain amount of agriculture and they also had some domestic animals. They were dressed in the skins of reindeer, and lived on the meat of wild animals that they hunted, on fish, milk, and cheese. Strictly speaking, they were no longer nomads, for they knew how to make dairy products, and had established themselves on lands where they raised some crops. They had magistrates of their own, and each clan was ruled by a chieftain, although well-ordered government had not yet been established. On the whole they held the cultivated fields in common, for Caesar states that no one could hold a piece of land with fixed boundaries for more than one year at a time.

The Protection of the Frontier along the Rhine. The Romans resembled the French in their anxiety to preserve the Rhine as an inviolable frontier against the Germans. For that reason they established strongly fortified places along the course of that river. Among the cities that they established were Coblenz, Cologne, Mainz, Utrecht, and Leiden. In the Netherlands the Romans subjugated the native Celts and made the Frisians their friends and allies. They taught the natives to draw up dikes along the rivers and sea coast, to drain marshes, and to clear the forest. Augustus hoped for a time to invade Germany and to annex a larg part of the country as a province of the Roman Empire. But when in the year A.D. 9 his legions were defeated under Varus by Arminius (Hermann) in the Teutoburger Forest, he became discouraged and gave up his plans for the conquest of Germany. Today a huge statue of Hermann stands upon one of the hills in the Teutoburger Forest, to commemorate the exploits of the first great leader of the Germans.

The Frontier Between the Rhine and the Danube. The Romans, unwilling to surrender the lands which they had held on the east bank of the Rhine, constructed fortifications partly in the form of a stone wall and partly in the form of a ditch and palisade which connected seventy forts. The fortified line extended from the Rhine just below the confluence of the Rhine and the Main southeastward across the Main for 228 miles, and from that point eastward for another 108 miles to a point on the Danube. In recent years the Germans have reconstructed one of these forts at a place near the city of Frankfort among the lower regions of the Taunus Mountains, and called it the Saalburg. Near the main gate stands a temple dedicated to Mithras, who, as we saw above, was worshipped by many of the Roman soldiers. Inside the fort may be seen one of the Roman camps, and beyond the gate in the rear one may follow a path for a distance of three hundred feet to a ditch and palisade. This palisade was made of wood and resembled the fortifications used by the settlers in the English colonies when they protected themselves from attacks by the Indians. But whereas in America the civilized persons of European descent were to win the final victory over the natives, in the case of the Romans in western Germany their high degree of culture and intelligence was no match for the physical power possessed by the Germans in the centuries following.

The Defense of the Lower Danube. It was also necessary for the Romans to entrench themselves along the banks of the Danube up to the shores of the Baltic Sea. Here, along the lower Danube was constructed a province called Dacia. The province had been established by Emperor Trajan about the beginning of the second century. At this time it had become customary to reward veterans of the army with grants of land, which were located to the west and south of these lines of fortification. Here the Roman soldiers settled after a career of fighting, cultivating the fields and bringing up their children. The latter eventually intermarried with the Germans who from time to time crossed the frontiers.

The Germans Described by Tacitus. The Germans who lived at the end of the first century differed considerably from those described by Caesar. In the time of Tacitus they had learned much about the art of cultivation and the use of domestic animals. They had for some time been trading with the Romans and had taken over from the Romans certain characteristics of settled and civilized life. This must be borne in mind when we consider the valuable description left by Tacitus of the Germans who lived nearest the frontiers of the Roman Empire. It is impossible to say how these Germans differed from those who settled several hundred miles to the east and north of them.

Tacitus Was a Bit Partial to the Germans. It is unfortunate that the only important source regarding the Germans in the period 50 to 400 is the treatise called *Germania* by Tacitus, because the writer's aim was to contrast the simple manners and integrity of the Germans with the luxurious mode of living and the vice that was prevalent in Rome at the close of the first century of our era. But when this fact is borne in mind, the reader will get an excellent picture of the Germans by reading Tacitus.

Description of the Country in Which the Germans Lived. Tacitus tells us that the country was covered for the most part with forests and swamps, which is no doubt correct. This region was suitable for the growing of grain, but not for the production of fruits. Flocks of cattle and herds of sheep were plentiful, but the animals were not very large, which again is correct, for we know that all through the Middle Ages the cattle of western Europe were frightfully small and undernourished. But cattle constituted the chief wealth of the people, exactly as had been the case with the earliest inhabitants of Italy, as we saw previously. As far as Tacitus knew, there were no deposits of gold and silver in Germany. This may have been because, as he stated, the Germans were not interested in the possession and use of precious metals. Although from time to time certain Roman officials had presented the Germans with articles made of silver, the Germans did not esteem them, preferring pottery of clay. But Tacitus was struck by the fact that the Germans who lived nearest to the frontier did show marked interest in implements made of gold or silver. These Germans could use such implements and articles in trading with the Romans. Those who lived in the interior of Germany did not have use for precious metals in commerce, but they practiced only barter.

Weapons Employed by the Germans. The Germans used battle-axes of stone or iron and swords or long spears, though they generally preferred javelins. They employed both infantry and cavalry forces. Afterwards they were protected with shields and helmets of leather.

Political Institutions. The Germans chose kings from among the nobility, but they selected the generals for their bravery upon the battlefield. The kings possessed great power, but they did not rule as absolute monarchs. From time to time the freemen assembled in a meeting called the Popular Assembly. Here important matters of state were settled by the assembly at large. The men attended these meetings only when they were fully armed. After they had been commanded to be silent by the king or priests, the king or a chieftain would address them. They showed approval by shouting, and disapproval by the clashing of spears. In matters of justice, the priests had more power than the kings. A person might make an accusation within the assembly, where it usually was decided that traitors and deserters should be hanged, while weaklings and cowards, together with those that had been convicted of various infamous deeds, had to be thrown into the swamps with a hood over their head. It was felt by the Germans that infamous crimes ought to be hidden, and the culprits quietly removed from sight. Crimes of a lesser nature were punished in an appropriate manner, the punishment being in the form of fines that had to be paid not in cash but in heads of cattle. The injured persons received part of the fine, while the rest went to the king or the tribe as a whole. In the Assembly the magistrates were selected who had to decide the civil suits in the counties and villages. The chief officials were each assisted by one hundred associates.

Functions of the Priests. The priests, as was said, exerted considerable power in the administration of justice and in addressing the political assemblies of the Germans. They derived much of their power from their alleged ability to forestall events through the use of omens, such as the flight of birds, or the behavior of the sacred horses that they kept in their groves.

Division of the Land. Many of the Germanic tribes were divided into units called *hundreds,* which were made up of approximately one hundred, or ten dozen, free families. Each hundred had a government of its own. The Franks applied the word *mark* to a corresponding unit within their tribe. But the Saxon preferred the use of the word *hundred*. For centuries the English people retained these small units inside their counties. The highest court employed by the Saxons came to be called *witenagemot,* which was the council of the wise men.

The Custom of Comitatus. The Germans had a custom that resembled in many details the later custom in western Europe called *chivalry*. A young nobleman was not considered of rank until he had received the right to arm himself. He went through a regular ceremony, which later was called *knighting*. These young nobles used to attach themselves to greater nobles and became regular members of the households of these greater nobles. This custom of becoming part of a nobleman's household was called by Tacitus *Comitatus* and later passed on into the system of society in Europe called *feudalism*.

Home Life of the Germans. As in the time of Caesar, so in the days of Tacitus, the Germans continued to hunt a great deal, and the men spent much of their time doing absolutely nothing, while the women were required not only to take care of the house work, but also of the agricultural labor. It is interesting to note that many of the German women of recent times have continued the old practice of assisting the men in the fields. The Germans constructed villages that consisted of about twenty to forty separate houses, each of which was surrounded by a plot of ground. These houses were all built of wood, and it is remarkable that even today in Germany one may still see countless numbers of wooden houses in the rural districts. In France, the Netherlands, and Great Britain, on the other hand, houses constructed of brick or stone are more numerous. Each house was made up of one large room, with an annex for the cattle. There was an open fireplace or hearth, and in front of the fireplace there was a bench or one table or more. The nobles had larger houses than the others, with an additional hall decorated with trophies of war and hunting.

Farming. Unlike the American farmers, the Germans of ancient and medieval times, and even of early modern times, preferred to live in villages rather than upon the fields that they cultivated. Thousands of such villages still exist in southern and western Europe. Even now it is customary for many farmers to leave their homes in the morning and walk for one or two miles to their fields, and return late at night. The Germans knew very little about the fertilization of the soil, the use of manure, or the rotation of crops. It was their practice to let one-half or one-third of the fields lie idle, which is called the *fallow* system. They did not use winter crops, but were accustomed to plant their seeds in the spring only. Oats and barley were more widely grown than rye and wheat. Bread was made from barley or wheat, which was ground by hand. Much of the grain was consumed in the form of porrage, that is, a mixture of milk and grain. From the barley the Germans made their beer. They also grew hemp, from which coarse cloth or rope was constructed; and flax, which was grown for the manufacture of linen. The sheep provided the wool, while skins and hides were also used for clothing. Whereas the sheep and cows were kept in pastures, the hogs ran free in the forests where they found beechnuts and acorns. It seems that much of the land used to be held in common, but as the Germans became more highly civilized, they began to follow the practice of private property. On the other hand, it always remained customary for them to own the woods and pasture lands in common.

Clothing. The women spun garments from wool, but they were very partial to linen. For garments worn nearest to the skin, the Germans enjoyed the use of linen. But the outer garments, because the weather was often damp and cold, were usually made of wool. The men made use of jackets or short jerseys. The women were dressed in a manner somewhat similar to that of the Greeks and Romans of classical times. This may be gathered from some of the sculpture left by Roman artists in the city of Rome. Instead of wearing stockings or socks, the men were accustomed to cover their legs with cloth that was wound around their legs.

Commerce and Industry. The Germans learned much from the Romans in the fields of commerce and industry, perfecting excellent pottery and some metalwork. They sold to the Romans the amber which they found on the southern shores of the Baltic Sea, hides, skins, soap, goose feathers, and some timber. They exchanged these products for iron weapons, spices that the Romans had imported from the Orient, wine, glassware, and metalware.

Gambling. When the men were tired of hunting, or were kept indoors by inclement weather, they enjoyed gambling. Many times a man would gamble away his own liberty, in addition to his personal property and the liberty of his wife and children. This does not mean, however, that the Germans were immoral. They were strictly monogamists, as Tacitus carefully pointed out. They seem to have gambled with dice.

Slavery. Thus it becomes clear how the Germans instituted the practice of slavery among themselves. Persons would deliberately gamble away their own liberty. But the majority of the slaves had been captured in warfare. There apparently were no serfs among the Germanic tribes, although it is possible that a few of the tribes had those as well as slaves. It would seem, therefore, that the Germans had well-distinguished social classes, ranking from the king and higher nobility down to the lesser nobility and the freemen to the slaves. But it can not be said that the distinction of class depended upon the amount of property a person possessed. The different levels of society were determined rather by social prestige.

The Religion of the Germans. Like many peoples of the ancient world, the Germanic tribes worshipped deified forces of nature, including the sun and the moon. Our names for four days of the week have been derived unquestionably from Germanic gods, namely, Tiu, the god of war; Wodan, the chief god; Thor, the god of thunder; and Frigga, wife of Woden and often identified with Venus. The Germans had a curious conception of Walhalla, or heaven, thinking that to be a place reserved for their great warriors and brave men, who would enjoy themselves drinking wine from the skulls of defeated enemies. Since the Germans were not particularly attached to their gods and their religious beliefs, it was relatively easy for the Christian missionaries to convert them to the new faith.

The Germanic Law. The chief contribution made by the Germanic peoples to the growth of western civilization seems to consist in the perfection of Germanic law. This became the basis for the English Common Law, as well as for the laws of the Netherlands, Scandinavia, and Germany. On the other hand, Germany and the Netherlands have also taken over a large part of the Roman law as set forth in the famous Code of Justinian. The Germanic Law was unwritten, but nevertheless was transmitted from generation to generation. The most important collection of German laws is called the Salic Law, which will be discussed in another section.

THE ROMANO-GERMAN KINGDOMS

The Visigoths. Of all the Germanic tribes that invaded the German empire, it appears that the Visigoths covered the most territory. Between 200 B.C. and A.D. 350 they moved southeastward from southern Scandinavia past the eastern slopes of the Carpathian Mountains to what is now southern Russia. Here they might have remained indefinitely, had it not been for the invasion of the region by the Huns from central Asia. Thus they were pushed westward and southward, and migrated into the Balkan Peninsula, as we saw. In 378 they defeated the legions of Emperor Valens at Adrianople, after which they moved still farther southward about 395 when they occupied Athens and Corinth. Even then they were not satisfied; they started moving north, this time going around the Adriatic Sea until in 410 they sacked the city of Rome. Hardly had they completed this task when they turned north for a second time, crossed southern Gaul, and moved into Spain, where they established a kingdom that lasted until the first half of the eighth century when the Mohammedans moved into Spain from northern Africa. In Spain they found a highly civilized population that used the Latin language and was governed by Roman law. The Visigoths had a law of their own, while the Romans continued to abide by the laws of the old Roman Empire. But eventually the Germanic settlers lost their language and their laws, and in the end Spain became both Christian and Latin in culture. So it has remained until the present day.

The Ostrogoths. The Ostrogoths moved southward at about the same time as the Visigoths, and they also went to the same region in southern Russia. Likewise, they were disturbed by the Huns, but instead of moving into the Balkan Peninsula, they preferred setting up a kingdom of their own in Italy. They were led by a great general called Theoderic. He and his followers found in Italy another Germanic leader who had established a temporary kingdom. This was Odoacer, who was defeated during the course of the year 492-493 by the Ostrogoths under Theoderic the Great. Odoacer had removed from power the last of the Roman emperors, in the year 476. Much has often been made of the date 476, but it will be seen that it was only one of the many important dates during the course of the Germanic migrations and the establishment of their kingdoms. The Roman Empire did not really fall, but it declined during the course of two hundred years, and its decline merely culminated in the removal of its last emperor in the year 476. The Ostrogothic kingdom extended as far south as the southern coast of Sicily, as far west as southeastern France, and as far east as the eastern shore of the Adriatic Sea. Theoderic the Great established his capital in the beautiful city of Ravenna, where several famous churches of the Byzantine style of architecture were constructed shortly after his career. In 555 Belisarius, the general employed by Emperor Justinian, overthrew the Ostrogothic kingdom. For some time a large part of Italy belonged to the Byzantine Empire.

The Vandals. The Vandals moved from southwestern Germany through southern Gaul and Spain into northern Africa, where they established a kingdom that lasted from about 430 to 548. They were noted for a ruthless manner of destruction, and they shared with the Huns the opprobrium attached to the most barbarous and cruel races that wrecked the ancient world.

The Burgundians. The Burgundians came out of southwestern Germany but, unlike the Vandals, were content to move but a short distance from their homes. They established a kingdom in eastern France, which in 534 was conquered by the Franks. However, after some centuries of Frankish dominion, the Burgundians once more had a kingdom of their own, which during the Middle Ages was divided into two states, namely, the Duchy of

Burgundy in the west and the County of Burgundy in the east. During the fifteenth century the duke of Burgundy ranked among the greatest potentates in the West. But when in 1477 the last prince died, and was succeeded by a daughter only, the duchy was annexed by the king of France. It was not until 1678 that the county became a province under the name of Franche Comté.

The Franks. The Franks were far more successful than were the Goths or the Vandals. They were Orthodox Christians, while the Goths had been converted to the Christian religion by Ulfilas, who was an Arian. The Franks moved only a very short distance from their original homes on the banks of the middle Rhine, and they were careful to use the Netherlands as their base of operations. Here they were favored by fertile soil, long seasons for growing crops, an excellent system of water transportation, the support of the bishops of Rome, and the proximity of wealthy Gaul. They carefully took over from the Romans the highly organized system of government, the efficient management of armies, and the highly developed agriculture, commerce, and industry. Their greatest king before the seventh century was Clovis, who has already been mentioned. He ruled from 481 to 511, and he conquered northern and much of eastern France. The Franks are noted for having repulsed the Saracen hosts in central France in the famous battle of Tours in the year 732. Furthermore, they established a huge empire during the time of Charlemagne, and they laid the foundations of a new Roman Empire in western Europe.

The Angles and Saxons in England. During the fourth and fifth centuries large numbers of Angles and Saxons moved from northwestern Germany and the mainland of Denmark to England, where they established a half dozen kingdoms of their own. They subjugated the Celts, although many of the Celts removed to Wales, western Scotland, and Ireland. They were converted by Christian missionaries, and developed a high degree of civilization. Their political institutions and laws were mingled with the laws of the Roman Catholic Church and the Code of Justinian. Upon these foundations the famous parliamentary system of government was constructed during the closing centuries of the Middle Ages and the opening centuries of the modern period.

General Characteristics of the Romano-German Kingdoms in the West. In Italy, Spain, and France the Germanic tribes did not have enough man power to replace Latin and Roman civilization by the institutions and languages of their own. They lived among the highly cultured Romans as rulers, and they received a large portion of the real estate in the respective kingdoms. While on the one hand they became more cultured than they had been before, on the other hand the Romans lost much of their former culture. In this manner was introduced the period commonly referred to as the Dark Ages. The term implies that the art and learning of the Romans decayed, that many libraries were destroyed, that cities crumbled into ruin, and that commerce and industry declined to a marked degree. The political institutions of the Germans and Romans also became modified in both directions. Such peoples as the Franks gave up the frequent use of popular assemblies, adopting from the Romans the conception of absolute monarchy. Their kings became heads of their respective churches. Charlemagne used to send out his officials to the various provinces, in order to restrict local self-government. Through his imperial decrees he ruled both State and Church. In England, on the other hand, the situation was somewhat different, because England was separated from the Continent by the Channel. Here the leading nobles retained more of their power than was the case in some of the countries on the Continent. Here also the Roman Catholic clergymen continued to wield considerable power. In southern France, Roman law continued in operation, while in northern France the Frankish law replaced Roman law. In Spain the Germanic laws died out. In Italy for a time the Germanic law held a respected place in the north, but eventually it disappeared. During the twelfth century there occurred a tremendous revival of the study of Roman Law, not only in Italy, but also in France, Spain, and England. Many admirers of German culture have maintained that modern democracy goes directly back to the Germans, but their theory is difficult to prove. It can at least be stated that the Germans left a certain heritage that modified the conception of the Romans in the field of politics.

The Salic Law. One of the Frankish tribes, called the Salians, developed the celebrated Salic Law, according to which the government took over from private individuals the administration of justice. This law classified the people into various ranks, so that the life of a Frank was worth twice as much as that of a Roman. Again, the person employed in the court of the king was worth three times as much as an ordinary freeman. The law also prescribed that crimes be punished in accordance with the age of the wounded person, the nature of the wound that had been inflicted upon him, the importance of the limb that had been cut or wounded, and even in the cases where cattle were stolen the age and the condition of the cattle in question. The Salic Law stated further that women could not inherit property in their own right and name, for which reason it was never possible in the history of France for a woman to inherit the throne.

CHAPTER XIV.

THE END OF
THE ANCIENT WORLD

It is difficult to say exactly where ancient history ends and where medieval history begins. The fourth and fifth centuries no doubt mark the borderline between these two great periods of history. It was an age of transition, in which the Roman Empire in the West disappeared, and in which the Roman Empire in the East revived. At the same time occurred the establishment of the Germanic kingdoms upon the ruins of the Roman Empire of the West. While one of these kingdoms was being enlarged, becoming eventually an outstanding empire of the Middle Ages, another empire was being constructed in the Near East, where Mohammed founded a religion. Inspired by his remarkable personality, his followers conquered the Byzantine rulers in the provinces of Syria and Egypt, as well as those of Persia, northern Africa, Spain, and Sicily. This empire rose during the course of the seventh century. It witnessed the ruin of Greek culture in the Near East, but it was not able to disturb the Frankish kingdom and its subsequent empire. In the meantime great nations were being built in the Far East, where a remarkable civilization flourished during the period under consideration. Although it has often been customary to ignore these countries and civilizations completely, the present work includes their early history.

TRANSITION IN THE NEAR EAST

The Vitality of Constantinople. There are textbooks of ancient and medieval history that pay practically no attention to the marvelous civilization that was constructed in and near the city of Constantinople at the very time that Rome was falling into ruins. It was assumed that Byzantine civilization was decadent and made no contribution to the growth of civilization in the west. It was not generally known during the course of the nineteenth century that the Byzantine Empire staged a revival in practically every field of human endeavor. The capital of the Byzantine Empire possessed such vitality that it withstood the onslaught of the greatest armies and navies. It saw the Seljuk Turks pass by its frontiers from time to time, and it witnessed the decline and fall of all the Germanic kingdoms in the West, including the great empire constructed by the Franks. It saw the papacy in Rome rise to tremendous heights, and come to a time of marked decline during the close of the Middle Ages, long before Constantinople itself fell before the hosts of the Ottoman Turks. When chaos prevailed in Spain, Gaul, Italy, and western Germany, the soldiers of the Byzantine Empire cleared the whole of the Balkan Peninsula of barbarians, reconquered a large section of Italy, rebuilt the civilization of Rome in northern Africa and Syria, and extended its commercial sway over ancient Mesopotamia.

The Buildings of Constantinople. Shocking though the story is of the decline of the population of Rome from about a million to a few thousand, sad though it is to hear the lamentations of the visitors who saw the greatest Roman buildings in ruins, no student of history can neglect to study the extraordinary rise of Constantinople to the position of the greatest city in the world when people spoke of the Dark Ages in the West. Certainly there were no Dark Ages in Constantinople between 500 and 800. When travelers came from Rome and the cities of ancient Gaul to visit Constantinople, they were impressed beyond measure by the famous market square, the so-called Augusteum, where stood the church of Hagia Sophia, the Imperial Palace, a huge vaulted monument from which started all the roads of the Byzantine Empire, and other buildings that looked out on the celebrated Hippodrome, where games were fought and exciting spectacles were held. In the open spaces and arcades around the Hippodrome, astonished travelers from the west could see a multitude of obelisks and statues that had been taken from Rome, Asia Minor, Greece, and Egypt.

The Commerce of Constantinople. Since Constantinople controlled the two great arteries of trade leading from Europe by land across the Straits into Asia Minor and the sea route from the Black Sea to the Mediterranean, it became immensely wealthy. Merchants from all quarters of the earth brought to Constantinople the luxuries of the Orient, slaves from Africa, skins, hides, and amber from the north, and grains and metals from the west. It was a great day when in approximately the year 550 two Christian monks returned from China with the secret of the manufacture of silk. For some four or five centuries after that date Constantinople controlled the monopoly of silk manufacturing in Europe. It imported cotton, pepper, cloves, precious wood, precious stones, glassware, rugs, carpets, and untold quantities of fruits and vegetables from the Orient. Especially active was the trade with Persia and Arabia, two countries which in the sixth and seventh centuries were highly cultured.

The Upper Classes. Much of the wealth that was derived from commerce and industry passed into the hands of nobles, who led lives of luxury, surpassing perhaps those that had scandalized Tacitus in Rome during the first century after Christ. Clad in silks, they entertained their guests in sumptuous homes and country estates. They controlled many of the posts in the administration, the army, and the church. They pursued hunting, horse-racing— and book learning. They were patrons of the arts and the professions. They were proud of the two universities that made Constantinople a leader in education. The professors were paid by the state, while the Church also had its great university. Even the middle class in Constantinople was very wealthy when compared with the conditions of similar classes of people in such cities as Rome, Paris, and London. There were many rich merchants and bankers among the middle class in this town. In the professions the bourgeois folk were also active, for the city was filled with lawyers, physicians, supervisors of hospitals, of aqueducts, water supply, and drainage.

The Government of Justinian. Emperor Justinian, as was noted above, was head of both the State and the Church. He controlled both the army and the navy. He established a huge bureaucracy, and through his famous code he affected the laws of untold peoples of medieval and modern times. During his reign the Byzantine Empire included areas in northern Africa, Italy, Spain, and western Asia. Also in Russia, northern Europe, Asia Minor, Syria, Mesopotamia, and Egypt, Byzantine art, law, scientific standards, and theology were widely copied. In this manner the Byzantine Empire preserved classical civilization in such measure that when it is properly studied the glory of Arab civilization and of the Renaissance of the fourteenth and fifteenth centuries will be considerably diminished.

The Peculiarity of the East Roman Empire. When we speak of the climax and fall or decline of ancient civilization, we often seem to overlook the extraordinary fact that amidst the decline of almost the whole of the ancient world around the Mediterranean Sea, Constantinople kept on rising upward and perfecting its art, its government, its universities, and its fighting machine. Those who love to speak of the Dark Ages, and apply them to the whole of the Mediterranean area, should be very careful not to overlook what was going on in Justinian's empire.

The Survival of the Greek Language. Justinian promulgated his code in Latin, his native language. He hoped that through his code he might be able to replace the Greek with the Latin. But he failed completely in this attempt, so that the later additions to the code all had to be written down in Greek. The language of instruction in the two great universities in Constantinople also continued to be Greek. The great works in history and science were likewise written in Greek. Thus down through the ages until the present time the Balkan Peninsula has remained Greek in culture as well as in language. But at the same time, Asia Minor, Syria, and Egypt were lost to Greek culture. Here the Saracens spread their language and the civilization that went with the Mohammedan religion. The time was to come when the Ottoman Turks even took Constantinople and turned Saint Sophia into a Mohammedan mosque, although today it is a public museum. In some sections of the Balkan Peninsula, notably in and near

Albania, there are still many tens of thousands of Mohammedans. But nearly the whole of the Balkan Peninsula has remained Christian and partly Greek. Nevertheless, the migration of numerous Slavic tribes into the peninsula during the sixth and seventh centuries, followed from time to time by other waves of migrations, altered the culture of the various peoples to such an extent that Greece alone remained exclusively Greek in language and in other characteristics. Serbia, Bulgaria, and Rumania may have retained many elements of Greek culture, but they also have adopted elements from other peoples, notably the Latins and the Slavs.

THE LATIN PEOPLES

The Dark Ages in the West. During the days of chaos and tumult, it seemed for a time as if the Germans would obliterate the classical culture of Rome. Time after time Rome was sacked by Germanic barbarians, first by Visigoths, then by Ostrogoths, and then by Lombards. Frankish armies also appeared from time to time to assist the bishop of Rome in his fight against either Lombards or Byzantines. At one moment the Pope was really at the mercy of the Franks, who saved him from Lombards and Byzantines alike. Thus the Papal States were created during the eighth century.

The Holy Roman Empire. In the year 962 Emperor Otto the Great, of the Germans, established an empire which later came to be known as the Holy Roman Empire. In his time Germany was still called East Frankland, while France was as yet West Frankland. But, whereas Germany remained German, West Frankland became thoroughly Latin in language and culture from the shores of the Mediterranean Sea in the south to the Netherlands, or Low Countries, in the north. The emperor in Germany continued to claim France as a part of his empire, and officially both the Netherlands and Switzerland remained a part of this empire until 1648. Western Switzerland and the southern half of Belgium are still French in speech and culture today. Italy freed itself from the rule of the emperors during the twelfth and thirteenth centuries.

Latin Europe is Saved from Conquest by the Saracens. Although the Saracens were able during the eighth and ninth centuries to occupy almost the whole of Spain and Portugal, as well as the island of Sicily, and although they frequently threatened the coasts of southern France and the mainland of Italy, western Europe was too far away from Arabia and Egypt to be held in subjection. The first important check received by the Saracens was that administered on the battlefield by the Franks in 732. During the eleventh century the Christians in Spain began to form kingdoms of their own, and gradually pushed the Saracens back farther to the south. Finally, in 1492, the Saracens lost their last stronghold in Spain. Long before that they had surrendered their hold upon Sicily, which nevertheless during the thirteenth century was still partly Mohammedan. In subsequent centuries the tide of conquest was reversed, and the Christians continued to pursue the Mohammedans, who eventually lost all of northern Africa to the Christian rulers of the West, besides almost all of the Balkan Peninsula. Today even Palestine and Syria are mandates under the respective control of Great Britain and France.

THE GERMANIC PEOPLES

In Great Britain. The half dozen states of the Saxons and the Angles were united during the course of the eighth and ninth centuries. Thus the kingdom of England was established, while to the north another kingdom was founded that was called Scotland. For some centuries Wales remained independent of England, but eventually it became a province. The same fate befell Ireland, which did not recover its independence until a few years ago.

Influence of the Germans in Latin Europe. Although, as we saw, the Germanic conquerors in Italy, Spain, France, and what is now southern Belgium, were not able to impose upon their subject populations the Germanic language and Germanic political institutions, these victorious peoples contributed somewhat to the shaping of both the languages and the institutions. The Italian language, as well as French and Spanish, contains a relatively large number of words that are clearly of Teutonic origin. It is also likely that the tradition of popular assemblies among the Germans never completely disappeared from the minds of the people at large. The time was to come when England would establish a parliamentary form of government, in which the House of Commons wrested from the king and the nobles nearly all of their political powers. Thus the House of Commons was in a way a revival of the popular assemblies of the Saxons and the Franks. But one must be careful to remember that this system which developed in England does not go back entirely and directly to the Germans of old. During the course of several centuries various peoples contributed to the making of this British parliamentary system of government. But it is true that this system of government was imitated by the peoples of Italy, France, and Spain. Italy had a popular assembly until it was removed in 1936 by Mussolini. France until 1940 had two houses that formed the national legislature. Spain for ages had its *Cortes*. In early modern times France retained the national legislature under the name of Estates-General.

The Low Countries or Netherlands. During the Middle Ages this region did not become a united nation, but was made up of a number of principalities called duchies and counties respectively. But at the close of the Middle Ages they were controlled for the most part by the duke of Burgundy. Today in the kingdom of the Netherlands and in northern Belgium the literary language of the people is the Frankish tongue.

Germany. Only the extreme west and south of Germany was dominated by the Romans, so that Germany upon the whole escaped the process of Romanization that occurred in such countries as Spain and France. The language remained always German, although in the universities until the eighteenth century the language of instruction was Latin. For some centuries the emperor of the Holy Roman Empire issued a large number of decrees in the Latin language. Church hymns and chronicles were also written in that language, while at the end of the Middle Ages and in early modern times scholars frequently composed their treatises in the same language. But the masses were never affected by this habit on the part of the scholars. Owing to the process handed down by the Franks and other Germanic peoples of old, who were accustomed to divide their property among their children, the relatively small number of states that were formed in Germany at the close of the period under consideration grew in number so that at the end of the Middle Ages there were more than two hundred such states. Strictly speaking there never was a country called Germany until the year 1871, when a little more than twenty states became the German Empire.

Scandinavia. During the fourth and fifth centuries the region to the north of Germany was still inhabited by the same sort of folk that·used to migrate through Germany and assume various names, as we saw. During the eighth and ninth centuries three kingdoms were formed in what we call Scandinavia, namely, Sweden, Denmark, and Norway. In 1397 these three kingdoms were united into one under a common ruler. But in 1523 Sweden broke away and established a kingdom of its own. Denmark and Norway remained united until 1815, when Norway was taken from Denmark by the great statesmen of Europe and joined with Sweden. But in 1905 Norway again became an independent state, so that until 1940 there were the three independent kingdoms of Sweden, Norway, and Denmark. The languages of these three peoples are very closely related, having no doubt been derived from a common source, which may be called the Gothic language. The Scandinavian nations are seldom mentioned in our history textbooks, for the simple reason that they have always followed a course of peace and order, as far as seemed possible to the rulers and leading nobles in those countries. All the noble qualities of the German tribes of old may be seen reflected today in the Scandinavians.

ANCIENT INDIA

The Land. India is a peninsula in the shape of a rough triangle, about two-thirds as large as the United States. Its long regular coast line has few harbors. North of it lie the world's tallest mountains, the Himalayas, which act both as a barrier and as a protection. The richest and most populous part of India is the fertile plain of the Ganges River. In contrast is the Deccan plateau, a broken rocky region covering the southern half of the country. The seasons are alternately wet and dry. The hot damp climate has had an enervating effect upon the inhabitants.

The People. The population of India in 1940 was about 380,000,000, and consisted of a number of races. Of these the Dravidians, a short dark people, scattered from Ceylon to the

Ganges, are aboriginal. There are numerous Mongolians also, especially in the provinces of Nepal and Bhutan. The Indo-Aryans, descendants of the Aryan invaders, are most prominent in Punjab and Kashmir.

Religions and Castes. India is a land of many religions. Chief among these is the Hindu or Brahman, a polytheistic belief, with Brahma as the supreme deity, and with the *Vedas,* or sacred books, written in Sanskrit. Four castes were originally recognized: 1. The Brahmans; 2. the nobles and warriors; 3. the peasants and traders; 4. the Sudras. These have changed until now there are more than two thousand groups, of which the lowest, the "untouchables," comprise 30 per cent of the population. Brahmans believe in the transmigration of souls and ultimate absorption of the pure into Brahma. In the sixth century B.C. there arose a reformer named Buddha, who taught that salvation came through honesty, purity, and charity, and that all classes could attain perfection. His creed, triumphant at first, was later crowded out, so that today only about ten million people in India follow his teachings. It spread elsewhere, though, and now numbers more followers than any other non-Christian religion. Seventy-odd million people, chiefly of Arab and Turkish descent, profess Mohammedanism. Christianity has gained only a few million followers.

Invasions Between 3500 and 1500 B.C. Recent excavations in northern India have revealed remains of peoples who were either Sumerians, having come from Mesopotamia, or tribes that were closely related to them. The sites of two ancient cities have been excavated in that part of northwestern India called the Punjab. Although these cities (Mohenjo-daro, on the Indus, and Harappa on the Ravi) were 400 miles apart, their civilization was "astonishingly homogeneous," according to a distinguished British archeologist. Here seems to have been constructed a state that was four times as large as Egypt and twice as large as Mesopotamia.

Punjab Civilization from 3000 to 2000 B.C. The cities in this state differed from those of ancient Egypt and Sumeria in that no great temples or palaces were erected in them to glorify some god or king. It seems that here a democratic bourgeoisie ruled, and controlled industry and commerce. One great public building was a bath of immense proportions. The size of the cities compares favorably with those of ancient Babylonia or Egypt. Like the cities of the Sumerians, they were constructed of kiln-dried brick. The streets were wide and carefully laid out. The homes were provided with bathrooms and running water.

Agriculture, Commerce, and Industry. Irrigation was resorted to, as in Egypt and Sumeria. Among the crops grown were bread wheat, barley, dates, rice, and cotton. Such domestic animals as cows, buffaloes, sheep, chickens, and elephants were kept. The swine may have been wild, however. Since saddles were used, the horse or mule may have been kept also. Commerce evidently flourished. Two-wheeled carts, identical with some of those used in India today, facilitated transportation. The boats also resemble modern vessels. Metalware was abundant, as gold, silver, lead, and copper were widely used in making household goods or implements. Chisels, axes, daggers, spearheads, single-edged knives, razors, pruning hooks, arrowheads, sickles, and tweezers were manufactured, but less skilfully than in Sumeria. The goldsmiths knew how to solder. But pottery was even more popular than in Sumeria. The potter's wheel was swift.

Writing. Many seals have been found showing a style of writing that differs from cuneiform and from the pictorial. It has not yet been deciphered.

Later Invasions. At the time of the Indo-Aryan dispersion, perhaps about 1500 B.C. or earlier, the Aryans penetrated India as far as the Ganges River, and imposed their civilization on the natives. Alexander the Great in the fourth century B.C. also invaded a part of India, introduced Greek civilization, founded cities, and developed commerce. Various Mongolian tribes from Central Asia have entered India from time to time; most notable of these were the Huns in the fifth century. Arab Moslems conquered the province of Punjab, and other Mongol followers of the Prophet under the leadership of Baber (1525) established the Great Mogul Empire, which lasted until the English overthrew it two or three centuries later.

ANCIENT CHINA

The Land. China is a land somewhat larger than India and with greater natural resources. It has fertile valleys, navigable rivers, rich minerals, and a varied climate. High mountains protect it from invasions. These factors have tended to make China a great nation and to isolate it from other peoples.

The People. The Yellow River valley was inhabited almost five thousand years ago by probably an aboriginal people. They gradually conquered and absorbed surrounding territories and peoples. This ability to fuse with other races has given the Chinese a marked physical sameness possessed by few other people.

Earliest History. There was a long mythical period when China was ruled by heroes, and concerning which there is little reliable information. Wu Wang, founder of the Chow dynasty (1122-249 B.C.), emerges as a real character. He perfected a feudal system, and established schools and hospitals. His successors gradually lost control over their feudal lords. During this period the reformer Confucius lived (551-478 B.C.). He made no claims to miraculous power, but taught obedience to parents, reverence for ancestors, and the golden rule, negatively stated. Mencius (272-289 B.C.), a disciple of Confucius, exerted an influence second only to that of his teacher.

Religions. The Chinese are ancestor and nature worshippers. Connected with this worship are two divinities, Shangti (heaven), and Ti (earth). There are five sacred mountains and four sacred streams but no priests. Taoism, founded by the philosopher Lao-tzu, also has many adherents. It is a mystical nature worship which features many superstitions. Confucianism, which includes the moral philosophy of its founder, has many followers. Buddhism spread into China in the fourth century B.C. It borrowed much from the native religions.

The Empire. After the collapse of the Chow dynasty, Shih Hwang-ti (246-221 B.C.) founded an empire. He divided China into 36 provinces, each ruled by a governor-general and a treasurer, whom he appointed. He broke with the past, ordered the works of Confucius and other classics to be burned, and built the Great Wall to keep out the Huns. After his death there was a period of disorder, followed by the rulers of the Han dynasty (206 B.C.-A.D. 221), who extended their dominion over Korea and elsewhere. Several centuries of confusion followed the decline of this dynasty, then came the T'ang dynasty (618-907), during which time China became the most powerful state in the world.

Civilization. The Chinese reached the phonetic state of writing by 2000 B.C., but have not yet developed a simple universal alphabet. They also printed books from movable type as early as the tenth or eleventh century of our era. The Nine Classics, which Confucius collected and which taught his beliefs, have exerted a potent influence on Chinese thought. Until 1905 they formed the basis for civil service examinations. There are many old colleges, academies, and other schools. In art, architecture, and related fields of culture the Chinese have made great advancement.

ANCIENT JAPAN

The Land. The Japanese archipelago consists of a number of islands off the eastern coast of Asia with a total area of about 175,000 square miles. It is a region of short rivers, volcanoes, and numerous lakes and harbors. Its rather poor soil nevertheless produces valuable forests and, under careful cultivation, large quantities of rice, barley, wheat, tobacco, and other crops, while the nearby waters abound in fish. The climate is temperate and bracing. The mineral supply, especially iron, is limited.

The People. The Japanese are of mixed origin. There are Mongolians, Koreans, North Chinese, and aborigines. Some are Malays. As a whole, the Japanese are frugal, polite, patriotic, and imitative. Their high birth rate has caused Japan to be the home of eighty-odd million people, and has given rise to serious problems of emigration and expansion.

Religions. The Japanese, like the Chinese, worship their ancestors. To them, the dead are very real and living. Their Mikados are generally deified. Shintoism, the national faith, emphasizes nature and ancestor worship, and features many spirits, gods, and deified men. Ameratsu, the sun goddess, is regarded as the ancestor of the Mikado. Shintoism pays little heed to morality or immortality and has no sacred book. There are many temples, though, each with a prayer hall and a sanctuary, where priests offer daily sacrifices. Buddhism was introduced in the sixth century and soon became the most prominent religion. Indeed, many

Japanese are both Shintoists and Buddhists. The land is filled with beautiful Buddhist temples and statues. Christianity was introduced in the sixteenth century, but the Mikado frowned upon it and persecuted its followers. Only a small proportion of the Japanese are Christians.

Early History. While it is difficult to separate myth from history, it appears that Jimmu Tenno made conquests in Japan in 660 B.C. and established the dynasty that still exists. In the third century the Empress Jingu invaded and conquered a part of Korea and, more important, brought the Japanese into contact with Chinese civilization, much of which they adopted and improved. In the seventh century of our era an official called the Shogun became the active hereditary ruler and the Mikado went into seclusion. Late in the thirteenth century the Chinese ruler, Kublai Khan, made an unsuccessful attempt to conquer Japan. Three centuries later the Japanese made a counter attack on China and, although they continued to claim Korea, they failed in their major purpose.

Civilization. The Japanese have developed a syllabic writing system that approaches an alphabet. In literature they have followed Chinese leadership, but have some historical novels, dramas, and poetry of their own, not to mention translations of Western authors. There is a state supported system of education from the elementary schools to the universities. Taking Chinese arts as a model, they have generally improved upon it. Feudalism was long an established institution, with its land-owning nobles, its knights and its serfs, but this has been abolished with the coming of Western influences.

Significant Dates

5000-525 B.C.

4500—First cities constructed in Sumeria
3400-3000—Merging of city-states of Egypt into Old Kingdom
3200—Menes, first Pharaoh
3000—Founding of Assyria
3000—Building of great cities in northwestern India
2980-2475—Pyramid age in Egypt
2900—Khufu (Cheops), Pharaoh
2900-2750—Old Kingdom in Egypt
2850—Khafre, Pharaoh
2800—Menkure, Pharaoh
2776—Invention of Egyptian calendar
2630—Sargon I, ruler of Akkad
2475-2160—Feudal age in Egypt; Heracleopolis capital
2300—Ur revolts under King Dungi
2160-1778—Middle Kingdom in Egypt; Thebes, capital
2150—Amenemhet, Pharaoh
2100—Founding of Babylonia
2050—Seostris I, Pharaoh
2000—Early Cretan culture
2000—Age of Hammurapi, king of Babylonia
2000—Amenemhet II, Pharaoh
1950—Seostris II, Pharaoh
1950—Abraham leaves Ur for Canaan
1900—Seostris III, Pharaoh
1850—Amenemhet III, Pharaoh
1800—Achaeans invade Aegean area
1800—Amenemhet IV, Pharaoh
1800—Sebeknefure, Pharaoh
1785—Kassites invade Babylonia
1778-1580—Hyksos in Egypt
1580-1350—Egyptian Empire; capital, Thebes
1580-1577—Ahmose, Pharaoh
1577-1501—Amenhotep I and Thutmose I, Pharaohs
1501-1447—Thutmose II, Queen Hatsheput, and Thutmose III, Pharaohs
1500—Hittite kingdom in Asia Minor
1447-1420—Amenhotep II, Pharaoh
1420-1411—Thutmose IV, Pharaoh
1411-1375—Amenhotep III, Pharaoh
1375-1358—Amenhotep IV (Ikhnaton), Pharaoh
1358-1350—Tutankhamon, Pharaoh
1350-1315—Harmhab, Pharaoh
1315-1314—Ramses I, Pharaoh
1314-1292—Seti I, Pharaoh
1300-1200—Greeks begin to invade Aegean area
1292-1225—Ramses II, Pharaoh
1290-1260—Shalmaneser I, king of Assyria
1275-1175—Hittite empire in Asia Minor and Assyria
1225-1215—Merenptah, Pharaoh
1215-1205—Seti II, Pharaoh

1205-1167—Ramses III, Pharaoh
1169—Fall of Kassite kingdom in Babylonia
1167-1090—Ramses IV-XII, Pharaohs; rapid decline of Egypt
1150—Fall of Hittite empire
1150—Philistines enter Palestine
1150—Hebrews conquer Canaan
1150-1100—Greeks conquer Mycenaean kingdoms; fall of Troy
1100-800—Phoenicians dominate Mediterranean commerce
1020-975—David, king of Hebrews
975-935—Solomon, king of Hebrews
937—Hebrew kingdom divided
900-800—Homeric age; writing of Odyssey and Iliad
900—Age of Hebrew prophets Elijah and Elisha
900—Reign of Shalmaneser II in Assyria
860-825—Reign of Shalmaneser III in Assyria
854—Battle of Quarqar
785-745—King Jeroboam II of Israel
745-605—Assyrian Empire
745-727—Reign of Tiglath-Pileser of Assyria
732—Fall of Aramaean kingdom
722—Fall of kingdom of Israel
722-705—Sargon II, Assyrian Emperor
672-662—Egypt under Assyria
650—Reign of Assur-bani-pal in Assyria
650—Height of Lydian kingdom
800-600—Greek kingdoms
625-604—Nabopolassar, king of New Babylonia
612—Fall of city of Nineve
606—Fall of Assyrian Empire
604-561—Rule of Nebuchadnezzar in New Babylonia
586—Fall of Judah and Jerusalem
546—Persians annex Lydia
538—Fall of Babylon
536—Hebrews are permitted to return to Palestine
525—Persians conquer Egypt

525-336 B. C.

521-485—Reign of Darius in Persia
509—Reforms of Cleisthenes
509—Founding of Roman Republic
493-486—War of Darius against Greeks
490—Battle of Marathon
485-465—Reign of Xerxes I in Persia
594—Reforms of Solon
480—Battle at Thermopylae
480—Naval battle at Salamis
479—Battle of Plataea
469-399—Career of Socrates
457-445—War of Spartans and Boeotians against Athens
450—Twelve tablets of Roman law

215

445—Thirty Years' peace established between Athens and Sparta
444-429—Athens under Pericles
431-404—Peloponnesian wars
415-413—Expedition of Athenians against Pericles
406—Battle of Arginusae
405—Battle of Aegospotami
404—End of Athenian empire
404-371—Spartan empire
399-387—War between Persians and Spartans
395-387—War between Sparta and Corinth
394—Battle of Cnidus
387—Gauls attack and sack Rome
379-362—War between Sparta and Thebes
371-362—Thebes at height of power
367—Licinian laws passed
362—Battle of Mantinea
343-341—War between Romans and Samnites
338—Battle of Chaeronea
340-338—Latin war; dissolution of Latin League

336-31 B. C.

336-323—Reign of Alexander the Great
334—Battle of Granicus
333—Battle of Issus
331—Battle of Arbela or Gaugamela
327—Alexander invades India
326—Battle of the Hydaspes
324—Alexander returns from India
323—Death of Alexander the Great
282-272—War between Rome and Tarentum
264-241—First Carthaginian (Punic) war
227—Passing of Hortensian law
218-201—Second Punic war
218—Hannibal invades Italy
218-211—War in Spain
217—Battle of Lake Trasimene
214-205—First Macedonian war
214-210—War in Sicily
212—Syracuse captured; death of Archimedes
203—Scipio defeats Hasdrubal, brother of Hannibal
202—Battle of Zama
201—Rome makes peace with Carthage
200-197—Second Macedonian war
190-189—War between Rome and Antiochus III of Syria
171-168—Third Macedonian war
149-146—Third Punic war
148-146—Fourth Macedonian war
146—Carthage destroyed
146—Macedonia and Greece become Roman provinces
133—Rome annexes Pergamon
133-121—The Gracchi and Their Reforms
113-101—Romans defeat Teutones and Cimbri
102—Battle of Aquae Sextiae
100—Marius consul for sixth time
91-88—Social or Marsian (Marsic) war
88-82—Civil war between Marius and Sulla
88-81—Two wars against Mithridates

82-79—Sulla dictator in Rome
73-71—Further civil war
60—First Triumvirate
58-51—Gaul conquered by Caesar
49-46—Caesar and Pompeius engage in civil war
48—Battle of Pharsalus
44—Caesar assassinated
43—Second Triumvirate
42—Battle at Philippi
31—Battle at Actium
31—Rome annexes Egypt

27 B.C.-A.D. 284

27—Augustus (Octavian) establishes Roman Empire
9 A.D.—Varus defeated by Arminius in Teutoburger Forest
14-37—Reign of Tiberius
14-16—Expeditions against Germans near mouths of lower Rhine
37-41—Reign of Caligula
41-54—Reign of Claudius
54-68—Reign of Nero
64—Great fire in Rome
64—First persecution of Christians
68-69—Rule of Galba, Otho, Vitellius
69-79—Reign of Vespasian
70—Destruction of Jerusalem
79-81—Reign of Titus
81-96—Reign of Domitian
96-98—Reign of Nerva
98-117—Reign of Trajan
111—Dacia becomes province of Roman Empire
117-138—Reign of Hadrian
130—Wall constructed in northern Britain
138-161—Reign of Antoninus Pius
161-180—Reign of Marcus Aurelius
162-165—War against Parthians
180-192—Reign of Commodus
193-211—Reign of Septimius Severus
211-217—Reign of Caracalla
212—Roman citizenship extended to all provincials
217-218—Reign of Macrinus
218-222—Reign of Elagabalus (Heliogabalus)
222-235—Reign of Severus Alexander
235-238—Reign of Maximinus the Thracian
243-249—Reign of Philip the Arab
249-251—Reign of Decius
250—Persecution of Christians
251-253—Reign of Gallus
253-258—Reign of Valerian
258-268—Reign of Gallienus
268-270—Reign of Claudius II
270-275—Reign of Aurelian
276-282—Reign of Probus
282-283—Reign of Carus

284-565

284-305—Reign of Diocletian
292—Diocletian appoints two caesars named Constantius and Galerius
303-311—Last great persecution of Christians
311, or 312—Edict of Milan

313-323—Constantine and Licinius rule Empire
323-337—Reign of Constantine the Great
325—Church council at Nicea
330—Founding of Constantinople
337-361—Reign of Constantius
361-363—Reign of Julian
364-375—Reign of Valentinian I
364-378—Reign of Valens
367-383—Reign of Gratian
378—Battle of Adrianople
379-395—Reign of Theodosius
395—Visigoths take Athens and Corinth
395-423—Reign of Honorius
406—Burgundians found kingdom on Rhine
406-407—Vandals invade Gaul
410—Visigoths sack Rome under Alaric
412—Visigoths in Gaul
419—Visigoths establish kingdom in Spain
425-455—Reign of Valentinian III
429—Vandals establish kingdom in northern Africa

430—Death of St. Augustine
430-440—Angles and Saxons invade Britain
439—Vandals take Carthage
451—Battle of Chalons (Mauriac Plain)
440-461—Leo I, Pope
455—Sack of Rome by Gaiseric
476—Odoacer removes Romulus Augustulus as last emperor in West
486—Clovis defeats Syagrius
481-511—Clovis king of Franks

Byzantine Emperors

395-408—Arcadius
408-450—Theodosius II
450-457—Marcian
457-474—Leo I
474—Leo II
474-491—Zeno
491-518—Anastasius I
518-527—Justin I
527-565—Justinian

Bibliography

Abbott, F. F., *A History and Description of Roman Political Institutions*, Third ed., 1911.

Agard, W. R., *What Democracy Meant to the Greeks*, 1942.

Albright, W. F., *The Archaeology of Palestine and the Bible*, 1935.

Allen, T. W., *Homer: The Origins and the Transmission*, 1924.

Baikie, J., *Egyptian Antiquities in the Nile Valley*, 1932.

Baikie, J., *History of Egypt from the Earliest Times to the End of the XVIIIth Dynasty*, 1929.

Baikie, J., *The Sea Kings of Crete*, 1936.

Bailey, C., *The Greek Atomists and Epicurus*, 1928.

Barker, E., *Greek Political Theory: Plato and His Predecessors*, Fourth ed., 1951.

Barrow, R. H., *The Romans*, 1953.

Bell, H. I., *Egypt from Alexander the Great to the Arab Conquest*, 1948.

Bevan, E. R., *A History of Egypt under the Ptolemaic Dynasty*, 1927.

Bevan, E. R., and Singer, C., *The Legacy of Israel*, 1928.

Bewer, J. A., *The Literature of the Old Testament in Its Historical Development*, Rev. ed., 1933.

Boak, A. E. R., *A History of Rome to 565 A.D.*, Fourth ed., 1955.

Boissier, G., *Cicero and His Friends*, 1925.

Botsford, G. W., *Hellenic History*, Fourth ed., 1955.

Breasted, J. H., *Ancient Records of Egypt*, 5 vols., 1906-1907.

Breasted, J. H., *Ancient Times: A History of the Early World*, Second ed., rev., 1944.

Breasted, J. H., *The Dawn of Conscience*, 1933.

Breasted, J. H., *History of Egypt*, Second ed., 1909.

Browne, E. G., *Literary History of Persia*, 4 vols., 1928.

Buchan, J., *Augustus*, 1937.

Budge, E. A. W., *Book of the Dead*, 1949.

Burkitt, M. C., *The Old Stone Age.*, Third ed., rev., 1956.

Burn, A. R., *Minoans, Philistines, and Greeks*, 1930.

Burton, H. E., *The Discovery of the Ancient World*, 1932.

Bury, J. B., *A History of Greece to the Death of Alexander*, Third ed., rev., 1951.

Bury, J. B., *The Hellenistic Age*, 1923.

Butterfield, H., *Christianity and History*, 1950.

Cambridge Ancient History, ed. J. B. Bury, *et al.* 12 vols.

Cameron, G. G., *History of Early Iran*, 1936.

Carleton, P., *Buried Empires*, 1939.

Carcopino, J., *Daily Life in Ancient Rome*, 1940.

Carter, H., and Mace, A. C., *The Tomb of Tut-ankh-Amen*, Vol. I, 1923; Vol. II, 1927; Vol. III, 1933.

Cary, M., *History of Rome to the Reign of Constantine*, 1935, Second ed. 1954.

Cary, M., *The Legacy of Alexander: A History of the Greek World from 323 to 146 B.C.*, Second ed., 1952.

| Ceram, C. W., *Gods, Graves and Scholars,* 1951.

Chapot, V., *The Roman World,* 1928.

Charlesworth, M. P., *The Roman Empire,* 1951.

Childe, V. G., *The Dawn of European Civilization,* 1925.

Childe, V. G., *New Light on the Most Ancient East,* Fourth ed., 1952.

Cochrane, C. N., *Thucydides and the Science of History,* 1929.

Code of Hammurabi, The, ed. by R. F. Harper, 1904.

Collingwood, R. G., *Roman Britain,* 1934.

Contenau, G., *Everyday Life in Babylon and Assyria,* 1954.

Cooper, L., ed., *The Greek Genius and Its Influence: Select Essays and Extracts,* 1952.

Cornford, F. M., *Before and after Socrates,* 1932.

Cough, H. N., *Greece,* Second ed., 1940.

Cowley, A. E., *The Hittites,* 1926.

Croiset, M., *Hellenic Civilization,* 1925.

Day, J., *An Economic History of Athens under Roman Domination,* 1942.

Debevoise, N. E., *Political History of Parthia,* 1938.

De Burgh, W. G., *The Legacy of the Ancient World,* 2 vols., 1953.

Declareuil, J., *Rome the Law-Giver,* 1927.

Delaporte, L., *Mesopotamia,* 1925.

Dentan, R. C., ed., *The Idea of History in the Ancient Near East,* 1955.

Dickinson, G. L., *The Greek View of Life,* 1925, 1949.

Diehl, C., *History of the Byzantine Empire,* 1945.

Duchesne, L. M. O., *Early History of the Christian Church,* 1922-1926.

Duff, J. W., *Literary History of Rome,* Third ed., 1953.

Edwards, I. E. S., *The Pyramids of Egypt,* 1954.

Evans, Sir A. J., *The Earlier Religions of Greece in the Light of Cretan Discoveries,* 1932.

Evans, Sir A. J., *The Palace of Minos,* Vols. I-IV, 1921-23.

Farrington, B., *Greek Science,* 1953.

Ferguson, W. S., *Greek Imperialism,* 1913.

Ferguson, W. S., *Hellenistic Athens,* 1911.

Finegan, J., *Light from the Ancient Past,* 1946.

Flickinger, R. C., *The Greek Theatre and Its Drama,* Third ed., 1926.

Fowler, H. N., *A History of Ancient Greek Literature,* Rev. ed., 1923.

Fowler, H. T., *A History of the Literature of Ancient Israel,* 1912.

Fox, W. S., *Greek and Roman Mythology,* Rev. ed., 1928.

Frank, T., *A History of Rome,* 1923 .

Frank, T., *Roman Imperialism,* 1914.

Frankfort, H., et al., *The Intellectual Adventure of Ancient Man,* 1946.

Frankfort, H., *The Birth of Civilization in the Near East,* 1951.

Frankfort, H., *Kingship and the Gods,* 1948.

Gadd, C. J., *History and Monuments of Ur,* 1929.

Gardner, E. A., *A Handbook of Greek Sculpture,* Second ed., 1915.

Garstang, J., *The Hittite Empire,* 1929.

Geer, R. M., *Rome,* Second ed., 1950.

Ghirshman, R., *Iran,* 1955.

Gibbon, E., *The History of the Decline and Fall of the Roman Empire,* 1776-88 and reprints.

Gittler, J. B., *Social Thought among the Early Greeks*, 1941.
Glanville, S. R. K., *Daily Life in Ancient Egypt*, 1930.
Glotz, G., *The Aegean Civilization*, 1927.
Glotz, G., *The Greek City*, 1930.
Glover, T. R., *The Conflict of Religions in the Early Roman Empire*, 1920.
Glover, T. R., *Democracy in the Ancient World*, 1927.
Godolphin, F. R. B., ed., *The Greek Historians*, 1942.
Goodenough, E. R., *The Church in the Roman Empire*, 1931.
Gordon, C. H., *The Living Past*, 1941.
Graham, W. C., *The Prophets and Israel's Culture*, 1934.
Grant, Michael, *Ancient History*, 1952.
Grote, G., *History of Greece*, 1845-56 and reprints.
Gurney, O. R., *The Hittites*, 1952.
Guthrie, W. K. C., *The Greeks and their Gods*, 2 vols., 1951.

Hall, H. R. H., *The Ancient History of the Near East*, Eleventh ed., 1936.
Halliday, W. R., *The Pagan Background of Early Christianity*, 1925.
Halliday, W. R., *The Growth of the City State: Lectures on Greek and Roman History*, 1923.
Hamilton, E., *The Great Age of Greek Literature*, 1942.
Hamilton, E., *The Greek Way*, 1930, 1949.
Hamilton, E., *The Roman Way*, 1932.
Harnack, A., *The Expansion of Christianity in the First Three Centuries*, 1904-05.
Harrison, J. E., *Mythology*, 1924.
Haskell, H. J., *This Was Cicero*, 1942.
Heidel, A., *The Babylonian Genesis: The Story of Creation*, Second ed., 1951.
Hitti, P., *History of the Arabs*, Sixth ed., rev., 1956.
Hogarth, D. G., *The Kings of the Hittites*, 1926.
Holmes, T. R. E., *The Roman Republic and the Founder of the Empire*, 3 vols., 1923.
Holsapple, L. B., *Constantine the Great*, 1942.
Homo, L., *Roman Political Institutions from City to State*, 1929.
Hooton, E. A., *Up from the Ape*, 1931, Rev. ed., 1946.
Huart, C., *Ancient Persia and Iranian Civilization*, 1927.

Jardé, A., *The Formation of the Greek People*, 1926.
Jones, T. B., *A Short History of Ancient Civilization*, 1941.
Jouguet, P., *Macedonian Imperialism and the Hellenization of the East*, 1928.

Keith, A., *The Antiquity of Man*, Rev. ed., 1931.
Keith, A., *New Discoveries Relating to the Antiquity of Man*, 1931.
Kent, C. F., *A History of the Hebrew Commonwealth*, Rev. ed., 1949.
Kidd, B. J., *A History of the Church to A.D. 461*, 1922.
King, L. W., *A History of Babylon*, 1915.
King, L. W., *A History of Sumer and Akkad*, 1923.
Kitto, H. D., *Greek Tragedy: A Literary Study*, Second ed., rev., 1950.
Kitto, H. D., *The Greeks*, 1952.

Laistner, M. L. W., *Greek Economics*, 1923.
Laistner, M. L. W., *Greek History from 479 to 323 B.C.*, 1949.
Lang, Andrew, *The World of Homer*, 1910.
Lewis, N. and Reinhold, M., *Roman Civilization*, 1951.

Lods, A., *Israel*, 1932.
Lot, F., *The End of the Ancient World*, 1953.
Lucas, A., *Ancient Egyptian Materials and Industries*, Third ed., 1949.

Marsh, F. B., *A History of the Roman World from 146 to 30 B.C.*, Second ed., rev., 1953.
Marsh, F. B., *Modern Problems in the Ancient World*, 1943.
Maspero, Sir G. C. C., *The Dawn of Civilization: Egypt and Chaldaea*, Rev. ed., 1922.
McCown, C. C., *The Ladder of Progress in Palestine*, 1943.
Mercer, S. A. B., *Horus, Royal God of Egypt*, 1942.
Mommsen, T., *The History of Rome*, 1854-1855 and reprints.
Moore, R., *Man, Time and Fossils*, 1953.
Moret, A., *The Nile and Egyptian Civilization*, 1928.
Muir's Atlas of Ancient and Classical History, 1956.
Muller, H. J., *The Uses of the Past*, 1952.
Murray, G., *Five Stages of Greek Religion*, Third ed., 1952.
Myres, J. L., *The Dawn of History*, 1911 and reprints.
Myres, J. L., *The Political Ideas of the Greeks*, 1927.

Neugebauer, O., *The Exact Sciences in Antiquity*, 1952.
Newbigin, M. I., *The Mediterranean Lands*, Rev. ed., 1950.
Nilsson, M. P., *A History of Greek Religion*, Second ed., 1949.
Nock, A. D., *Conversion: The Old and the New in Religion from Alexander the Great to Augustine of Hippo*, 1933.

Olmstead, A. T., *History of the Persian Empire*, 1948.
Ormerod, H. A., *Piracy in the Ancient World*, 1924.
Osborn, H. F., *Men of the Old Stone Age*, Third ed., 1934.

Parker, H. M. D., *A History of the Roman World from A.D. 138 to 337*, 1935.
Peake, H., and Fleure, H. J., *The Corridors of Time*, 1927-1936.
Pearson, L., *Early Ionian Historians*, 1939.
Peet, R. E., *Egypt and the Old Testament*, 1922.
Pendlebury, J. D. S., *The Archaeology of Crete*, 1939.
Petrie, Sir W. M. F., *Arts and Crafts of Ancient Egypt*, 1923, reissue 1932.
Petrie, Sir W. M. F., ed., *History of Egypt*, Tenth ed., 1924-1927, 6 vols.
Petrie, Sir W. M. F., ed., *Prehistoric Egypt*, 1920.
Petrie, Sir W. M. F., *Social Life in Ancient Egypt*, 1923.
Pritchard, J. B., *Ancient Near Eastern Texts Relating to the Old Testament*, Rev. ed., 1955.

Raphael, M., *Prehistoric Cave Paintings*, 1946.
Reymond, A., *History of the Sciences in Greco-Roman Antiquity*, 1927.
Robin, L., *Greek Thought and the Origins of the Scientific Spirit*, 1928.
Robinson, C. A. Jr., *Alexander the Great*, 1947.
Robinson, T. H., and Oesterly, W. O. E., *A History of Israel*, 2 vols, 1932.
Rogers, R. W., ed. and tr., *Cuneiform Parallels to the Old Testament*, 2 vols., Second ed., 1926.
Rogers, R. W., *A History of Ancient Persia*, 1929.
Rose, H. J., *A Handbook of Greek Literature from Homer to the Age of Lucian*, 1934.
Rose, H. J., *The Mediterranean in the Ancient World*, Rev. ed., 1935.

Ross, Sir E. D., ed., *The Art of Egypt through the Ages*, 1931.
Rostovtzeff, M., *A History of the Ancient World*, 2 vols., 1926-1927.
Rostovtzeff, M., *Social and Economic History of the Hellenistic World*, 3 vols., 1941.
Rostovtzeff, M., *The Social and Economic History of the Roman Empire*, 1926.
Runciman, S., *Byzantine Civilization*, 1933.

Sachar, A. L., *A History of the Jews*, Rev. ed., 1953.
Sarton, G., *A History of Science*, Vol. I, 1952.
Schmidt, E. F., *Anatolia through the Ages: Discoveries at Alishar Mound*, 1931.
Schneider, H., *The History of World Civilization from Prehistoric Times to The Middle Ages*, German, 1927; tr. by M. M. Green, 2 vols., 1931.
Scramuzza, V. M., *The Emperor Claudius*, 1940.
Scullard, H. H., *A History of the Roman World from 753 to 146 B.C.*, 1935.
Semple, E. C., *Geography of the Mediterranean Region: Its Relationship to Ancient History*, 1931.
Setton, K. and Winkler, H., eds., *Great Problems in European Civilization*, 1954.
Shepard, A. M., *Sea Power in Ancient History*, 1924.
Shepherd, W. R., *Historical Atlas*, Eighth edition, rev. and enl., 1956.
Showerman, G., *Eternal Rome*, 1924.
Smith, W. S., *A History of Egyptian Sculpture and Painting in the Old Kingdom*, 1946.
Steindorff, G., and Seele, K. C., *When Egypt Ruled the East*, 1942.
Starr, C. G., *The Roman Imperial Navy*, 1941.
Syme, R., *The Roman Revolution*, 1939.

Tarn, W. W., *Hellenistic Civilization*, 1930.
Taylor, H. O., *Greek Biology and Medicine*, 1922.
Toutain, J., *The Economic Life of the Ancient World*, 1930, reissue, 1951.
Toynbee, A. J., *Greek Historical Thought from Homer to the Age of Heraclius*, 1924, reissue, 1950.
Toynbee, A. J., *A Study of History, Vol. III*, 1935.
Turner, R., *The Great Cultural Traditions: The Foundations of Civilization*, 2 vols., 1941.

Ullman, B. L., *Ancient Writing and Its Influence*, 1932.
Ure, P. N., *Justinian and His Age*, 1951.

Vasiliev, A. A., *History of the Byzantine Empire*, 1952.

Warden, C. J., *The Evolution of Human Behavior*, 1932.
Weidenreich, F., *Apes, Giants and Men*, 1946.
Weigall, A. E. P. B., *History of the Pharoahs*, 3 vols, 1925-1929.
Wilcken, U. E. E. F. W., *Alexander the Great*, tr. by G. C. Richards, 1932.
Wilson, J. A., *The Burden of Egypt*, 1951.
Winlock, H. E., *The Rise and Fall of the Middle Kingdom in Thebes*, 1947.
Woolley, C. L., *A Forgotten Kingdom*, 1953.
Woolley, C. L., *Ur of the Chaldees*, 1934, reissue 1954.
Woolley, C. L., *Digging up the Past*, 1933, reissue 1954.

Zeuner, F. E., *Dating the Past*, Third ed., 1952.
Zimmern, A. E., *The Greek Commonwealth*, Fifth ed., 1951.

INDEX

Abraham, 8, 12, 35, 36, 145
Academics, 161
Achaean League, 89, 111
Achaeans, 62
Acropolis, 73, 79, 168
Acropolis Museum, 145
Actium, 116
Adrianople, 156, 197
Adriatic Sea, 197
Aediles, 107
Aegatian Islands, 109
Aegean Sea, 26, 51, 58, 60, 62, 86, 104
Aegenas, 62
Aegina, 74, 75
Aegospotami, 75
Aeneid, 132
Aeolians, 63
Aeschines, 87
Aeschylus, 73, 80
Aethelbert, 172
Aetolian League, 89, 111
Agamemnon, 80
Age of Iron, 63
Age of the Kings, 63
Age of the Nobles, 65
Age of the Tyrants, 66, 68
Agriculture: Assyrian, 47; Babylonian, 16;
  Egyptian, 3, 25; German, 190, 195;
  Greek, 77; Indian, 211; Mesopotamian,
  3; Roman, 116, 117, 129; Sumerian, 11
Agrippa, 133
Ahura-Mazda, 51, 54
Akkadians, 14, 15
Alaric, 156
Alcibiades, 75
Alexander the Great, 22, 25, 44, 86-89,
  102, 211
Alexandria, 88, 90, 91, 119, 140, 184
Alphabet, 30, 96; Egyptian, 29, 30;
  Hebrew, 41; Japanese, 214; Roman,
  120
Ambrose, St., 174, 184
Amenembet III, 22
Amenhotep III, 22
Ameratsu, 213
Ammianus Marcellinus, 143
Amon, 23, 29; Temple of, 26
Amorites, 14
Anabaptists, 184
Ananias, 183
Anatolian Greeks, 68
Anaximander, 68, 161
Angles, 5, 158, 188, 199, 207
Anthony, St., 177
Antigonus, 89
Antioch, 89, 168, 184
Antiochus, 111
Antoninus Pius, 123, 127
Antony, 116
Aphrodite, 64, 122
Apollo, 64; Temple of, 84
Appeles, 91

Appian Way, 119
Aquinas, St. Thomas, 96, 181, 182
Arabia, 9, 127
Arabs, 98
Aramaeans, 42-43, 45
Archelaus, 161
Archimedes, 91
Architecture: in Age of Tyrants, 68; As-
  syrian, 19; Byzantine, 198; Cretan, 60;
  Early Byzantine, 146; Egyptian, 26;
  Greek, 79; Persian, 53; Roman, 119,
  131, 155; Sumerian, 12
Archons, 71
Ares, 122
Arginusae, 75
Argos, 65
Arians, 181, 199
Aristarchus, 91
Aristophanes, 73, 80, 81, 91
Aristotle, 64, 82, 87, 92, 93, 94, 98, 100,
  161
Arius, 170
Armenia, 63, 127
Arminius, 125, 149, 191
Army: Byzantine, 158; Roman, 124, 138,
  149
Arno, 104
Art: Assyrian, 47; Athenian, 73; Chris-
  tian, 144; Egyptian, 26; Roman, 144;
  Sumerian, 12, 13
Artemis, Temple of, 79
Asceticism, 177, 178, 187
Ashur, 47, 48
Asia Minor, 59, 89; conquered by Assy-
  rians, 45
Asiatic Plague, 127
Assembly, 115, 124
Assur-bani-pal, 48
Assyria, 8, 18-19, 25, 44-50
Astrology, 14, 50
Astronomy, 13, 81
Athena, 64, 73, 80, 122
Athenagoras, 161
Athenian Empire, 70
Athens, 63, 65, 67, 69-79, 89, 99, 116,
  147, 168, 197
Athos, Mt., 69
Atrium, 119, 120
Attica, 75
Attila, 156, 173
Augusteum, 203
Augusti, 137
Augustine, St., 96, 98, 99, 147, 160, 172,
  174, 178, 180, 181, 184
Augustus, 89, 117, 123, 131, 133, 135, 149,
  190
Aurelius, 161
Austrasia, 158
Avesta, 56

Baal, 42
Babel, Tower of, 12, 49

223